Modern Passings

Modern Passings

DEATH RITES, POLITICS, AND SOCIAL CHANGE IN IMPERIAL JAPAN

Andrew Bernstein

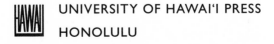

UNIVERSITY OF HAWAI'I PRESS
HONOLULU

Library of Congress Cataloging-in-Publication Data
Bernstein, Andrew.
    Modern passings : death rites, politics, and social change in
Imperial Japan / Andrew Bernstein.
        p. cm.—(Studies of the Weatherhead East Asian Institute,
Columbia University)
    Includes bibliographical references and index.
    ISBN-13: 978-0-8248-2874-5 (hardcover : alk. paper)
    ISBN-10: 0-8248-2874-7 (hardcover : alk. paper)
    1. Death—Social aspects—Japan—History—19th century. 2. Death—Social
aspects—Japan—History—20th century. 3. Funeral rites and ceremonies—
Japan—History—19th century. 4. Funeral rites and ceremonies—Japan—
History—20th century. 5. Japan—Social life and customs—1868–1912.
6. Japan—Social life and customs—1912–1945. I. Title. II. Series.
DS827.D4B47 2006
306.9'0952'0904—dc22

                                                    2005022845

Studies of the Weatherhead East Asian Institute
Columbia University
The Weatherhead East Asian Institute is Columbia University's center
for research, publication, and teaching on modern and contemporary
Asia Pacific regions. The Studies of the Weatherhead East Asian Institute
were inaugurated in 1962 to bring to a wider public the results of
significant new research on modern and contemporary East Asia.

University of Hawai'i Press books are printed on acid-free paper and meet the
guidelines for permanence and durability of the Council on Library Resources.

Designed by the University of Hawai'i Press Design & Production Department
Printed by The Maple-Vail Book Manufacturing Group

For my parents,
Eva and Richard Bernstein

Contents

Acknowledgements

It is a pleasure to recount the generosity that made this book possible. I would first like to thank Carol Gluck, whose expert guidance and warm encouragement sustained this project from start to finish. I am also grateful to my other professors at Columbia, especially Henry Smith II, Angela Zito, and Gregory Pflugfelder, for their advice and support.

David Howell, Anne Walthall, and Sarah Thal provided invaluable feedback on the manuscript, helping me to both broaden and deepen the analysis. Richard Jaffe, Mark Jones, Beth Katzoff, Duncan Williams, Mark Rowe, Susan Glosser, David Campion, Rebecca Copenhaver, Bruce Suttmeier, Lisa Claypool, Keith Vincent, Andrew Hicks, and Michael McCorkle made insightful suggestions. I would also like to thank Zenno Yasushi, Iwasaki Haruko, Suzuki Hikaru, Tsuji Yōko, Elizabeth Kenney, Jane Hunter, Robbie Roy, Margo Ballantyne, Marshall Hammond, and Shinohara Michie for their assistance.

Research in Japan was made possible by a Fulbright Fellowship, and I was given an institutional home at Meiji University, thanks to Tamamuro Fumio. I am particularly grateful to Professor Tamamuro for introducing me to Yamamoto Akiko, who taught me how to read antiquated, handwritten Japanese. I cannot thank her enough for the many hours spent huddled over obscure documents. Mori Kenji provided further support, first steering me to key documents and then helping me to decipher them. I received various other forms of assistance from Fujii Masao, Murata Antoku, Murakami Kōkyō, Shimazono Susumu, Isomae Jun'ichi, Hiasa Hidenori, Aoki Toshiya, Inoue Haruo, Kotani Midori, and Yamada Shin'ya.

Thanks also go to the extremely helpful staff members of the Meiji University Library, the Tokyo Metropolitan Archives, the National Diet Library, and Tokyo University's Meiji Shinbun Zasshi Bunko. I am further indebted to those companies and individuals who provided access to funeral ceremonies and shared firsthand insights about them. These include Himonya Hajime, Yokoyama Kiyoshi, Tomatsu Yoshiharu, Kōekisha, Sugimoto K.K., Ceremony Miyazaki, and the funeral department of Co-op Tokyo. During my time in Japan I was also fortunate to rent an apartment from the Moris—Akira and Masako—who provided warm friendship along with a solid roof.

In the United States I received financial support from the Whiting Foundation, Columbia University, and Lewis and Clark College. Many thanks go to Madge Huntington at the Weatherhead East Asian Institute of Columbia University, as well as to Patricia Crosby and Cheri Dunn, at the University of Hawai'i Press, and Margaret Black, my copy editor, for shepherding this book into print. An earlier version of Chapter Three appeared as "Fire and Earth: The Forging of Modern Cremation in Meiji Japan" in the *Japanese Journal of Religious Studies* 27, 3–4 (Fall 2000).

Finally, I want to thank the members of my family—my grandmother, May-Britt, my mother, Eva, my father, Richard, my sister, Marian, my brother, Robert, and my partner, Jeffrey—for their love and support. They are the foundation of all my pursuits.

Abbreviations

CKKS   Chiso Kaisei Shiryō Kankōkai. *Chiso kaisei kiso shiryō.* 3 vols. Tokyo: Yūhikaku, 1953.

DJR   *Dajō ruiten.* Records of the Council of State, 1868–1881. 5 vols. Microfilm at Meiji University, Tokyo.

KD   Masugi Takayuki. *Kurowaku no dorama: Shibō kōkoku monogatari.* Tokyo: Sōyōsha, 1985.

MKS   Irokawa Daikichi and Gabe Masao, eds. *Meiji kenpakusho shūsei.* Tokyo: Chikuma Shobō, 1986–.

MSBS   Tsuji Zennosuke, Junkyō Washio, and Murakami Senshō, eds. *Meiji ishin shinbutsu bunri shiryō.* 1926. New Edition. 10 vols. Tokyo: Meicho Shuppan, 1983.

RR   Naimushō Chirikyoku, ed. *Reiki ruisan.* Records of Home Ministry Land Office, 1872–1887. Reprint in 10 vols. Tokyo: Tachibana Shoin, 1981. Footnotes refer to original volumes, some of which were compiled in 1884 and others in 1887.

SD   Katō Takahisa, ed. *Shinsōsai daijiten.* Tokyo: Ebisu Kōshō Shuppan, 1997.

SKH   Fujita Yukio, ed. *Shinbun kōkokushi hyakuwa.* Tokyo: Shinsensho, 1971.

SSM   Nakagawa Yasuaki, ed. *Shinbun shūsei: Meiji hennenshi.* 15 vols. Tokyo: Honpō Shoseki, 1982.

TKS   *Tōkyōto kōbunshokan shiryō.* Records of the Tokyo Metropolitan Government Archives.

TSS   Tōkyō Shiyakusho, ed. *Tōkyōshi shikō.* 1911–.

INTRODUCTION

*N*othing seems so unmodern as death. Modernity presents itself as newness continually renewed, casting aside worn-out pasts and extending into far-flung futures. Death, however, remains a steadfast check on worldly ambitions, no matter how extended our life spans become, no matter how limitless the future may appear. In the end, death exacts its due, and all societies, modern or not, face the inevitable question: what to do with the dead?

THE FUNERAL

It is a hot summer morning at a Buddhist temple in suburban Tokyo, 1997.[1] The air is filled with the scent of incense, together with the sound of cicadas and the sonorous chanting of two Buddhist priests. Tomiko, born nine decades earlier, has been dead for two days. She now lies in a coffin, her body surrounded by items traditionally marking a Buddhist pilgrim: a white robe, a walking stick, and a rosary. Keeping her cool on her voyage into the beyond are blocks of dry ice. An imposing altar *(saidan)*, constructed for the occasion by an undertaker and consisting for the most part of artfully arranged flowers, both fronts and flanks the coffin, hiding it from view. Wooden plaques rise from the flowerbeds at carefully planned intervals, displaying the names of family members, neighbors, and friends who have helped defray the cost of the funeral. Placed at the center of the altar, directly above the coffin, is a photograph of the deceased. It looms over a wooden mortuary tablet *(ihai)* displaying the characters that make up Tomiko's Buddhist name *(kaimyō)*, conferred posthumously to signify her entrance into the clergy and, it is hoped, into a

1

state of buddhahood. Throughout the proceedings of the day, she is, in fact, referred to as a "buddha" *(hotokesama)*, as are most of the dead in Japan.

Two priests, dressed in brilliantly colored robes, sit directly in front of the altar with their backs to the attendees. To one side of them sit Tomiko's children and grandchildren, who, like almost everyone in attendance, understand very little of the Buddhist scriptures and prayers that the priests are chanting. Unlike the priests, they do not face the altar. Instead, they are seated at an angle so that they can return small bows to the guests, all dressed in black and many grasping rosaries, who walk, one by one, up the temple stairs. At the entrance to the temple hall, its enormous doors flung open, each attendee quietly approaches a cloth-covered stand holding a censer and a box of powdered incense. Once there, each person adds a pinch of incense to the smoking censer, bows toward the "buddha," then bows toward the family members. Afterward, each one walks down the steps, wipes his or her hands on a towel offered by one of the undertaker's staff, and either leaves the temple grounds or waits quietly at the base of the stairs.

Some of these guests, including the members of Tomiko's flower-arranging club and neighborhood association, knew the dead personally. Most, however, are there not for the deceased but for the chief mourner *(moshu* or

Funeral altar. Photo by the author.

seshu), Tomiko's daughter, who is a respected university professor. Many of those offering incense are her colleagues, and it is her students who staff the tent-covered reception desk at the base of the stairs, collecting the gifts of cash (*kōden*, "incense offering" or "incense money") that each attendee hands over before proceeding up the temple steps. The students, four men and two women in their late teens and early twenties, carefully record the names of the donors and the amounts given by each. This is an important responsibility, since it will determine the value of the "return gift for incense money" *(kōden-gaeshi)* to be given to each attendee, which often takes the form of different grades of green tea delivered either days or weeks after the funeral. Also, if a family member of one of today's guests dies in the future, knowing how much the guest gave at Tomiko's funeral will help the members of Tomiko's family decide how much money they should give as attendees.

After about fifty people have paid their respects, the priests conclude their chanting by repeating several times, "Hail Amida Buddha" *(namu Amida Butsu)*,[2] the central figure in the Pure Land (Jōdo) sect to which this temple belongs. According to scripture, Amida resides in a paradise located to the west, where he welcomes into salvation those who recognize and call upon his grace. The priests take their leave, and the undertaker, a middle-aged woman wielding a microphone, announces over a loudspeaker the name and professional title of the chief mourner, a middle-aged woman herself. The undertaker then proceeds to read telegrams sent by people who could not attend the ceremony, after which she directs her three-man staff to dismantle the altar and open the lid of the coffin. Next, she invites relatives and close friends to approach the coffin and place flowers inside. Once they have done this, the coffin is nailed shut and carried by the students and funeral staff to a "shrine-style" *(miyagata)* hearse waiting just inside the gate to the temple. Its chassis is constructed of wood and gold and topped with an elaborate roof like those found on shrines and temples throughout Japan.

Attendees bow as the coffin is placed in the hearse, and before it drives away, the chief mourner, now holding the mortuary tablet with both hands, tells them that her mother is surely glad to be joining her husband in the after-life and honored that everyone has attended her funeral. The chief mourner's brother, standing at her side with their mother's portrait in hand, offers a brief word of thanks to the attendees. This is the cue for people to leave the temple grounds and for the family members, including distant relatives, to follow the hearse in several vans to the crematory.

At the municipal crematory, the undertaker's staff takes care of the bureaucratic paperwork required by law while the family assembles in front of the doors to a gleaming steel oven. One of the priests from the temple has accompanied them, and he resumes chanting as family members bow their heads, clutching rosaries. Free at last from the obligation of greeting guests, several of them, including the chief mourner, begin to weep, then openly sob, as the coffin is placed into the oven by a member of the crematory staff, who is attired in an official-looking hat and a starched white uniform. Once the doors are closed, the family members are ushered by the undertaker to a room where they eat, drink, and reminisce as Tomiko's body is cremated. An hour and a half later, they reassemble in front of the oven, and the remains are presented to them on a stainless steel cart together with a ceramic urn. Now calm and collected, the mourners step forward two by two and, under the watchful eye and direction of the crematory's uniformed staff member, lift the shrunken bones with large chopsticks and deposit them in the urn. The staff member

The chief mourner, holding the mortuary tablet, and her brother, holding the photograph, thank attendees for coming to their mother's funeral. Photo by the author.

collects the remaining bones and ash and puts them in the urn, which is enclosed in a carefully wrapped box and handed to the family.

It is mid-afternoon when the family returns to the temple where the funeral took place. At the gate stand two members of the undertaker's staff. They sprinkle the mourners with salt and offer them a ladle and a bucket of water so they may cleanse their hands as they enter the temple grounds. This is done to purify them of the death pollution *(kegare)* encountered at the crematory. Once inside, they take seats in the temple, this time facing a much more modest altar holding the box of remains. The priests chant once more, in a ceremony that had, for centuries, occurred seven days after the funeral to mark the first stage of the deceased's passage into the afterlife. The seventh-day ceremony is still eponymous in some regions, actually occurring on the seventh day after the funeral, but in a world where time equals money and relatives are often far-flung, it is increasingly performed on the day of the funeral itself.

Several weeks later the urn will be placed in a family grave behind the temple, joining the remains of Tomiko's husband and his parents. The grave is topped with a rectangular tombstone displaying the family name, standing in

A family visits a grave at a temple cemetery in Tokyo. The wooden slats behind the tombstone, called *tōba*, signify the stupas, or pagodas, that house the relics of the Buddha Shākyamuni and venerated Buddhist clerics across Asia. Placed at gravesites on designated holidays and death anniversaries, they display the Buddhist names of the dead. Photo by the author.

a line of similar tombstones all covering their own concrete cubicles that hold the urns of other temple parishioners. To these graves family members come at appointed times: once in the spring and fall and once during the summer "ghost festival" *(obon)*, when, it is said, the spirits of the deceased return to their families. Relatives also visit the graves at times determined by the individual deaths of those interred within them. It is customary to make visits to comfort the recently departed at forty-nine and then one hundred days after they have died. In fact, in much of Japan, it is at forty-nine days, the end of the Buddhist period of limbo between this life and the next, that the remains are placed in the grave, having been kept on an altar at home since the funeral. Rituals aimed at both comforting and honoring the dead occur at increasing intervals thereafter.[3] When asked whether she would regularly visit her mother in the years to come, Tomiko's daughter replied with a teary-eyed smile, "Of course. Sometimes she'll need a break from my father—and especially my grandmother."

PRESENTING THE PAST

The funeral rites just described are representative of those held in hundreds of towns and cities throughout Japan on any given day. Coordinated by professional undertakers, most are officiated by Buddhist priests and most incorporate the offerings of money and incense that cast social relations between family members and attendees into sharp relief. Moreover, virtually all funerals end in cremation, with family members expected to take on the ritual work of placing the remains in an urn and interring them in a family grave. Each death is handled according to individual circumstances—including the social position of the deceased, local customs, and religious beliefs—but it is possible to speak of a standardized, Japanese "way of death,"[4] a way that achieved its present form in the twentieth century.

This is not to say that key elements have not been long in the making. The practice with the longest pedigree is the use of water and/or salt to counter the dangers posed by death pollution. According to a Chinese document written in the third century, the inhabitants of Wa (the term then used to describe the Japanese islands) immersed themselves in water after each funeral as an act of purification.[5] When Buddhism entered Japan several centuries later,[6] it introduced a host of new rituals to cope with the danger of death. According to Buddhist priests, this danger confronted not only survivors but also the dead, who could (and probably would) pass into a hellish afterlife if not given proper care. Today's funerals feature Buddhist rituals that were embraced by the imperial court as early as the seventh century, and popularized among commoners in the centuries that followed, in order to guard against such a fate. These include, as we saw in the case of Tomiko, dressing the dead as a Buddhist pilgrim, devising a posthumous name, and offering incense.

Funerals have also long performed the function of displaying and negotiating social relations. From earliest times, in Japan as elsewhere, funerals have been conspicuous occasions to display wealth and status, to build or challenge communal solidarity, and to perpetuate lineages, biological and otherwise. Tomiko's death activated a social network whose main nexus was the chief mourner, her daughter. Her students staffed the reception desk to the funeral, and her colleagues at the university where she teaches comprised the bulk of the guests.

The central role played by Tomiko's daughter perpetuated tradition in one form even as it undermined it in another. Had this funeral occurred before the U.S. occupation of Japan (1945–1952), the role, indeed the duty, of chief mourner would almost certainly have fallen to her brother, who would have been mandated by law to inherit his family's assets and don the mantle of "lineage head" *(ienushi)*. Even at the end of the twentieth century, many Japanese continued to honor a ritual system favoring the eldest male, now under the aegis of custom instead of law. By assuming the position of chief mourner in place of her brother, Tomiko's daughter broke with that system. Yet, on a deeper, structural level, Tomiko's funeral continued the tradition of making the most socially powerful member of a mourning family—in this case, a daughter who was a well-respected professor at a prestigious university—the chief mourner. It was precisely *because* the longstanding social function of funerals was still intact in Japan at the end of the twentieth century that Tomiko's daughter, not her son, assumed the most honored role at the funeral.

Just as the old persists within the new, the new frequently passes for the old, a phenomenon created through a process that historians now commonly refer to as the "invention of tradition."[7] Impressed by the antiquity of many of its ritual elements, Japanese accept as tradition a way of death relatively recent in origin. Central to this way is the practice of cremation, today the taken-for-granted endpoint of virtually every Japanese. Cremation has been practiced in some form throughout Japan's recorded history, but this manner of dealing with the dead, now nearly universal, became dominant only in the twentieth century. In fact, for a short time in the 1870s, the government then ruling Japan outlawed the "barbaric" practice of cremation, a little-known piece of history that tends to surprise Japanese who learn of it. Although many communities embraced cremation only decades ago, burning the dead is now accepted as a national tradition that reaches far back into the past. The same can be said of the shrine-style hearse, a prominent feature at many funerals, including Tomiko's. Invented in the 1930s to replace funeral processions— made impractical by streetcar, then automobile, traffic—it was consciously clad in the material trappings of Buddhist and Shinto tradition. This legacy also inspired the design of increasingly elaborate altars that, together with the hearse, perpetuated the splendor formerly embodied by processions.

Thus, while elements of Japan's modern way of death arose in a premodern past, others date to the nineteenth and twentieth centuries, shaped by the same political, economic, and social forces that transformed Japan into an industrialized nation and a world power. Even those customs that passed relatively intact through the centuries, such as the offering of incense and the reading of Buddhist scriptures, were resituated and reconfigured by rapidly changing circumstances. Priests increasingly came to perform their time-honored function in settings controlled less by themselves than by commercial providers, who forced the clergy to make adjustments along the way.

Constituting the funeral rites of Japan, then, is an evolving negotiation of the new and the old, of traditions perpetuated and invented. Reaching as far back as the seventh century and as far forward as the 1990s, the following chapters trace this dynamic process over the sweep of Japanese history. While touching on both the recent and the distant past, they focus especially on the imperial period (1868–1945), when Japan underwent its rapid transformation into a global power. Initiated by the Meiji Restoration and terminated by Japan's defeat in World War II, these turbulent decades witnessed change on an unprecedented scale, and this was as true for the handling of death as for the conduct of daily life. As a confederated hierarchy of samurai domains metamorphosed into a constitutional state and an agricultural economy turned into an industrialized one, various groups pursuing differing and often conflicting aims—including Buddhist priests, Shinto nativists, journalists, intellectuals, bureaucrats, businessmen, and, of course, mourning families— struggled to find places for the dead, and the past, in a world continually on the move.

The conflicts and compromises that made up this struggle not only generated a national way of death, one that reached its maturity among the urban middle class by the 1930s and became increasingly popular in the decades that followed, they also contributed to a wider negotiation of the shifting boundaries between private and public, native and foreign, civilized and barbaric, religious and secular, local and national, superstitious and rational, traditional and fashionable. Examining how these categories were generated, separated, and joined through the changing practices surrounding death helps us to make sense of the "human shuffling of social feet"[8] that constituted modern Japan. The result is a tale of Japanese death rites that is, at the same time, a story of Japanese modernity.

MODERN DEATH IN GLOBAL PERSPECTIVE

From the eighteenth through the twentieth centuries, bureaucratic and commercial forces isolated the consequences of death from the business of everyday life. In industrializing nations around the globe, including Japan, dead city-dwellers were exiled to suburban cemeteries and outward displays of mourning were abolished so as not to disrupt the work of creating a future without delay. The modern restructuring of age-old death practices provoked a nostalgic response that was also global in scope: from the late nineteenth century, folklorists in various countries scrambled to record customs on the brink of extinction, producing "discourses of the vanishing"[9] that offered continuity in prose if not in practice.

Historians were slower to turn their attention to death, but they made up for lost time beginning in the 1960s. Two main factors explain the timing of this trend. One is the boom in social history, whose practitioners rejected political narratives of the elite in order to analyze changes to the everyday lives of ordinary people. Studying death was an attractive way to study those lives for the simple fact that death strikes everyone. A mid-century upsurge in studies about contemporary death also motivated historical research on the subject. Especially influential for historians was the work of British sociologist Geoffrey Gorer, who in 1955 coined the provocative phrase "the pornography of death" to describe the marginalization not only of funerary rites but also the very subject of mortality among the English middle and upper classes, arguing that it had replaced sex as a social taboo.[10] No sooner had Gorer proclaimed this taboo, however, than a succession of works concerning death began to fill bookshelves in England and elsewhere. In fact, international criticism of the funeral business reached a high water mark with the 1963 publication of Jessica Mitford's scathing and bestselling exposé of the U.S. death industry, *The American Way of Death*. In Japan too, intellectuals loudly advocated streamlined funerals shorn of "useless" excess. Five years after Mitford's book was released, for example, a group of Japanese doctors published a book bluntly called *Sōshiki muyōron* (On the uselessness of funerals).[11]

Countering the utilitarian reformers, pioneers of the history of death, like the folklorists, bemoaned the corrosive effects of modernity, writing works that adhered to a story line of decline and loss. A prominent example is Haga Noboru's *Sōgi no rekishi* (1970), which roundly condemns the rationalization and secularization of modern times for perverting what were supposedly heartfelt funeral rites of the past into empty spectacle. Haga exhorted his contemporaries to appreciate "the goodness of Japan that has been lost amid rapid [economic] growth,"[12] writing that what motivated him to study the historical origins of mortuary customs was to help his fellow Japanese discern "what should be preserved, what should be passed on. . . ."[13] The nostalgic tone in Haga's scholarship also pervades the work of French historian Philippe Ariès, who ambitiously charted changing attitudes toward death in Western Europe over the course of a thousand years. In the final chapter to *L'Homme devant la mort,* this scholar of the *longue durée* highlighted the recent decline of mourning practices, such as the donning of "crepe and voluminous black veils," that had been prevalent during his youth.[14] Agreeing with and building upon Gorer's thesis, Ariès introduced the expression *"la mort inversée,"* or "death reversed," to describe what he perceived to be a modern tendency to banish death from mind as well as sight.[15] Histories declaring death to be a fundamental "taboo" of modern life continued to appear over the next couple of decades. A notable Japanese example is Inoue Shōichi's *Reikyūsha no tanjō,* which invokes Gorer's concept of "the pornography of death" (via Ariès) to explain the replacement of funeral processions with motorized hearses in early- to mid-twentieth-century Japan.[16]

Since the 1990s a growing number of works have challenged the "denial of death" thesis, which had proved to be of limited utility to those seeking to understand not only the *dis*placement but also the *re*placement of death in the modern world. Writing about the history of cremation in America, for example, Stephen Prothero stresses that "death and its processes still demand ritual and stimulate meaning-making," despite the fact that "many steps in the American way of death have been taken out of the hands of family members and clerics. . . ."[17] Recent ethnographers of Japanese funerals also emphasize the positive creation of new approaches to death, providing a counterbalance to tales of decay and loss.[18] They do not deny that certain facets of death have been displaced from day-to-day living. Yet their work demonstrates that this phenomenon must be understood within a larger context, one in which people both create and perpetuate death practices as actively as they discard them. If this were not the case, funeral providers would have closed shop long ago.

Paying attention to the creative and not merely the destructive interaction between locally embedded practices and the standardizing forces of modernity helps us to avoid the common trap of reducing "modernization" to "Westernization." This is not to say that the latter did not play a role in the former. For example, during the reign of the Meiji emperor (1868–1912), the Japanese upper class adopted the European and American practice of publishing obituaries with black borders; and in planning the state funeral of Iwakura Tomomi (1825–1883), government officials consulted English military procedure to determine the appropriate number of gun salvos. The spread of cremation, however, took on a very different meaning in Japan than it did in England. Cremation became the dominant method of disposing bodies in both countries over the course of the twentieth century. Yet in England today it is common to scatter the ashes,[19] while in Japan cremation is a step to ensuring permanent resting places for the deceased in family graves.

It is also important to keep in mind that Japan does not stand in binary opposition to a unified "West" represented by England or by any other "Western" country. Rates of cremation versus full-body burial differ dramatically from one European country to another. And when it comes to the handling of remains, it is America—frequently portrayed as the modern nation par excellence—that is the exception rather than the rule among its (post-) industrialized peers. Ariès was flummoxed that America, "the most fertile center of modernity," had devised "ridiculous" rites centered on the embalming of the corpse,[20] a practice popularized during the Civil War to transport dead soldiers to their families. At the start of the twenty-first century, the American funeral industry continues to generate profits based on the nineteenth-century technology of embalming, radically distinguishing itself from its counterparts in both the "East" and the "West."

Modern societies, then, do not deny death so much as remake it, and how they do this is determined by a complex mix of global forces and parochial aims. Simply put, wherever it takes place, modern death has a history. This book tells how it happened in Japan.

POLITICS AND SOCIAL CHANGE

A person dies not in the singular, but in the plural. When Tomiko passed away at the age of ninety, she was at once a mother, a neighbor, a parishioner, and a friend. She was also many things to the different people who met her only in death or at the verge of it. To her doctors and nurses—who, according to convention, acknowledged their brief connection to Tomiko by making incense offerings in front of her dead body before it left the hospital—she was, first and

foremost, a patient. To the students of the chief mourner she mattered insofar as she was the mother of a professor who expected their logistical support.
To the undertaker she was the centerpiece of a funeral that contributed, along
with other such ceremonies, to the livelihood of herself and her staff. Finally,
to unseen bureaucrats who never came in direct contact with Tomiko, alive or
dead, she was a statistic to be counted and a corpse to be regulated.

The practices surrounding Tomiko's death reflected her multiple identities
and the interests attached to them, both differentiating and uniting those who
had known her in life while satisfying the impersonal demands of a capitalist
economy and centralized state. The funeral rites put attendees into ritual
motion according to conventions—such as the offering of sums of money
determined by one's relationship to the mourning family, or the exclusion of
nonfamily members from the crematory—that made clear each person's place
in a hierarchy governed, for the most part, by social proximity to the deceased
or the chief mourner. At the same time, the rituals provided an income to the
undertaker and her staff, and conformed to bureaucratic rules designed to
keep track of the population and guard public health against the improper disposal of corpses. What resulted was not only the public acknowledgement of
an individual death but also a display of social, commercial, and legal relations
between the living and the dead and among the living themselves, whether
they attended the funeral or not.

The following chapters show how these relations and the powers they entail
changed with and through death rites over time, especially in the nineteenth
and twentieth centuries. This dynamic process, in which the ritual and the
social mutually constructed each other, was driven by a variety of interests—
ranging from the saving of souls to the building of a nation-state—that could
be complementary but were often in conflict. Writing at the close of the Meiji
period, Hozumi Nobushige, the most influential architect of the imperial civil
code (1898) and one of the most prominent advocates of primogeniture and
ancestor reverence, made the following observation about the "blending of
the Past and Present" in ceremonies designed to honor and comfort the dead:

> To the Western eyes, the sight must appear strange of a Japanese family
> inviting their relatives, through the medium of telephone, to take part in
> a ceremony of this nature. Equally incongruous may seem the spectacle
> of members of a family, some of them attired in European and others in
> native costume, assembled in a room lighted by electricity, making offer-
> ings and obeisances before the memorial tablet of their ancestor. The

curious blending of the Past and Present is one of the most striking phenomena of Japan.[21]

This passage depicts modernity, the "Present" with a capital "P," in the form of material goods (the telephone, electric light, and European clothing) that appear to have been smoothly, albeit curiously, integrated into existing practice without substantively altering it. In reality, the combining of past and present was far more troubled, involving open clashes between parochial interest groups advancing distinct agendas. Buddhist clerics attempting to perpetuate their beliefs and practices and Shinto competitors trying to popularize "purely" native forms of worship fought bitterly over ritual turf. Bureaucrats trying to standardize Japan by using Euro-American methods collided head-on with the defenders of local tradition. Families competing to outdo each other in mortuary splendor, together with the burgeoning funeral industry that serviced them, faced attacks from advocates of thrift both in the government and outside it.

The history of Japanese death rites is composed of the interactions between these different groups, each of which made particular claims on the dead and gained or lost influence at particular junctures in time. Complicating the picture is the fact that these groups changed in composition and character as they pursued their different agendas, making the study of what changed in Japanese death rites inseparable from a study of the transformations undergone by those who made change happen. This twofold analysis provides the structural framework for the following chapters, each of which shows how death, the most intimate of events with the most public of consequences, was implicated in a reordering of relationships within and between the familial, communal, official, and civil spheres.

Providing a measure of stability throughout this historical process were the aims and expectations of mourning families and Buddhist priests, but they and the social networks in which they lived and died changed significantly over the centuries. During the Tokugawa period (1600–1868), a combination of government policy and social striving increasingly grouped extended families into corporate patrilines *(ie)*, lineages determined mainly by biological descent from a common ancestor although often sustained through the practice of adoption. From the mid-seventeenth century, the ruling shogunate required these lineages to register their affiliations with Buddhist temples, legally binding them to priests who were themselves regulated by a system of privileges and punishments specific to their clerical status.[22] This does not mean that priests and parishioners were placed into a simple relationship of dominators and dominated, for it was partly through their voluntary and lavish spending on Buddhist funerary ritual that patrilines vied for position in their communities—to the chagrin of Tokugawa officials who encouraged frugality and passed sumptuary laws—generally with limited success.

Patrilineal identity remained strong in the post-Tokugawa world, and was, in fact, reinforced by the Meiji civil code designed by Hozumi and other conservatives. Yet its demographic foundations perceptibly shifted as increasing numbers of Japanese established nuclear families in urban areas far from their villages of origin. For generations Buddhist temples had maintained a hold on the lineages affiliated with them. Yet after the early years of the Meiji period, when the imperial government instituted a number of measures that firmly separated Buddhism from the state—such as abolishing the requirement that Japanese register with Buddhist sects, seizing vast tracts of land donated to temples by the shogunate and daimyo (*daimyō,* domain lords), and demoting clerics to the status of commoners—their influence derived more from custom than from law. Given a choice not available under the shogunate, many of the freshly minted urbanites of imperial Japan did elect to maintain ties with ancestral temples in the countryside, sending cremated remains to be interred in the graveyards attached to them even if this attempt to maintain tradition on one level required a large number of Japanese to part with it on another, since most came from areas where full-body burial, not cremation, was the norm. Other Japanese who had moved from the countryside to the city chose, in contrast, to bury their dead (cremated or not) near their new homes, a trend that generated parishioners for urban and suburban temples while draining them from rural ones. Finally, whether or not they chose to send the dead back to ancestral communities, Japanese transplanted to urban areas, and particularly those who joined the growing middle class, produced funerals that both reflected and created new social networks—formed in schools, workplaces, and other locations in the modern landscape—that quickly grew as dense as those that had been in the making for generations, eventually eclipsing and displacing them.

As families, communities, and the Buddhist clergy changed, new groups emerged on the ritual scene, making their own contributions to the management of death. Some did so directly and others indirectly, some to greater and others to lesser effect. The one with the most radical and active ritual agenda was composed of anti-Buddhist, pro-Shinto nativists *(kokugakusha)* who desired to "return" Japan to a mythical state in which the emperor, his subjects, and native deities *(kami)* harmoniously interacted via "purely" Japanese forms of worship.[23] Nativism arose in the eighteenth century and came into its own in the nineteenth, when its practitioners mined the earliest imperial histories (dating to the eighth century) in order to construct an indigenous alternative to the widely accepted systems of belief and ritual that had long combined worship of deities particular to Japan with devotion to buddhas venerated across Asia.[24] The combinatory systems, which typically treated *kami* as the local manifestations of universal buddhas and were for the most part controlled by Buddhist temples, were unacceptable to the nativists, who worked hard at convincing fellow Japanese to embrace forms of Shinto ritual free of Buddhist taint. Although differing from one subset of nativists to another, these ritual formats were anchored by the imperial house, the ultimate this-worldly authority descended from, and in communication with, the otherworldly sun *kami* Amaterasu. Central to the nativist cause was the development of Shinto funerals: no easy task, since *kami* were thought to abhor the pollution generated by death. Moreover, because ancient Japanese texts provided only fragmentary evidence of pre-Buddhist death rituals, those seeking to invent a native funerary tradition drew upon, ironically, the Chinese teachings and protocol advocated by Confucian scholars, who themselves had long attacked the "unfilial" and "barbaric" practices of Buddhism, especially cremation.

Until the end of the Tokugawa period, campaigns against Buddhism, and against Buddhist death rites in particular, made little headway against a status quo enforced by the shogunate. So when the shogun's government fell to the leaders of the Meiji Restoration, the promoters of Buddhist-free funerals eagerly seized the opportunity to match a political revolution with a ritual one. Nativists numbered among the decision-makers of a new state that declared itself hostile to Buddhism and quickly enunciated the principle of the "unity of rites and rule" *(saisei itchi),* a policy that put the imperial house at the ritual center of governance and established the ideological foundation for a system of Shinto ritual sponsored and controlled by the state. In the years following the Restoration, prominent nativists and their allies worked to rid state ceremony and, ultimately, the entire nation, of Buddhism, making the replacement of Buddhist death rites with Shinto ones a cornerstone of their efforts.[25]

Consequently, nativists made history, but not as they had hoped. First, their anti-Buddhist campaign met strong resistance from the population at large, which was less interested in reviving a putative, pre-Buddhist antiquity that in ensuring the well-being of dead family members. To most Japanese, Buddhism was not a "foreign" teaching, but an integral part of their lives and deaths. Second, the Meiji state, particularly in its early years, was not a unitary entity; it was, rather, a collection of diverse officials pursuing goals frequently at odds with one another. While nativists sought to cast the new Japan in a supposedly ancient mold, other officials focused first and foremost on revising the so-called "unequal treaties" that had been signed by the shogunate with the United States and Europe in the wake of Commodore Matthew Perry's uninvited visit to Japan in 1853.[26] To counter gunboat diplomacy meant building a "wealthy country, strong army" *(fukoku kyōhei)*, to quote a popular slogan of the day. Bureaucrats in the Finance and Home ministries (Ōkurashō and Naimushō) accommodated the pro-Shinto, nativist agenda to the extent that it contributed to this task, which it did mainly by augmenting the charisma and authority of the emperor. When it did not, however, they forced it to take a back seat to the material aims of an industrializing nation-state. In dealing with the consequences of death, their overriding goal was not to promote Shinto belief and ritual. Instead, it was to keep the immediate reality of corpses from interfering with ambitious plans for the future.

This pragmatic approach towards death, more prophylactic than proactive, was starkly evident in the events leading up to and surrounding the Meiji state's prohibition on cremation. Instituted in 1873, only to be repealed in 1875, the ban was justified by supporters as a way to protect public health from the baneful effects of crematory smoke while putting an end to what nativists and Confucian scholars had long reviled as an immoral Buddhist practice. The ban proved to be unpopular, however, just like the Shinto funerals that were being promoted by nativists and sympathetic officials. Buddhist priests, intellectuals, and journalists used petitions and newspapers to pressure the government to overturn the ban; they argued that rotting corpses were far more deleterious to people's health than crematory smoke and that reducing bodies to bones and ash and placing them in family graves furthered the filial goal of keeping family members together after death. They were joined by pragmatic officials in the Meiji regime like Kanda Takahira (1830–1898), one of the originators of Japan's modern land tax system and at the time of the ban the governor of a major prefecture. He and other modernizers recognized that full-body burial required more space than the interment of cremated remains, consuming land that could be put to economically productive use. They were also converted to the position that cremation protected public health more than damaged it, swayed, in part, by scientific studies coming out of Europe on the dangers posed by rotting bodies. The ban was therefore rescinded, its ironic legacy being a broad-based consensus among the official and civil elite that cremation was good for families and good for the nation.

In responding to the cremation ban, both those for and those against the policy incorporated the modern concern for hygiene into the pursuit of their parochial aims. As a result, the new consensus in favor of cremation not only provided a starting point for growth in the cremation rate, eventually transforming what had once been a minority practice into a majority one, but also established that the protection of public health would be central to all future discussions of death and the disposal of human remains. It also contributed more broadly to the post-Restoration dialogue developing between officials (the *kan*) and self-appointed representatives of the "people" (the *min*).[27] The latter consisted of prominent clerics, intellectuals, journalists, and other members of the literate public who increasingly voiced their opinions not only by submitting petitions directly to the government, a practice inherited from the Tokugawa period, but also through newspapers founded after the Restoration. The fight over cremation was, in fact, one of the earliest debates chronicled by Japan's burgeoning national press, "creating a public" in the process.[28]

Notably, this debate and others did not weaken state control so much as strengthen it. Continuing a Tokugawa tradition of active but loyal opposition, the early Meiji elite tried as much as possible to change the hearts and minds of officials, not to oust them from power or undermine their authority. Although the cremation ban was a policy failure, the public appeals of its detractors reinforced acceptance of the fledgling imperial state as a legitimate arbiter for competing interests. Intent on working through official channels, cremation boosters ultimately succeeded in authorizing their agenda through the conversion of a hostile bureaucracy, thereby also fostering acceptance of the Meiji government as a forum for social change. The more fights that occurred in this forum, including the one over cremation, the more indispensable the forum became, setting the parameters for building the nation as a whole.[29]

After the fiasco of the cremation ban, the Home Ministry led the effort to disentangle the practical operations of nation-building as much as possible from the ritual agenda of the nativists. Choosing to secularize daily governance, officials from the late 1870s onward regulated cremation and burial almost solely in line with pragmatic aims such as efficient land use and the protection of public health, and they did so with approval from a civil sphere that, for the most part, considered such aims to be positive manifestations of "civilization and enlightenment" *(bunmei kaika),* a catchphrase for the Euro-American technologies, institutions, and practices that were rapidly remaking Japan.

This did not mean that government policy no longer clashed with popular opinion and practice. Bureaucrats and "enlightened" supporters encountered strong resistance to their modernizing, homogenizing policies when they undermined local practices that had been honored for generations. It was particularly difficult for the new order to accommodate the self-determination of communities whose burial customs were tied to deeply entrenched sectarian identities, most of them Buddhist in one form or another. The Meiji state recognized the autonomy of religious belief, explicitly conferring this liberty in its constitution (promulgated in 1889), but officials understood this concept, imported only recently from Christian nations, not to grant "freedom of religion" so much as to relegate people's faith to a private realm separate from, and, more importantly, subordinate to, a public interest determined by bureaucratic reason. To illustrate: municipal officials in Tokyo and the state officials who backed them saw it as within their rights to seize control of graveyards in the capital, declaring that they belonged to the city, not to the temples and their parishioners who had traditionally controlled them. Their purpose was not to interfere in the ritual life of Tokyoites, though that is, in the end, what happened. Instead, it was to ease the path of urban development. To defend their autonomy against encroachment by the state, the temple communities in Tokyo and communities across the nation invoked their religious liberty, although usually with the understanding that this liberty was a communal one conferred by tradition, not a personal one bestowed by nature. Because our ancestors did it this way, we need to do it too: that was the gist of their argument.

This line of reasoning gained increasing respect and force from the late 1880s and especially into the 1890s, when there developed a conservative backlash among officials and the wider public against the sweeping pace of change in the preceding decades.[30] The example was set on high. In 1890 advisors to the emperor drafted the widely disseminated Imperial Rescript on Education, which enjoined his subjects to "render illustrious the best traditions of your forefathers,"[31] a sentiment also enshrined eight years later in the patrilineal civil code. The positive reappraisal of tradition was also reflected in the government's approach to death rituals. Some bureaucrats, such as those in Tokyo, did not hesitate to meddle directly in the burial customs of the "people," but others defended communal traditions, and not so much for their content as for their status *as* traditions.

The desire to preserve notwithstanding, after Japan's entrance into the twentieth century, new developments advocated by no one in particular forced changes that were as influential as they were unplanned. A major case in point is the traffic jam, the unwelcome result of rapid urbanization combined with the industrialization of transport. Nobody asked for it, but this unwanted child of the modern world did more to cause mourning families in urban areas to abandon mobile funeral processions in favor of geographically fixed funeral ceremonies than any other factor, permanently changing the character of mortuary rites in metropolitan and, eventually, rural Japan.

There to facilitate and direct the change was a funeral industry that had been growing hand-in-hand with a largely urban, status-seeking middle class for several decades. Initially hired to outfit elaborate processions, undertakers adapted to the changing times by taking on ritual tasks once performed by relatives and neighbors. Transferring the splendor of defunct processions onto altars erected in homes and temples, undertakers not only built the ritual stage, but increasingly determined what was performed on it, putting them in an awkward yet lucrative partnership with Buddhist clerics.

None of this is to say that undertakers were merely heartless profiteers or that families were insincere in their mourning, as finger-wagging moralists claimed. The personal feelings that may or may not have been experienced in the context of particular death rites are, nevertheless, beyond the scope of this study. While acknowledging the power of emotion, it is important to clarify that a history of funerary practices and the public debates surrounding them entails questions, sources, and interpretations dramatically different from a history designed to analyze personal reactions to death, which are as numerous as the individuals who experience them. Although they intersect, "the history of dying, of death, of grief, of mourning, of bereavement, of funerals and of cemeteries are all distinct subjects, the relationship between which is at best complex and at worst obscure," observes David Cannadine, who adds, "any attempt to trace the evolution over time of an emotion like grief, or even to generalize about such an emotion at a given time in a given society, is an extraordinarily difficult, if not impossible task."[32] Private feelings do play a role in the pages ahead, but only insofar as they were transformed into public acts with public consequences.

"What to do with the dead?" In Imperial Japan, as elsewhere in the modernizing world, answering this perennial question meant continuing to rely on ancestral solutions. Even in times of turbulent change, as during the decades after the Meiji Restoration, few practices were as entrenched as those surrounding death. Funerals, burials, and other mortuary rites had developed over the previous centuries with the aim of building continuity in the face of loss. As Japanese coped with the economic, political, and social changes that radically remade their lives, they clung to the local customs and Buddhist rituals—such as sutra readings and incense offerings—that had, for generations, given meaning to death.

Yet death, it turned out, was not impervious to nationalism, capitalism, and all the other "isms" that constituted and still constitute the shape-shifter we call modernity. As Japan changed, so did the handling of the inevitable. Cremation grew from a minority practice into a majority one; urban traffic drove funerals off public streets and into private spaces; commercial funeral providers took over tasks once performed by community and kin. As these and other changes created new contexts for old rituals, Japanese faced the problem of how to fit them all together. "What to do with the dead?" was thus a question tied to a broader predicament, one that haunts all societies committed to rapid change: "What to do with the past?" This puzzle is at the heart of the modern experience, and how Japanese tried to solve it through their dealings with the dead is, in the end, the subject of this book.

CHAPTER I

OF BUDDHAS AND ANCESTORS

𝓕unerary rites in contemporary Japan are overwhelmingly Buddhist, and the performance of these ceremonies is the primary function of temples and their priests. This does not mean that most Japanese today understand the teachings of Buddhist sects or literally believe in their heavens or hells. When surveyed about religious attitudes, most Japanese tend to deny belief in a particular cosmology or doctrine. Nevertheless, the majority of these professed unfaithful regularly participate in religious activities and rituals, making them doers if not necessarily believers.[1] This especially holds true when it comes to Buddhist mortuary rituals, not only those occurring immediately at death, but also those taking place years thereafter. In one survey of Japanese adults taken in 1997, for example, 56.1 percent of respondents claimed not to believe in any religion at all.[2] Yet according to the same survey, 87.3 percent of respondents performed regular grave visits, while 77.5 percent offered incense and flowers to their ancestors at the family Buddhist altar *(butsudan)*.[3]

This powerful and enduring link between Buddhism, the living, and the dead was forged in the distant past, long before the late-nineteenth and early-twentieth-century developments that are the main concern of this book. Because we cannot make sense of those relatively recent developments without knowing what preceded them, this chapter reaches much further back in time to explain how Buddhism came to dominate Japanese death rites, tracing a history that begins with the ancient imperial court and ends in the Tokugawa period (1600–1868), commonly referred to as Japan's "early modern" age. Despite the apparent disconnect between belief and practice in contemporary Japan, the fact that Buddhism provided compelling explanations of the afterlife and specific procedures to navigate it was central to this history, as was the ability of Buddhism to transform polluted corpses, via cremation or sanctified burial, into lasting objects of reverence. In the process, Buddhism and its rituals also served the critical social function of creating and maintaining corporate patrilines *(ie)*, which structured familial relations initially among aristocrats, then samurai, and, eventually, commoners.

SAVING SOULS

It is impossible to isolate a single moment when Buddhist beliefs and practices entered the Japanese islands, but according to one of Japan's earliest chronicles, the eighth-century *Nihon shoki* (also known as the *Nihongi*), Buddhism was officially transmitted from the Korean peninsula in the year 552, when the king of Paekche presented to the imperial court a statue of Shākyamuni Buddha[4] along with a number of Buddhist scriptures *(sutras)*.[5] Several aristocratic clans opposed the introduction of foreign worship, arguing that it would anger the native *kami* (deities).[6] But one, the Soga, threw its support behind Buddhism, and over the next several centuries Buddhist practices were integrated into the court's ceremonial complex.

At the center of this complex was the Yamato clan, the imperial lineage that traced its origins to the sun *kami*, Amaterasu. This clan consolidated its power from the fifth to eighth centuries,[7] and it did so by exerting military force, manipulating native *kami* worship, and adopting institutions, technologies, and belief systems—including Buddhism—from the continent. What we know about death rites in early Japan comes mainly from records, the *Nihon shoki* foremost among them, whose chief aim was to legitimate this process of creating a court-centered state.

These records tell us little about the practices of commoners, but they do reveal that the imperial court began embracing Buddhist teachings and rituals concerning death as early as the seventh century. Facilitating this process was the fact that native *kami* worship lacked systematic explanations of the afterlife that could compete with the elaborate cosmology and soteriology of Buddhism. In fact, the term Shinto (the way of the *kami*) in ancient and medieval Japan did not stand for an independent religion with explicit doctrines, but simply referred to those matters that concerned the *kami*, who, for most of Japanese history, were interpreted to be avatars of buddhas.[8]

Of the Buddhist rituals designed on behalf of the dead, the one that Japanese courtiers seem to have practiced first is *urabon*,[9] commonly rendered into English as the "ghost festival."[10] Celebrated as early as 538 C.E. by Emperor

Wu (r. 502–549) of China's Liang dynasty,[11] the ghost festival amalgamated the Chinese cult of filial devotion and ancestor worship with the cosmology and ritual practices of Buddhism. When this teaching from India entered China during the first several centuries C.E., it encountered a highly articulated system of rites and values centered on reverence for one's parents and more distant ancestors. Asked what it meant to be filial, Confucius (551–479 B.C.E.) reportedly said, "When your parents are alive, comply with the rites in serving them; when they die, comply with the rites in burying them; comply with the rites in sacrificing to them."[12] The Han dynasty classic *The Book of Filial Duty (Xiao jing)* also underscored the importance of offering sacrifices to one's ancestors, and especially one's dead parents, who, in turn, would repay the favor with their benediction.[13] Indian Buddhist teachings encouraged those seeking enlightenment to leave their kin and join communities of clerics *(sangha)*, an act that could potentially sever the mutually beneficial ties between descendants and ancestors. But the ghost festival, which required participants to make offerings of food and other items to their dead relatives via living clerics, instead made monks "an essential party in the cycle of exchange linking ancestors and descendants," placing them at "the very heart of family religion." By renouncing the everyday world of family relations, Buddhist clerics were able to acquire spiritual technology that could then be channeled back into the cult of the dead. It is significant that the timing of the festival in the seventh lunar month put it right after the summer meditation retreat, taking advantage of the "store of power" generated over that period.[14]

With this power, monks were able to direct benefits more efficiently to ancestors than could descendants themselves, particularly if the dead were condemned to a miserable existence. In fact, the presumption underlying the ghost festival was that ancestors were, or very well might be, suffering in the afterlife, a belief contingent upon a Buddhist universe richly furnished with punishing underworlds. Buddhist scriptures commonly recognize six major existences, or "paths,"[15] into which beings are continually reborn—that is, unless they have attained perfect enlightenment. These are the realms of heavenly beings, humans, titans, animals, hungry ghosts, and hell dwellers. The logic of the ghost festival, articulated through a vast literature featuring the efforts of the disciple Maudgalyāyana[16] to rescue his mother from hell, is that deceased relatives are most likely not enjoying the fruits of paradise, but are in desperate need of salvation. This threat of damnation fueled not only the spread of the ghost festival, which is today one of the most popularly observed holidays in Japan, but also encouraged the incorporation of clerics into the mortuary rites determined by individual deaths.

When Buddhist monks and nuns began participating in aristocratic funerals during the seventh century, their merit-generating powers were drawn into a local variant of "double burial."[17] For deceased members of the imperial family, at least male ones, this entailed constructing a court of temporary interment *(mogari no miya),* where the dead were installed for a period of months or years before final entombment. Inside, women who had engaged in sexual relations with the deceased performed rituals designed to call back the spirit of the deceased. Meanwhile, in the vicinity of the temporary structure, courtiers delivered politically charged eulogies aimed at securing advantages during the succession process.[18] After the death of Emperor Temmu (?–686), Buddhist monks and nuns reportedly "made lament" in this structure over a four-day period.[19] What their "lament" actually entailed in this context is unclear, but their involvement can be viewed as an extension of the role they played in trying to stave off the death of the emperor in the first place. When Emperor Temmu had first fallen ill, prayers were directed to Yakushi, the medicine buddha, in hopes of a cure. Orders followed in subsequent weeks to clean pagodas and temple halls, distribute alms to priests, recite sutras, and induct new monks and nuns into the clergy.[20] Buddhist activity also extended beyond the period immediately following Temmu's demise. Exactly one year after the emperor died, a "national feast of vegetable food was given in the Temples of the capital," and another Buddhist feast celebrating Temmu was held eight years from the day of his death.[21]

In this fashion Buddhist clerics were integrated into a long-term process of both assisting and honoring the dead. Over the centuries following Temmu's death, this process was systematized according to an explicitly Buddhist paradigm of belief and ritual that displaced the former "double burial" system along the way. Central to this paradigm was the forty-nine-day Buddhist limbo (*chūin* or *chūu* in Japanese) separating one lifetime from the next. This indeterminate state, which began with death and ended in rebirth in one of the "six paths," provided an extended opportunity for the living to intercede on behalf of the dead with sutra readings and ritual offerings. For example, after the death of Emperor Shōmu in 756, records show that special services were held every seven days for forty-nine days, each one marking his progress through limbo.[22]

One could hope that the deceased's own store of merit would propel him or her into a heavenly state, but Buddhism thrived wherever it took root by implanting the fear that the dead were not enjoying the fruits of paradise, but were, rather, in desperate need of salvation. Over the centuries that followed, ceremonies that channeled the transfer of merit (*ekō*) through ritual offerings *(kuyō)* spread through descending levels of society. The author of one thirteenth-century work noted that it was commonplace for even "miserably poor men and women" to offer incense, flowers, and light to lead dead spirits to salvation.[23] As the practice of merit transfer filtered down from the aristocracy to commoners, so did the belief in the "ten kings," deities of both Indian and Chinese origin who presided over underworld courts through which the dead were required to pass. Belief in the ten kings emerged in China in the tenth century, it seems, and was soon adopted in Japan as well.[24] Seven of the kings and their courts corresponded to the original seven weeks of Buddhist limbo, becoming the focus of offerings made in that period, but the three others were appeased at intervals of 100 days, one year, and three years after death. The belief in the ten kings also generated devotion to the bodhisattva Jizō,[25] who was thought to help the dead in their journey through the purgatorial court system. From the twelfth to fourteenth centuries the period of intercession was extended in Japan even further by the addition of seven-year, thirteen-year, and thirty-three-year services. The ten kings were said to be the avatars of different buddhas, and the three extra services were associated with buddhas in their original forms.[26] Incorporated into a system designed to boost the standing of the dead at regular intervals, the mortuary practices immediately following a death comprised just one step—albeit a crucial one—in managing the afterlife.

It is important to note that those who assisted the dead were not motivated purely by filial devotion. Funerary rituals also functioned as a defensive measure against the possibility of *tatari*—retribution from the spirit realm. An unhappy ghost equaled an angry ghost, and literature from the Heian period (794–1185) and beyond is replete with stories of vengeful spirits *(onryō)* attacking the living. Samurai warriors who seized the reins of political power from the imperial court at the end of the Heian period and placed Japan under different versions of samurai rule until the Meiji Restoration in the nineteenth century, found it just as important to appease dead enemies as well as dead kin, so they worked to ensure their escape from a hellish existence and facilitate their rebirth, ideally, in the Pure Land.[27] Victorious samurai did this by sponsoring Buddhist services on behalf of their slain foes and erecting markers in their honor.[28]

Until the middle of the Kamakura period (1185–1382) the mortuary rites immediately following death, whether for enemies or loved ones, were cobbled together from a number of sources since there were no authoritative liturgies to structure them.[29] Over the next several centuries, however, different Buddhist sects began adopting standardized funeral services, with the Sōtō and

Rinzai Zen lineages leading the way. This was accomplished by importing formats for clerical funerals systematized in Song China (960–1279). These funerals combined Buddhist elements such as cremation, sutra readings, and incense offerings with age-old Confucian norms, including ritualized washing and dressing of the corpse and the carving of a mortuary tablet *(ihai)* for enshrinement of the deceased.[30]

Like their counterparts in medieval Europe, wealthy lay patrons of temples —consisting of courtiers and powerful samurai—desired elaborate obsequies for themselves. They therefore planned to be ordained just before they died, which would entitle them to the same honors accorded a Buddhist monk and would, in effect, embed the worldly family lineage that they either hoped to found or perpetuate in a sacred lineage extending back to Shākyamuni himself.[31] One could even join the clergy after death via postmortem ordination. Under this increasingly popular scheme, the deceased received the precepts and were presented with Buddhist names *(kaimyō)* and lineage charts *(kechimyaku)*.[32] Eventually, the postmortem ordination was taken as evidence that the dead had become a full-fledged buddha, or *hotoke,* which is today the most common way to refer to a dead person in Japan.

Once clerical funerals were adopted by lay people, they did not stay con-

Giving the tonsure to the deceased. From *Sketches of Japanese Manners and Customs,* by J. M. W. Silver.

fined to the rich and powerful. Several collections of Sōtō Zen funeral sermons from the fourteenth and fifteenth centuries indicate that most, in fact, were performed for commoners of relatively low social status.[33] Naturally their funerals did not include all the finery accorded to wealthy patrons, but they featured shared elements that form the ritual backbone of the Japanese funeral ceremony as we know it today: choosing an ordination name *(kaimyō)* and inscribing it on a mortuary tablet *(ihai);* offering incense, food, and light *(kuyō);* and chanting sutras and *dhāranis* (magical formulas).[34]

FROM POLLUTED CORPSES TO SACRED REMAINS

The dead consisted of not only souls but also bodies, and saving the former entailed dealing with the latter. To do this, in turn, meant confronting a deep-rooted aversion to the pollution *(kegare)* generated by death, an aversion explained in large part by the material reality of rotting corpses.

This unpleasant fact is made explicit in the myth of Izanagi and Izanami, the two *kami* who together created the Japanese islands. According to the *Kojiki*—a compilation of imperial mythology written, like the *Nihon shoki,* in the eighth century—Izanami died after giving birth to the fire *kami* and was consigned to the land of Yomi, an ill-defined netherworld comparable to the Hades of Greek mythology. Her distraught husband Izanagi decided to follow her there and bring her back to the world of the living. He was initially welcomed by his wife, on the condition that he not look upon her; but despite the warning he lit a fire and saw maggots "squirming and roaring" in her body. Horrified, he fled, and the shamed Izanami dispatched the denizens of Yomi to chase him, in the end joining the pursuit herself. Escaping the underworld, Izanagi blocked access to it with a large boulder, afterwards declaring, "I have been to a most unpleasant land, a horrible, unclean land. Therefore I shall purify myself." He then proceeded to perform ablutions in a river, in the process creating more *kami,* including the sun goddess, Amaterasu.[35]

Izanagi's mythical act reflected historical practice. According to a Chinese account written in the third century, it was customary for Japanese to immerse themselves in water after funerals.[36] In the centuries that followed, they also devised ways to reduce the exposure of *kami* to death pollution. Court and shrine rules established in the Heian period (794–1185), for example, required those in mourning, or those who had simply come in contact with the dead, to refrain from serving the punctilious *kami* for at least a month.[37] These rules contributed to a larger system of fastidious codes designed to shield *kami* from *kegare* in all its forms, whether it was caused by the death of a person or by blood-tainted events such as the butchering of an animal, childbirth, or menstruation.

Buddhist priests also subscribed and contributed to prevailing notions about *kegare*. During the Kamakura period (1185–1382), monks of the Ritsu sect who participated in funerals did not touch corpses, leaving their disposal to "lower-class affiliates."[38] But Buddhist clerics in Japan also took active measures to confront the danger of *kegare*, drawing on teachings of universal compassion and salvation to develop a niche as pollution-management experts.

This was evident in funerals for women, who, according to Buddhist doctrine, were polluted due to childbirth and menstruation, making them unfit to attain buddhahood. In response, Japanese clerics devised strategies to counteract the ill effects of this distinctively female form of *kegare*. One commonly used by Sōtō priests was to incorporate copies of the *Ketsubonkyō* (Menses scripture) into funerals held for women on the premise that it could save them from the torments of "blood pool hell"—to which they would ordinarily be doomed because of menstruation during their lifetimes.[39] Measures taken to "rescue" women from this fate served, of course, to reinforce its threat, perpetuating the lucrative intervention of priests in a continuous cycle of hope and despair.

Also, while some Buddhist clerics avoided physical contact with dead bodies—male or female—other priests, fortified by their faith in the saving power of the buddhas, took the opposite approach. According to Kamo no Chōmei's (1155–1216) early-thirteenth-century devotional memoir, the *Hōjōki*, when a famine struck the capital toward the end of the Heian period, so many dead bodies were left to rot by the banks of the Kamo River that "there was not even room for horses and cattle to pass." In response, "the Abbot Ryūgyō of the Ninnaji, grieving for the countless people who were dying, gathered together a number of priests who went about writing the letter A on the forehead of every corpse they saw, thus establishing communion with Buddha."[40]

Buddhist teachings and rituals were also incorporated into the regular disposal of the dead, especially through the practice of cremation, which transformed rotting bodies into sacred relics that could be installed in reliquaries. According to the eighth-century history *Shoku Nihongi*, cremation was introduced to Japan by the Buddhist priest Dōshō (629–700), who was burned on a funeral pyre in 700. The cremation of Empress Jitō (645–703) followed three years later, establishing a precedent among the aristocracy.[41] Recent archeological evidence shows that cremation was practiced in Japan well before

Dōshō's time, and the written record suggests that not all cremations in the centuries immediately following Dōshō's funeral were motivated by Buddhist beliefs.[42] By the middle of the Heian period, however, cremation had become closely tied to Buddhist belief and ritual.[43]

There is no scriptural injunction within the Buddhist canon requiring cremation. In fact, Buddhist texts commonly recognize four different ways to dispose of a corpse: earth burial *(dosō),* water burial *(suisō),* exposure in the wild *(fūsō,* literally, "wind burial"), and cremation *(kasō).*[44] Nevertheless, because it was believed that Shākyamuni Buddha had been cremated, aristocrats and then commoners came to regard the practice as particularly meritorious, a means to "becoming a buddha" *(jōbutsu).*[45] Just as the relics of Shākyamuni were enshrined, so too were the cremated remains of those aspiring toward buddhahood (or at least a Buddhist paradise). Some were transported long distances to locations considered particularly sacred, such as the temple complex on Mt. Kōya.[46]

The cremation itself served a pedagogical function. While the remains produced by cremation may have been invested with a measure of immortality, burning bodies starkly exhibited the Buddhist teaching of *mujō,* the impermanence of all things. In his miscellany *Tsurezuregusa* (ca. 1340), Zen monk Yoshida Kenkō (1283–c. 350) made the following poetic reference to the cremation grounds at Toribeyama, near Heian (Kyoto): "Were we to live on forever—were the dews of Adashino never to vanish, the smoke on Toribeyama never to fade away—then indeed would men not feel the pity of things. . . . Truly the beauty of life is its uncertainty."[47]

Funeral sermons were more direct, containing "vivid references to the burning flames of the cremation fire, forcing the audience to confront the finality of death."[48] Believers were exhorted not to fear death but to accept it as the natural complement to life. A positive function was therefore ascribed to the cremation fire, making it a source of spiritual transformation. "Where the red fire burns through the body, there sprouts a lotus, blossoming within the flames," reads one sermon.[49] Lay observers often interpreted the transformative power of cremation in more literal terms. For example, "many laymen who witnessed the Zen funeral of Prince Yoshihito [d. 1416] . . . reportedly believed that the cremation fires liberated his spirit *(tamashii)* from his body."[50] Englishman Richard Cocks took note of this belief in the early seventeenth century. After describing the arrangements that had been made for a cremation, he mentioned in his diary, "And they verely think that, when the body is consumed, the sole flieth directly for heaven. . . ."[51]

It appears that cremation remained limited primarily to the imperial family and to aristocratic clans like the Fujiwara until the Kamakura period (1192–1333). But from this time on, it spread among commoners along with popular Buddhism, and by the seventeenth century it was prevalent enough for one Confucian scholar to note (disapprovingly), "there are very few places in the sixty-odd provinces that do not perform cremation."[52] Because of the example set by Jōdo Shinshū founder Shinran (1173–1262), who asked to be cremated upon his death and whose remains were later interred at the sect's head temple *(honzan),* it took a particularly strong hold in regions with a high percentage of Shinshū believers, including present-day Niigata, Toyama, and Ishikawa prefectures. The funeral of Shinshū patriarch Rennyo (1415–1499) demonstrated the religious fervor that cremation could unleash among followers of the sect. According to contemporary accounts, once the fire consuming his body had cooled, crowds of believers vied over Rennyo's charred remains, some even stuffing their mouths with his ashes. Those less fortunate apparently had to be satisfied with the surrounding earth and stones.[53] By the middle of the Tokugawa period, it had become commonplace among many Shinshū families to send cremated remains to the head temple in Kyoto for interment alongside Shinran, Rennyo, and other luminaries. Consequently Shinshū believers often did not bother to build individual graves at home.[54]

Notable funerals, like Rennyo's, warranted the building of enclosed structures in which to burn the dead. For ordinary cremations a shallow pit filled with brush and wood sufficed. These cremations were often performed by the relatives of those who had died, assisted by fellow villagers who acted according to local traditions. For example, in one village located in what is now Akita prefecture, it was customary during the Tokugawa period for every family to place two bundles of straw under the eaves of their houses whenever someone in the community died. These would then be collected and brought to the cremation ground to be used as fuel. Gender was frequently a factor in determining the roles involved in cremation. In a village in the northern section of today's Fukui prefecture, for example, convention dictated that only men accompanied the body to the cremation grounds and only women went to collect the remains.[55]

Cremations in many regions were performed by ordinary villagers according to communal traditions, but in those where the concern about death pollution was particularly strong—near Heian (modern-day Kyoto) and Nara, for example—the task was performed by a professional class of crematory and graveyard caretakers called *onbō.* Two sets of characters can be used to write this term. One refers simply to a Buddhist monk or his residence, while the other roughly translates into "shadowy death." This dual meaning is appropriate for a group of people who were viewed as quasi-religious figures but also shunned as outcasts contaminated by their regular contact with death. Living in settlements segregated from nearby villages, in many respects, *onbō* were treated as ordinary *kawata* (leather workers), outcastes who were defiled through occupations such as butchering animals and collecting night soil that brought one in contact with *kegare*. In legal documents from the Tokugawa period, *onbō* were consistently mentioned alongside the *kawata*, known derogatorily, and legally, as *eta* (highly polluted).[56] *Onbō* sought to distinguish themselves by tracing their roots back to the Nara-period monk Gyōki (668–749), who, in addition to his work in building the great temple Tōdaiji, was also known for establishing graveyards throughout western Japan. Based on the authority of this lineage, these *onbō*, also known as *sanmai hijiri*,[57] consolidated their control over cremation and burial in western Japan during the Tokugawa period. They may have been segregated from ordinary villagers, but by the same token, their settlements were free from taxation. Creating a network of guilds centered on the great Nara temple Tōdaiji, in many villages they enjoyed monopolistic privileges over the handling of the dead and defended these privileges fiercely when they were challenged.[58] Elsewhere, cremations were performed in temple precincts or in special "cremation temples" *(kasōdera)* affiliated with them. In these places, such as the cremation grounds clustered in the Senju district of Edo, *onbō* seem to have functioned more like temple employees than as independent monopolists.[59]

Thus in the centuries after its introduction from the continent, Buddhism was firmly linked to the remains, as well as the souls, of the dead. This was achieved not only through cremation but also through the more straightforward and less resource-consuming practice of full-body burial, which, despite the merit supposedly conferred by cremation, was the more popular choice for disposal in Japan until the twentieth century.[60] To make sure that the dead received adequate care, families and communities situated temples by graveyards and graveyards by temples. Whether above ground or below, in temples or near them, resting places of the dead thus became ritual sites supervised either by Buddhist priests or their lay followers, matching fear of pollution with respect for remains. As in medieval Europe, where the desire to be buried in consecrated ground undermined the old Roman law of burying the dead beyond town limits, the idea that saving souls meant maintaining contact with bodies drew the deceased into villages and urban areas, where they coexisted with the living. Rotting corpses, in addition to cremation remains, invaded even Heian, despite the fact that eighth-century burial regulations had explicitly banned dead bodies from the imperial capital.[61] Sacralization thus won out over sanitation, regardless of persisting concerns about the *kegare* generated by death.

LAW, LINEAGE, AND LUXURY

Funeral ceremonies differed according to sect and region, incorporating local beliefs and practices. But it is fair to say that, through standardized funeral ceremonies, the cremation and burial of corpses, and long-term care for the deceased, the Buddhist clergy created a comprehensive framework for ritualized death management that encompassed all of Japan by the start of the Tokugawa period. Caring for the dead, both body and soul, was, in fact, one of the chief reasons for the temple-building boom between the late fifteenth and early seventeenth centuries that solidified the presence of Buddhist sects in even the remotest villages.[62]

The Tokugawa shogunate (1600–1868) took advantage of this reach as it established its political hegemony, enforcing measures designed to ensure that Japan would not devolve again into a collection of warring samurai as it had during the sixteenth century. In order to weaken their local power base and drain their coffers, and thereby head off potential revolts against Tokugawa rule, the shogunate transformed daimyo into officials who were required to live in Edo every other year and to leave their families behind when they returned to the domains *(han)* under their control. It also instituted a policy of restricting foreign trade to the Dutch, Chinese, Koreans, Ainu, and Ryūkyūans, and limited their operations to the domain of Tsushima (an island between Japan and Korea), portions of Hokkaido (controlled by the Matsumae domain in northern Honshu), and Nagasaki, in Kyushu. Except under very limited circumstances, no Japanese was permitted to leave the home islands.

As part of its efforts to consolidate power, the shogunate also asserted its authority over Buddhist temples, some of which had accumulated enormous wealth and influence over the prior millennium. Early in the seventeenth century the regime ordered that all temples be officially divided into sects, each headed by one main temple; demanded that these sects clarify their doctrines and rituals; imposed an exam system for the selection of head priests; and established the Office of Temples and Shrines (Jisha bugyō) to ensure that the shogunate's policies were enforced.[63]

In the mid-1600s an even more intrusive and, for the history of death rites, more significant, policy was put into effect: the enforced registration of every family in Japan at a local Buddhist temple. The so-called "parishioner household system" *(danka seido)* was devised in response to the perceived threat of Christianity, introduced to Japan by Portuguese missionaries in the sixteenth century. The first of the pre-Tokugawa "unifiers," Oda Nobunaga (1534–1582), treated the confreres generously, and during the 1500s several daimyo and thousands of ordinary Japanese converted to the teaching of Deus, especially in Kyushu. But Nobunaga's successor Hideyoshi Toyotomi (1537–1598) viewed the Christian mission as a threat to his sovereignty and in 1587 banished the foreign padres from Japan, outlawing Christianity entirely in 1591. After the Tokugawa prevailed, the new regime adopted the anti-Christian policy, expanding it into a full-fledged persecution after restive Christians instigated the Shimabara Rebellion of 1637–1638. In the wake of this insurrection in Kyushu, the shogun ordered all Japanese to register with a particular Buddhist temple to prove that they were not Christians.[64]

Over the following decades this "rectification of sect" *(shūmon aratame)* policy developed into a standardized system of surveillance, making Buddhist priests agents of a regime focused, to an unprecedented degree, on making the entire population of Japan "legible"—in other words, observable and therefore vulnerable to the mechanisms of government.[65] An important step in accomplishing this was the shogunate's 1664 order to daimyo to set up their own shrine and temple offices, primarily to make sure that those living (and dying) in their domains were properly registered as the parishioners of specific temples. Then, in 1671, the shogunate provided them with guidelines specifying that local officials should record not only the sectarian affiliation of each family but also the age and sex of its members, as well as their deaths, births, and any changes of residence.[66]

For the remainder of the Tokugawa period Buddhist temples participated in this registration system both by certifying sectarian affiliation and by reporting deaths to domain and/or shogunate officials. Before it was implemented, individual members of a particular family might belong to different sects, but the policy coming out of Edo forced them to affiliate with temples by corporate patriline, each one headed, ideally, by a male. These affiliations were then frozen without regard to personal beliefs, as parishioners were obligated by Buddhist clerics—under the threat of being labeled Christians or adherents of other doctrines deemed dangerous[67]—to participate in the ghost festival and other communal, yearly rituals of their designated temples. They were also required to pay the priests who monitored them for the performance of funerary rites for both the recently and long departed, facing sanctions if they did not.[68]

Grouping all Japanese into ancestor-venerating family units registered with specific temples contributed to the larger Tokugawa project of constructing and enforcing a status system *(mibunsei)* meant to put each person—whether samurai or peasant, merchant or outcaste—in clearly designated "containers" determined by occupation and birth.[69] This meant not only reinforcing the legitimacy of those at the top but also the place of those at the bottom. The most obvious and odious way in which Buddhist temples did this was to assign outcastes insulting posthumous names, using Chinese characters meaning "beast" or "less than human."[70] This fate was shared by the *kawata,* who inherited their place in society from birth, as well as the *hinin* (literally, "nonpersons"), registered beggars who had become outcastes due to crime or misfortune.[71]

The irony is that although the parishioner household system did help the government to enforce the status quo, by fostering a sense of lineal descent among all strata of society, it also undermined that very goal. There were those who strained under the financial burden of forced contributions to their temples, but others took advantage of the mandated affiliations and their attendant rituals to seek higher status, challenging the stability sought after by the government. Indeed, funerals and the erection of tombstones boasting impressive posthumous names became important tools in the competition for social prestige, powered by Tokugawa economic trends that generated increasing levels of wealth among broadening segments of the population.

Commoners seeking models for luxurious funerals looked to those of the courtier and samurai elite. By the beginning of the Tokugawa period, a mentality of "more is more" had generated sumptuous funeral processions that were as much expressions of economic and political power as they were instances of filial piety and spiritual devotion. In 1565 the Catholic missionary Luis Frois wrote a letter in which he described one such procession in Kyoto. Translated into English by Richard Willes in 1577, it reads in part:

> About one hour before the dead body he [sic] brought forth, a great multitude of his friends, apparelled in their best array, go before unto the [cremation] fire. . . . Each woman hath with her also, according to her ability, all her family trimmed up in white silk moccado: the better sort and wealthier women go in litters of cedar, artificially wrought, and richly dressed. In the second place marcheth a great company of footmen sumptuously appareled. Then afar cometh one of the Bonzii [Buddhist priests], master of the ceremonies for that superstition, bravely clad in silks and gold, in a large and high litter excellently well wrought,

accompanied with 30 other Bonzii, or thereabout, wearing hats, linen albes, and fine black upper garments.

Frois also describes the mortuary tablet and the "gorgeous litter" in which the corpse, "clothed in white, hanging down his head, and holding his hands together like one that prayed," was carried.[72] Following the dead man, in addition to the children, were

> well near 200 Bonzii . . . singing the name of that devil[73] the which the party deceased chiefly did worship by his life time, and therewithal a very great basin is beaten, even to the place of fire, instead of a bell. Then follow two great paper baskets hanged open at the staves ends, full of paper roses butterfly colored: such as bear them do march but slowly, shaking ever now and then their staves, that the aforesaid flowers may fall down by little and little, as it were drops of rain, and be whirled about with the wind. This shower say they is an argument that the soul of the dead man is gone to Paradise.[74]

Of course those of lower status could not afford such sumptuous affairs. Frois writes, "great rich men do spend in these funerals, 3,000 ducats or there-

A daimyo funeral procession. From *Sketches of Japanese Manners and Customs*, by J. M. W. Silver.

about, the meaner sort two or three hundred," but that "[s]uch as for poverty be not able to go to that charges, are in the night time, darkelong without all pomp and ceremonies, buried in a dunghill."[75] The difference between burial of the poor and the great was, quite literally, the difference between night and day. Apparently, the ideal set by the rich was so high that those who could not measure up quietly buried their dead under the cover of darkness.

The pressure to meet high standards intensified in the Tokugawa period, as the expansion of a money economy fueled the desire and created the means to advance one's status through displays of conspicuous consumption. This caused no end of hand-wringing among the ruling elite. Especially troublesome for the shogunate were well-to-do townspeople *(chōnin)*, especially the upstarts in Edo and Osaka, who dared to sponsor grand funerals that aped and even trumped those of high-ranking samurai. The gaudiness of their funerals was rebuked in a short story that appeared in a popular volume published in Edo in 1752, the *Imayo heta dangi* (Awkward lessons of this world).[76] The story consists of two parts. The first is a mock leaflet distributed by the owner of a palanquin business *(shirokoshiya)*[77] to advertise services for funeral processions. Sōshichi, as the owner is called, begins his flier by thanking the *nembutsukō* and *daimokukō*[78] who have supported his business and made it a success. He then announces that he has plenty of coffins in stock, and that, if a customer is not fully satisfied with his product mix and pricing, he is willing to make adjustments. Ceremonial clothes and implements and, if necessary, mourning women "who are rather skillful at weeping,"[79] are available as well. The consummate businessman, Sōshichi also warns, "Of course, depending on the distance to the temple, the price will go up. If by some chance it rains, there will be a hike in the previously decided price."[80]

The pamphlet is written tongue-in-cheek, intended to get a laugh from the reader, but the satire does point to the very real phenomenon of entrepreneurs, mostly palanquin shops and carpenters, catering to the mortuary needs of the well-off. The author chides the prosperous townspeople in the second part of his story, a criticism of the trend "in recent years" to sponsor funerals that are "extremely inappropriate to one's social standing."[81] If a samurai household has an income of over 1,000 *koku* of rice a year,[82] he writes, then it is proper for that household to have attendants march in its funeral processions. "But when vulgar townspeople and entertainers die, they have attendants dressed in light blue *kamishimo* (formal samurai dress) march through two districts *(chō)* in double file. Is this not shameful to see? . . . This is the wretchedness to be expected of the townspeople."[83] What made the townspeople so wretched was not simply that they "showed off" with their processions, but that they incorporated elements, like the ceremonial *kamishimo,* that were supposed to be reserved for the samurai class.

In their adoption of feudal pageantry, the townspeople of Tokugawa Japan behaved very like the growing middle classes of early modern Europe, a "whole new section of society" that "threw itself with enthusiasm into the previously forbidden delights of aristocratic mourning etiquette."[84] By the end of the eighteenth century the funerals of well-to-do families in England regularly incorporated footmen bearing black ostrich feathers, symbolizing esquires "bearing the shield and helmet of the deceased," and pages carrying wands, representing gentlemen-ushers.[85] These baronial displays cost a great deal of money. One undertaker's bill from 1824 shows that, for one English lady's funeral, just the amount spent to outfit twelve pages in silk hatbands and gloves "constituted half a year's wages of a domestic servant of the period."[86] As in Japan, funeral excesses in Britain became the object of harsh criticism. "The Grave," a poem by an Edinburgh clergyman published in 1785, was followed by an editorial comment that "*Pompous funerals* are as *ridiculous* as they are *unnecessary: Ridiculous* in respect to the *living,* except in the views of those who reap *pecuniary* advantage from them, and unnecessary respecting the *dead,* who are the principle subject and occasions for them."[87]

Funerals in North America, too, were sumptuous affairs. Families threw huge feasts and those of high standing liberally disbursed rings, scarves, and gloves to attendees. For the funeral of Andrew Faneuil in 1738, "three thousand pairs of gloves were given away and over eleven hundred persons accompanied the funeral cortège."[88] The General Court of Massachusetts tried to reign in funereal munificence, passing laws prohibiting "Extraordinary Expense at Funerals" in 1721, 1724, and 1742.[89] However, it took the American Revolution, which cut off the colonists' supply of finished goods from England, to make a dent in funeral spending.[90]

Like their counterparts in America, officials in Tokugawa Japan tried to restrain funerary extravagance through a combination of exhortation and fiat. As early as 1661 it warned that funerals and memorial services should be confined to modest levels.[91] But this proscription, like many others issued during the Edo period, served more to indicate a trend than to reverse it. Tokugawa officials in 1791 again proclaimed that funerals, although "meritorious," should not be "showy," noting that, despite the 1661 requirement to keep funerals modest, there were those who sponsored funerary rites "inappropriate to their status" *(mibun fusōō).*[92] This sentiment was expressed once again in 1831, when the government announced specific rules concerning funerals, this time stipulating that the number of clerics in attendance at funerals even for the wealthy should not exceed ten.[93]

Government regulations were dictated not only by the logic of keeping people in their place. They were also part of an attempt to encourage frugality for its own sake, since the flow of revenue depended on the financial health of corporate patrilines, at once the economic and biological building blocks of the Tokugawa order. In 1742, for example, shogunate officials banned the widespread practice of burying "coins for the six paths" *(rokudōsen)*,[94] stating explicitly in their order that the practice of burying these coins was "unprofitable" *(mueki)*. Acknowledging that it was difficult to change longstanding customs, the shogunate called upon temple priests to lecture to their parishioners about the wastefulness of burying money.[95] It is unclear to what extent clerics obliged, but there are hints that the policy may have had an impact, at least in Edo and Osaka.[96]

The "keeping up with the Tanakas" phenomenon targeted by sumptuary regulations was reinforced by the custom of presenting gifts to mourning families, a practice formalized during the Tokugawa period that remains a central feature of Japanese funerary rites to this day. These gifts were theoretically intended to help families offset the significant expenses of hosting a funeral, but by the same token they bolstered expectations that there were such expenses to be met. In fact, much of the cost of the funeral included providing food and drink to the condolence callers. The gifts offered to a mourning family, called *kōden* (literally "incense offerings," but consisting mainly of rice and cash) also tied a family into long-term networks of reciprocity between corporate patrilines. If the representative of patriline A brought gifts to patriline B for funerals in patriline B, then patriline B was obligated to bring gifts to patriline A for funerals in patriline A. By exchanging gifts, families defined themselves against each other, periodically affirming the integrity of their lineages across the generations.

They kept tabs on one another by recording their gifts in registers known as *kōdenchō*. Designed to ensure that they did not breach etiquette, these registers developed in the Tokugawa period along with the patrilines who maintained them, making this social technology a common feature of Japanese death well before the Meiji Restoration.[97] When figuring out how much to give, one had to account not only for the relationships between patrilines, but also for the position of the dead within the hierarchy of the mourning patriline. In looking at registries from the mid-nineteenth century for one household in what is now Yamagata prefecture, for example, one sees that the amount of *kōden* differed in accordance with the age and gender of the deceased. When a seventy-year-old man died in 1847, gifts of white rice amounted to 84 *shō* (about 40 gallons) while cash presents added up to 3,900 mon. When a twenty-eight-year-old woman died four years later, however, the family received only 61 *shō* of white rice and 1,650 mon in cash.[98]

Status-mongering not only fueled the spread of lavish funerals, it also spurred the construction of imposing gravestones. Before the Tokugawa period the practice of erecting permanent markers for family members, an act that signified the durability of a patriline, was for the most part limited to aristocrats and samurai. But from the seventeenth century, the effort to cast lineages in stone began spreading to commoners, who until then usually had not bothered to erect permanent markers, and when they had, tended to make them collective monuments shared by entire communities. In a temple graveyard in the Nara prefecture village of Hayama, for example, the earliest extant memorial stone, dating from 1559, reads, "for the equal benefit of all spirits in the three realms" *(sankai banrei byōdō rieki).*[99] It was only during the Tokugawa period that stones dedicated to specific family members, whether buried individually or as married couples, gradually appeared in the graveyard.[100] This trend intensified as time passed, with old-fashioned stupas (miniature versions of the structures in which Shākyamuni's relics were housed) giving way to streamlined, rectangular slabs. These new gravestones prominently displayed family names and individual posthumous titles, a change that represented the intensification of patrilineal consciousness and ancestor reverence among the population at large.[101]

Social striving was especially apparent in the acquisition of posthumous names, which differed according to person, and, through the addition of special titles, according to rank.[102] Many Buddhist priests were happy to sell prestigious titles for the right price, regardless of a family's official status.[103] The sale of names grew so widespread that it prompted the shogunate in 1831 to prohibit farmers and townspeople from using the elite titles *ingō* and *koji*. At the same time the government banned the construction of gravestones taller than four *shaku* (about four feet).[104]

By the late Tokugawa period, then, the practices of Buddhist death had become firmly established, both through custom and through law, as the means not only to save souls and create sacred remains but also to compete for worldly status. From ancient times onward Japan's ruling families used mortuary rites to establish their legitimacy and to reconfigure power relations among them. The splendor of clerical funerals was incorporated into the politics of lineage-building, generating funerary practices—such as the granting of posthumous ordinations and the sponsorship of elaborate processions—that were eventually adopted by less powerful families looking to improve their own social standing. This trend rapidly accelerated during the Tokugawa period, when the shogunate made repeated efforts to restrain mortuary expenditures among the general population. The fact that these efforts were repeated is evidence that funerary excess played a social function that could not be ordered out of existence. It continues, after all, to this day.

CHAPTER 2

THE SHINTO CHALLENGE
TO BUDDHIST DEATH

*U*nder the Tokugawa shogunate, Buddhist temples registered, processed, and memorialized the deaths of captive parishioners, making the temples both enforcers of social control and enablers of social advancement. Meanwhile, there were those who criticized and challenged the power wielded by Buddhist clerics over the living and the dead. First Confucian scholars, then Shinto nativists *(kokugakusha)*, waged campaigns against Buddhist priests and their teachings, and out of this opposition arose a radical innovation, the Shinto funeral *(shinsōsai)*.

Confucian scholars promoted, for the most part, a ready-made package of death rites imported from China, but nativists sought to establish an indigenous alternative to Buddhist practices. To do this, they adopted protocols developed over several centuries by the Yoshida lineage of *kami* worship and scrutinized ancient Japanese texts for written remnants of homegrown death rites. Ironically, they also drew on the Chinese customs advocated by Confucian scholars, despite outwardly rejecting "foreign" Confucianism in favor of beliefs and practices imagined to be "purely" Japanese in origin. In fact, despite speculating about the makeup of the "other world" *(anoyo)*, those who promoted Shinto death rites (consciously or not) adhered to the pointedly earthbound logic of filial piety and lineage-building that undergirded Confucian thought. The formats devised for Shinto funerals differed in detail from one another, but they all shared the common goal of transforming the deceased into tutelary *kami* whose fates were not merely intertwined with the fortunes of surviving family members, but were inextricable from them.

Inventing and promoting Shinto death rites was no easy task, and there were four main reasons for this. First and foremost, nativists had to convince their fellow Japanese that to care properly for their ancestors meant breaking with the traditions of their ancestors, that being filial required casting off Buddhist practices and teachings that had successfully bonded one generation to the next. Second, the fastidious *kami* abhorred pollution *(kegare)*, especially death pollution, so combining funerals and *kami* worship was, for most Japanese, the ritual equivalent of mixing oil and water. Third, the attempt to glean information about indigenous death rites from the *Kojiki, Nihon shoki,* and other ancient Japanese chronicles—texts that had been produced only after the importation of a writing system, along with Buddhism and Confucianism, from the continent—yielded only ritual fragments, not a coherent system to handle death. Finally, all non-Buddhist funerals, whether Confucian or Shinto, made little headway during the Tokugawa period because of the requirement to register with Buddhist temples. During the seventeenth century, several daimyo did gain special permission to sponsor Confucian instead of Buddhist funerals, and from the late eighteenth century onward an increasing number of Shinto priests successfully petitioned the authorities to allow them to receive Shinto funerals. As long as the shogunate was in power, however, so was the Buddhist establishment, and even those Shinto priests who succeeded in freeing themselves from Buddhist death rites found their family members still bound to them.

The Meiji Restoration of 1868 eliminated this political obstacle, giving hope to the advocates of Shinto funerals. Inspired by nativist teachings, the early imperial government immediately took steps to disestablish Buddhism and institute the "unity of rites and rule" *(saisei itchi)* according to a putatively ancient Shinto blueprint. Nativists appointed to positions in the new state not only seized the opportunity to recast the rituals of the imperial house, the legitimating axis for the new regime, but also attempted to rework the ritual lives, and deaths, of ordinary Japanese.

For a brief time the future looked bright for Shinto funerals, whose Confucian values and native practices appeared to bolster the Meiji government's nation-building program. Acting on the assumption that the state should master death as well as life, nativists within the government centralized efforts to promote Shinto funerals, making it a key component of a larger "doctrinal instruction" *(kyōdō)* campaign designed to instill emperor-centered Shinto in the hearts and minds of all Japanese. They brought officiating priests under state control and published a manual to create a standard, national format for Shinto death rites. This government-supported format put the emphasis on filial piety front and center while downplaying concerns about death pollution and sidestepping any discussion of the "other world" *(anoyo)*. Nativist officials sought, above all, to transform the deceased into household-protecting—and, by extension, nation-protecting—ancestors, limiting their range to the territory of family and state.

What they discovered in the process was that most Japanese were unwilling to let go of Buddhism, even when told to abandon the "foreign" teaching by their leaders. How, then, were the nativists to replace a Buddhist reality with a Shinto dream—and do it without upsetting public order? This was the difficult, twofold question that nativists in the early Meiji period faced.

THE CONFUCIAN MODEL

Until the Tokugawa period Confucian teachings were situated in a Buddhist frame of reference, both within temples and outside them. But in the seventeenth century a growing number of intellectuals resolutely separated Confucianism from Buddhism, attacking the latter in the process. Founding scholarly lineages that drew heavily upon the neo-Confucian teachings of Zhu Xi (1130–1200) and other Song dynasty (960–1280) scholar-bureaucrats, Japanese Confucians, like their Chinese predecessors, saw it as their duty to contribute to the maintenance of a stable political and moral order, one that made no room for the world-renouncing tendencies of Buddhism.[1]

The Buddhist monopoly on death rites was particularly loathsome to Confucians ("neo" or not), who viewed funerals as occasions for the solemn expression of filial piety, not for the reinforcement of misguided beliefs in heavens and hells and the enrichment of venal priests. Buddhist clerics performed rituals that reinforced familial bonds at the same time that they preached the theory of transmigration, sending the message to parishioners that the fates of individuals and their families were intertwined and yet distinct. This two-pronged teaching was heresy to Confucians, who adamantly rejected the belief in individual rebirths and identified the afterlife exclusively with family life. No room was made for exotic heavens and hells in their scheme, which recycled the dead into this world at the expense of any other world.

A strong proponent of this viewpoint was Confucian scholar Kumazawa Banzan (1619–1691), who wrote an essay on funerals that sharply criticized Buddhist teachings and rituals and offered Confucian ones in their place. In fact he argued that ritual procedures thought to be Buddhist were originally Confucian, warning mourners not to be fooled by the Buddhist priests who had "stolen" these procedures. Take, for example, the practice of writing the name of the deceased on mortuary tablets. The original, Confucian purpose was to keep the dead close at hand, but the Buddhist clergy had perverted that intent by devising posthumous names unfamiliar to the dead, a practice criticized by Kumazawa's rhetorical question, "How will the spirit force *(reiki)* respond when a name unknown to the deceased is called out?"[2] Even worse, Buddhist measures to rescue one's parents of necessity cast them into hell. "How can a child bear to treat his parent like a sinner?" asks Kumazawa's essay, which instructs readers on how to honor the dead rather than save them.[3]

The relationship between children and parents is the main concern throughout Kumazawa's essay, to the exclusion of all other relationships between the living and the dead. Moreover, while the essay dwells at length on how children should mourn their dead parents, it mentions not once how parents should mourn their dead children. The reason is that children who did not produce their own successors ultimately played no role in perpetuating lineages from one generation to the next, which was, for Confucians, the most basic of filial duties.[4] This does not mean that Confucians in Tokugawa Japan felt no grief upon the deaths of their sons and daughters. The death of a child may have been emotionally devastating.[5] What made it ritually and rhetorically unimportant was the fact that such a loss had no place in a scheme whose ultimate goal was the production of ancestor-revering descendents. In contrast, the death of a parent required those in the succeeding generation to establish their legitimacy through the proper expression of grief, providing, in the process, a model of filial piety to *their* progeny.

To Kumazawa and other Confucians, how one did this was, in effect, to deny that the parent had truly departed or been transformed into another being. While the parent was still alive, filial piety was fulfilled in large part by the attention a child paid to the parent's physical comfort. In order to highlight the continuity of this devotion after death, the child was expected to treat the body of the dead parent with the same affection and consideration shown when the parent was still living. It was in this spirit that the child ought to offer food to the dead parent, wrote Kumazawa. Moreover, the posthumous title should incorporate the name that the deceased had used during his or her lifetime in order for the soul to recognize it; and instead of shaving the entire head and giving the dead the appearance of a world-renouncing Buddhist monk, mourners ought to wash the dead in a "habitual manner," then arrange the hair, shave the beard, trim the nails, and dress the body in clean clothes.

When writing about the coffin and burial, Kumazawa once more emphasized the continuity between life and death by likening the latter to sleep. Constructed of thick boards and varnished to keep out moisture, the coffin should be, in his words, "an instrument to allow the dead to lie in peace," a "sleeping chamber" in which one's parents could eternally rest.[6] The sturdy sleeping chamber advocated by Kumazawa contrasts sharply with the containers typically used to bury corpses in Tokugawa and even Meiji Japan. For the most part, these consisted of *hayaoke,* cheap barrels (or "quick tubs," as Isabella Bird [1831–1904] dubbed them)[7] into which bodies were crammed.[8] Kumazawa also instructed mourners to "worship the local *kami* of the earth" at the burial site, not in order to secure a place for the deceased in some far-off paradise, but to win divine protection for the grave in which he or she "slept."[9] Unfortunately, he observed, people were careless about burying the dead, consigning them to swampy temple land so as to facilitate "passage to the other world" rather than to preserve the integrity of their bodies in the here and now. It was pitiful to bury family members in coffins that fell apart, in locations where the dead were buried one on top of the other, he wrote.[10]

Even more heinous in the eyes of Kumazawa and other Confucian thinkers was cremation, a practice they roundly condemned as the most unfilial of acts. Buddhists celebrated its transformative power,[11] but Confucians, both in Japan and China,[12] viewed such a radical break between the treatment of the dead and that of the living as a profound threat to the filial devotion on which the fate of a family and the wider social order depended. Kumazawa compared burning the bodies of one's parents to slicing them up with a sword. Even if a parent specifically asked to be cremated in his or her last testament, the child should display true filial devotion by disobeying the "deluded order" and performing proper burial instead.[13] In the same vein, fellow Confucian Kaibara Ekken (1630–1714) wrote that the filial child "loves the flesh of his parent" and, "even though the parent has died, treats [the parent] as if still living." Therefore cremating a parent was even more reprehensible than "abandoning [the parent's] body in the fields and making it food for the foxes and badgers. . . . "[14] Yasui Sanesuke, in his essay "Hikasōron" (Against cremation), also emphasized that one ought to handle the corpse of a father or mother "as if it were still alive" and "not treat it roughly in any manner." Like other Tokugawa-period Confucians he labeled cremation an offense "contrary to natural feeling," citing the ancient Chinese use of cremation as a form of punishment to support this claim.[15] He also lamented that the perverse teaching of the Buddha had led filial children astray from their "natural" impulses. In bemoaning the spread of cremation into Japan, Yasui laid the blame squarely on the priest Dōshō, who, in Rasputin-like fashion, had beguiled the imperial family into adopting the hideous practice centuries before.[16]

Confucian scholars propagated their anti-cremation stance among the educated classes of the Tokugawa period; as a consequence, elite families who had burned their dead for generations, including the imperial family, gave up the Buddhist custom. Persuaded that banning cremation would, in the words of Ōtsuki Risai (1674–1734), "certainly generate morality and filial piety,"[17] several domains also tried to curb the practice among commoners, though it is unclear how successful they were. Leading the way in this effort was Nonaka Kenzan (1615–1663), the dynamic administrator of the Tosa domain. Nonaka apparently tried to ban the practice several times but was unable to halt it until he mandated the cremation of executed criminals. This stigmatization reportedly ended cremation—that is, of the voluntary sort—in Tosa.[18] In 1663 Hoshina Masayuki (1611–1672), daimyo of Aizu, also declared a ban on cremation in his domain, though it is unclear to what extent it was actually enforced.

Some tried not only to end cremation, but to replace Buddhist death rites entirely with Confucian ones. Ikeda Mitsumasa (1609–1682), daimyo of Okayama domain and Kumazawa's patron of ten years (1647–1657),[19] decided to enforce a registration system using Shinto shrines instead of Buddhist temples,[20] thereby opening the door for the adoption of non-Buddhist funerals. Judging from detailed domain records kept on formerly Christian families, it appears that Confucian funerals did make some headway. Between 1669 and 1687, documents show, eleven people from forcibly converted Christian families were given Confucian instead of Buddhist funerals. However, a much greater number of former Christians in this period, fifty-eight, were buried according to Buddhist rites;[21] and after Ikeda himself died in 1682, the Buddhist establishment applied pressure to reverse his policies. Accordingly, the temple registration system was reinstituted in 1687, snuffing out the spread of Confucian funerals in Okayama.[22]

Confucian-style funerals found favor among several other daimyo, perhaps the most notable being Tokugawa Mitsukuni (1628–1700) of the Mito domain. Mitsukuni was a strong advocate of both Shinto rites and Confucian teachings. Drawing from the tenets of Ise Shinto, which had traditionally excluded Buddhist influences,[23] Mitsukuni set out to purge shrines of Buddhist coloring, foreshadowing the Meiji policy of *shinbutsu bunri* (separation of *kami* and buddhas). Accordingly, when his wife died in 1658, she was buried according to the Confucian ceremony spelled out in Zhu Xi's *Kōbun karei* (Household rites).[24] Mitsukuni himself was given a Confucian funeral, as were later Mito lords; moreover, before he died, he established two cemeteries where retainers wishing non-Buddhist funerals could be buried. Nevertheless Mito commoners remained locked into the shogunate's system of temple registration, and even though Mitsukuni released Shinto priests and their families from Buddhist funerals, thirty-two years after his death, the shogunate once more bound them to their family temples.[25]

Other daimyo also had difficulty escaping the Buddhist death grip. Tokugawa Yoshinao, daimyo of Bishū domain, had indicated before his death in 1650 that he wanted to be buried according to Confucian rites, but in deference to the shogunate's policy, his family first sponsored a Buddhist funeral involving hundreds of priests before burying him according to Confucian norms.[26] Despite growing anti-Buddhist sentiment in the imperial court, emperors also continued to receive Buddhist obsequies throughout the Tokugawa period. In 1654 Emperor Gokōmyō was buried whole, breaking a centuries-long tradition of cremation in the imperial house,[27] and yet rituals were performed to make it appear as if he had been cremated. This initiated "the dissembling convention of faux cremation and secret corporeal burial" that was not exposed until the death of Emperor Kōmei in 1867, when it was finally rejected in favor of publicly acknowledged, full-body burial.[28]

GOING NATIVE

The Confucian tradition provided a ready-made template for funerals, and many of those who sought an alternative to Buddhist death rites chose to adopt the Chinese format without much alteration. Others decided to create syncretic "Shinto" funerals that incorporated elements of native *kami* worship while at the same time adhering to Chinese ritual conventions. To do so, they turned to a model provided by the Yoshida lineage of *kami* worship, which, in the decades leading to the establishment of Tokugawa rule, devised a series of death rites intended to transform the deceased into family-protecting *kami* rather than propel them into a faraway Buddhist paradise.

The Yoshida patriline was founded in the fourteenth century as an independent branch of the Urabe sacerdotal lineage that had exercised control of Kyoto's Yoshida shrine and other cultic centers since the ninth century. The founder of this branch, Yoshida Kanehiro (1348–1402), followed accepted practice by becoming a Buddhist monk as death approached, spending his last days chanting the *nembutsu*.[29] Kanehiro's descendants broke with this tradition, however, as they developed a "One-and-Only" Shinto (Yuiitsu Shintō) that crafted *kami* worship into a system of teachings and practices distinct from Buddhism. The great systematizer of Yuiitsu Shinto, Yoshida Kanetomo (1434–1511), famously declared buddhas and bodhisattvas to be avatars of *kami* and not the other way around, as was commonly believed.[30] There are no records revealing the procedures for Kanetomo's funeral, but he was enshrined after his death as the *kami* Shinryū Daimyōjin.[31] His successor, Kanemigi (1516–1573), also indicated in his will that he wished to become a guardian *kami* of the patriline. When he died, no Buddhist clerics participated in the initial funeral, although they did perform rites in the days that followed.[32]

The earliest work describing the steps of a Yuiitsu Shinto funeral has been attributed to the next Yoshida lineage head, Kanemi (1535–1610).[33] The ceremony described in his "Yuiitsu shintō sōsai shidai" (Protocol for Yuiitsu Shinto funeral rites) incorporated elements shared in common with Buddhist funerals, such as the offering of flowers, food, and incense. Yet it excluded Buddhist priests and, in dealing with the problem of death pollution, employed purification rituals and prayers specific to *kami* worship. Kanemi also posited an afterlife entirely independent of the Buddhist six paths by drawing upon a *Nihon shoki* passage concerning the fate of the *kami* Izanagi after he had lost his wife to Yomi. At one point, according to the chronicle, "Izanagi no Mikoto, his divine task having been accomplished, and his spirit-career about to suffer a change, built himself an abode of gloom in the island of Ahaji [Awaji], where he dwelt for ever in silence and concealment." This is not the cheeriest of endings. However, the *Nihon shoki* provides an alternate account, in which "Izanagi no Mikoto, his task having been accomplished, and his power great, ascended to Heaven and made report of his mission. There he dwelt in the smaller palace of the Sun (the larger palace being that of Amaterasu)."[34] Kanemi and later proponents of Shinto funerals seized on this second version, claiming that the enshrined dead, like Izanagi, resided in heaven and not in an "abode of gloom."[35] They thereby created an afterlife that could compete with the postmortem realms of Buddhism.

The procedures and teachings developed by the Yoshida lineage were adopted by pro-Shinto Confucians in the seventeenth century, one of the more famous being Aizu daimyo Hoshina Masayuki (1611–1672), who carefully planned his own funeral before he died. The shogun's advisors were initially opposed to the idea, but they were mollified by Yoshikawa Koretaru[36] (1619–1694), a member of the Yoshida lineage who had been appointed, through the offices of Masayuki himself, to the newly minted government post of *shintōkata* (Shinto intendant) in 1666.[37] It was in consultation with Koretaru that Masayuki chose the burial site where he was enshrined as a *kami*, his deification following Yoshida precedent.[38]

Combining Yoshida funerary rites with Chinese protocol reflected the view popular among seventeenth-century intellectuals that Shinto rituals and Confucian teachings mutually reinforced one another. For example, Yamazaki Ansai (1618–1682), a close associate of both Hoshina Masayuki and Yoshida Koretaru, was at once a prolific Zhu Xi scholar and an avid student of Yoshida and Ise Shinto. This neo-Confucian Shintoist, who founded his own sacerdotal lineage (Suika Shintō)[39] and built a shrine to himself while still living, argued, "In the universe there is only One Principle, [although] either Gods or Sages come forth depending on whether it concerns the country where the sun rises [Japan] or the country where the sun sets [China]. The [two] Ways [of Shinto and Confucianism] are, however, naturally and mysteriously the same *(onozukara myōkei suru).*"[40] To support this assertion, he noted that "Confucian funeral rites were the same as Shinto rites because the Ise teachings had always prohibited cremation."[41] Clearly, in the eyes of Yamazaki and his contemporaries, Confucianism and Shinto were united by what they did not do as much as by what they did do.

The complementarity of Chinese thought and Japanese Shinto taken for granted in the seventeenth century was challenged in the eighteenth century by *kokugaku,* "national studies" or "nativism," whose advocates sought to find an alternative basis for ritual and ethical behavior in a uniquely and purely Japanese tradition. In pursuit of this chimera, they hunted through classical texts —primarily the *Kojiki, Nihon shoki,* and *Man'yōshū*—volumes that supposedly expressed an untainted, indigenous Way, despite the fact that they had been written only after the importation of the Chinese writing system. For the nativists, Confucian teachings were forms of artifice that did not complement but instead corrupted an originally artless Japanese spirit. It followed that Buddhism, which had transformed *kami* into avatars and displaced native rites, was particularly loathsome.

One of the most eloquent and influential nativist scholars was Motoori Norinaga (1730–1801), who rejected the authority of even the *Nihon shoki* in favor of what he took to be the more authentic *Kojiki.* Consequently he also rejected the notion that, after death, the spirit, or even just a portion of the spirit, traveled to heaven. Drawing his conclusion from the *Kojiki,* he insisted that all, without exception, were destined for the gloomy netherworld of Yomi:

> Everyone in the world, noble or base, good or evil, must go to *yomi no kuni* at the expiration of his life. This is an extremely sorrowful thing. This statement may certainly sound very blunt and unreasonable, but is derived from the true tradition held since the age of kami and is based on a mysterious principle, so that man should not reason about it with his limited ordinary intelligence. In foreign countries many doctrines

have been contrived to explain the reason for man's life and death in attractive ways, but these are either mere human speculations, or contrivances cleverly made to appeal to people's credulity. Although they sound plausible, they are in fact not real but fabrications.[42]

Because the dead "must of necessity go to the foul *yomi no kuni*," it was natural to express extreme grief when loved ones passed away, said Motoori.[43]

This dim view of the afterlife did not translate into an indifference toward funeral arrangements. In fact, Motoori left behind very specific, and eccentric, instructions. It is not clear whether he was motivated more out of deference to Tokugawa regulations or to family tradition, but like the imperial family, he concocted a duplicitous set of death rites that both adhered to and departed from Buddhist protocol. Noting in his will that one must "maintain the family lineage without discontinuity," he asked that his funeral procession proceed according to custom to his family temple, the Jukyōji. He also designed his own posthumous Buddhist name (and one for his wife as well), ordering that it be carved onto his gravestone at Jukyōji and on his mortuary tablet, which was to be placed in the family's *butsudan* (Buddhist altar) and serve as the focus of the periodic memorial rites. What is striking about Motoori's plan is that the coffin destined for the Jukyōji temple was supposed to be empty. His body was to be placed in another coffin and secretly transported in the middle of the night to another location for burial. This true grave should be crowned by a cherry tree planted in a mound of earth, according to his directions, and the memorial stone must not feature his Buddhist name, but his secular name instead. He added that visitors from other regions looking to visit his grave ought to be directed to this latter one, which was located on a mountain looking out toward the Ise shrines.[44] Finally he asked that each year his disciples hang his portrait in his study and set the desk with a memorial tablet, flowers, a lamp, and a meal. To this day one can visit the tree-topped grave, but the funeral was not conducted exactly according to plan. Apparently, a local administrator balked at the idea of a secret burial, so he ordered the coffin holding the body to be carried in normal fashion to the Jukyōji temple and only after the funeral service to be transported to the designated gravesite.[45]

Although Motoori denied a heavenly afterlife, he put great store in being properly memorialized on earth and devised a funeral that would honor his personal beliefs while maintaining a front of conventional Buddhist ritual qua family custom. His successors, looking to bolster the appeal of Shinto cosmology, prized Motoori's actions over his words. The most famous of his disciples was Hirata Atsutane (1776–1843), who contended that his teacher was "inadvertently in error" by claiming that the dead reside in the "filthy realm of Yomi" and that his decision to fix on one spot as his eternal resting place constituted a final rejection of this view.[46] Atsutane argued that the corpse, made of water and earth, putrefies and thus belongs to the land of Yomi, but the soul "flies off with the air and fire." Rather than soar to a faraway paradise, however, the soul remains "eternally in Japan" to "serve in the realm of the dead governed by Ōkuninushi-no-kami." The world ruled by Ōkuninushi is invisible, but, according to Atsutane, "is not a specific place that exists separately from this Visible Realm. It refers to the divine court that [Ōkuninushi] set up within this Visible Realm, wherever it may be, to rule over hidden matters."[47] In other words, rather than transcend the mundane world, the dead enter into a deeper, concealed dimension of it. It was therefore possible for Atsutane to claim that Motoori resides at his gravesite while at the same time "dwells in peace and calm amid the spirits of scholars of former times, who wait in attendance on him."[48]

Other nativist scholars embraced the idea of an invisible realm for the dead that was *not* identified with Yomi, although they differed in explaining the precise makeup of this "concealed world" and the spirits that inhabited it.[49] They also devised varying death practices by drawing from the descriptions of mythical funerals in the *Kojiki* and *Nihon shoki*.[50] These bare-bones accounts left much to the imagination, thus granting a great deal of freedom to nativists looking to fill the ritual gaps, yet also inducing them to rely heavily on procedures already developed by the Yoshida lineage and, ironically, the ancient Chinese.[51] While outwardly disclaiming the "foreign" Confucian tradition, nativists also embraced the teaching of filial piety, making it a central tenet of nativist thought. By transforming the dead into family-protecting *kami*, and by positing an invisible realm coextensive with the visible one, nativists shared the Confucian commitment to minimizing the distance between the living and the dead.

RITUAL REBELS

From the late eighteenth to the mid-nineteenth century, a small but growing number of nativist priests petitioned authorities to divest themselves of temple affiliations and be buried according to Shinto rites. This movement was encouraged by the expansionist Yoshida lineage, which had already begun to grant licenses to shrine priests in the late sixteenth century and had benefited from a shogunal decree in 1665 that all shrines, with the exception of major shrines such as those at Ise and Atsuta, become its affiliates.[52]

The lineage used its format for Shinto funerals to make good on the government's order, pulling priests more tightly into its fold in emulation of the officially regulated hierarchies of the Buddhist sects. In 1732, for example, priests in Mito had been told to reattach themselves to Buddhist temples, but in 1766 the Yoshida lineage released a circular in Mito proclaiming a "revival" of Shinto funerals. The notice told the priests to honor the late Mitsukuni's wishes by applying for permission to conduct Shinto death rites from the domain authorities. The domain acquiesced, but only to a degree. Reaffirming the principle that families must be registered with temples, it limited the performance of Shinto funerals to priests and their immediate successors and forbade other members of their families to break free from Buddhist control.[53]

The Shinto funeral movement spread to other regions, but the going was not easy. Following Mito's example, certain domains allowed non-Buddhist death rites, but only for priests and their immediate successors and on the condition that they be licensed by the Yoshida lineage. The Buddhist clergy jealously guarded their shogunate-sanctioned privileges, so officials treated the requests for Shinto funerals gingerly, requiring petitioners not only to affiliate with the Yoshida lineage, but also to obtain permission from their family temples, which were reluctant to free priests from their control. In the sixth month of 1773, for example, twenty-eight priests in the Tsuchiura domain collectively submitted a petition for "self-managed funerals" (*jishin sōsai*) after having gotten permission from the Yoshida lineage. But in the ninth month, the twenty family temples of these priests lodged a protest with the Office of Temples and Shrines in which they refused to recognize the petitioners on the grounds that they, the temples, were defending the government's parishioner household system. Only after the priests stipulated in a written assurance that their family members would remain bound to the temples were they granted the right to handle their own funerals.[54]

The promotion of Shinto funerals accelerated somewhat during the Tenpō era (1830–1843), a period famous for a rash of economic, political, and social reforms mandated by individual domains and the shogunate itself. Tokugawa Japan had gone through two earlier paroxysms of reform, in the Kyōhō (1716–1735) and Kansei (1789–1800) periods, during which austerity measures and revised agricultural and financial controls were introduced. The reforms implemented in the mid-nineteenth century were similar in flavor, but they were infused by an additional urgency to strengthen Japan against the looming threat posed by empire-building Europeans and Americans. This threat took the form of repeated incursions into Japanese waters in the early nineteenth century and was brought into sharp focus by Britain's shocking defeat of the Qing dynasty in the Opium War (1839–1842).

As daimyo reevaluated existing policies and Japanese of various stripes began paying attention to the foreign danger, sympathy grew for nativist teachings, which provided an emperor- and *kami*-centered vision of a barbarian-expelling Japan. Yet even in an increasingly receptive environment, those seeking to escape Buddhist death rites continued to face obstacles. Shinto priests in the Hamada domain, for example, had to struggle for seven long years to win approval for a request originally made in 1839. In their first petition they expressed their desire to follow protocol from "the age of the *kami*," noting that many priests throughout Japan were "returning" to Shinto funerals in this "enlightened age" *(shōdai)*. They recognized that the parishioner household system that bound families to Buddhist temples had been put in place to control Christians, but being priests who "served the imperial land and the imperial *kami*," it was patently clear that they were not themselves Christian. Stepping over the line that had been established for such requests, they also asked that all the men and women in their families be permitted to shed their temple affiliations.[55] The request was consequently denied, fueling acrimony between the priests and their family temples. According to a subsequent petition submitted by the priests, when the mother of one of them died in 1840, the family temple spitefully assigned her a posthumous name that included characters meaning "disloyal" *(fuchūshin)*. The Shinto priests did not help their case by openly condemning their Buddhist counterparts for "ruining the chastity of women," indulging in drink, and otherwise breaking their precepts.[56]

Meanwhile Mito daimyo Tokugawa Nariaki (1800–1860) launched an all-out assault against Buddhism and its death rites, initiating a new, more aggressive phase in the nativist campaign. Mito was a hotbed for jingoistic scholars who responded to the threat posed by America and Europe by rallying under the slogan "Revere the emperor and expel the barbarian *(sonnō jōi)*."[57] For adherents of the "Mito school" (Mitogaku), the imperial family embodied an unbroken lineage descended from the age of the *kami* and was thus the natural focal point for a revitalized "national body" (*kokutai*, also commonly translated as "national polity").[58] Conversely, Buddhism was a corrupting force that weakened the loyalty of the emperor's subjects. Following in the footsteps of earlier Confucian and nativist scholars, Mito thinkers such as Aizawa Seishisai (1781–1863) reviled the Buddhist clergy for turning Japanese into followers of "Indian barbarism" and thereby dividing the "spiritual unity" of

the people.[59] Another Mito scholar, Fujita Tōko (1806–1855), coined a suc-
cinct slogan to complement *sonnō jōi:* "revere the *kami* and destroy the Buddha" *(keishin haibutsu)*.[60]

Accordingly, while Shinto priests in other domains struggled to disentangle themselves from Buddhist control, Nariaki spiked his Tenpō reforms with
lethal assaults against the Buddhist establishment and its death rites. In 1830
the Mito domain not only released Shinto priests from their Buddhist obligations, but ordered them—along with their entire families—to perform Shinto
funerals. In that year Nariaki also issued commands to rectify Buddhist abuses,
which included the sale of high-ranking posthumous names and the postpone-
ment of funerals for families who had failed to make sufficient contributions
to their local temples. Then in 1833 he banned cremation, a custom "intolerable to human feeling," and meted out punishments to those who defied this
order. He also ordered the melting of temple bells and the consolidation, relocation, and outright destruction of several hundred temples.[61]

The Mito campaign against Buddhist funerals reached its height in the early
1840s. In 1843 Nariaki banned the use of any "dharma titles" *(hōgo)* for the
mortuary tablets and graves of either samurai or commoners and decided that,
in place of Buddhist names, commoners would henceforth be allowed to adopt
surnames for their gravestones. He also promoted so-called "independent
funerals" *(jisōsai)* among the populace and settled upon a format that combined Confucian and Shinto elements.[62] The coup de grace in the nativist
offensive was delivered in early 1844, when Nariaki attempted to replace the
temple registration system with a shrine registration system. The domain
decreed that all villages switch from Buddhist to Shinto funerals, and an order
was given to establish shrine registries throughout Mito, with shrine priests
put in charge of recording births and deaths.[63]

That summer a manual was distributed throughout Mito to explain the new
format for what were alternatively called "independent" or "Shinto" funerals.
It was replete with Confucian sentiments, starting with the claim that the moti-
vating force for death rites is the grief that filial children feel upon the deaths
of their parents. The manual warned, "When someone dies, to ponder over
whether they went to a place of pleasure or pain and to think that they were
transformed into something else is wrong," and asserted that "the spirit of the
parent does not vanish, but eternally exists within the patriline *(ie).*" Mourners were told to construct a mortuary tablet to house the deceased-family-
member-turned-*kami*. They were then to dispatch the tablet, with a relative,
to the local Shinto shrine, where the date and place of death, as well as the
place of burial, would be recorded.[64]

No sooner had the domain begun implementing the new system, however, than Nariaki was forced into early retirement by the shogunate. Senior advisors in Edo had become alarmed at the radicalism of the Mito reform program, so in 1844 they placed the daimyo under house arrest. Reformist leaders were punished and participants in a movement to exonerate Nariaki were also jailed.[65] As a consequence, many of the Mito reforms—especially those targeted against Buddhism—were quickly annulled. In 1845 the shogunate put an end to "independent funerals" in towns and villages, and grassroots campaigns sprang up throughout Mito to revive destroyed or displaced temples, revealing the depth of popular attachment to Buddhism despite the nativist onslaught. Not surprisingly, the main reason given in petitions to rebuild temples was the performance of funerals and rites for family ancestors.[66] To what extent people believed in the cosmology and salvational efficacy of Buddhism is uncertain, but it is clear that they viewed their responsibility toward dead relatives through a lens of Buddhist ritual and temple affiliation.

The suppression of the nativist campaign in Mito provided a clear warning to radicals elsewhere in Japan. In 1846, for example, Shinto priests in Tsuwano, led by nativist scholar Oka Kumaomi (1783–1851), decided to antagonize Buddhist temples as little as possible in their campaign for Shinto death rites. They avoided overtly hostile language and included an assurance in their initial request to receive Shinto funerals that their families would remain temple parishioners and continue to honor the established memorial rites for their ancestors.[67] The approval process still required a series of negotiations via the office of shrines and temples, but permission was granted within a year's time.[68]

Despite his rehabilitation in 1849, Nariaki was unable to undo the reversals of his anti-Buddhist reforms. However, he had succeeded in establishing a model for attacking Buddhism that played out on a national level after the Meiji Restoration of 1868. Stymied by shogunal support for the Buddhist establishment, nativists staked their dreams on the political revolution that brought down the old in the name of the ancient. It seemed possible that, with the triumph of the forces to "revere the emperor," the imperial and "purely" Japanese practices of Shinto would finally gain the ritual day.

REVOLUTION AND RESTRAINT

At the ceremony where they formally swore their oath of loyalty to the emperor, the Restorationists who had ousted the shogunate stated for the record that they planned to discard "evil practices of the past,"[69] a sweeping declaration open to various interpretations. For radical nativists, who had won the sympathy of courtier Iwakura Tomomi (1825–1883) and other major figures in the new regime, it meant expunging Buddhism from the land of the *kami*. Only months after the Restoration, the newly minted Ministry of Rites (Jingikan)—directed in large part by Tsuwano daimyo Kamei Koremi (1825–1885) and the prominent Tsuwano nativist Fukuba Bisei (1831–1907)[70]— declared its commitment to the "unity of rites and rule" *(saisei itchi)*, subsequently issuing a stream of edicts aimed at "separating *kami* and buddhas" *(shinbutsu bunri).*[71] These included orders to laicize Buddhist priests serving as shrine intendants *(bettō or shasō),* abolish Buddhist titles for *kami,* and remove all Buddhist icons from shrine precincts.[72]

Shrines and temples were intertwined in centuries-old cultic centers that had, for the most part, never drawn a hard distinction between Buddhism and Shinto. Therefore the separation edicts forced clerics to decide whether a particular structure or institution was truly "Shinto" or "Buddhist" based less on historical precedent than on contemporary expedience.[73] Although the government did not officially sanction violence, its actions opened the door to a "destroy the buddhas, annihilate Shākyamuni" *(haibutsu kishaku)* movement in which radical nativist priests took the process of dividing Shinto from Buddhism into their own hands. They targeted what they deemed to be Shinto shrines and pillaged their syncretic contents, burning or selling Buddhist sutras, statues, and other treasures. A particularly vivid burst of nativist violence rocked Hiyoshi shrine, at the base of Mt. Hiei, where zealots decapitated statues and kicked their heads around for sport.[74] This was an extreme case, but it fell along a continuum of anti-Buddhist destruction wrought throughout Japan, including raids not only to rid shrines of Buddhist elements, but also to attack Buddhist temples proper. Forced laicizations and closures of Buddhist temples numbered in the thousands. Persecution of Buddhism was particularly severe in areas where domain officials actively encouraged and even systematized it, as in Satsuma, Tsuwano, Sado, and Kyoto.[75]

With anti-Buddhist sentiment at a fever pitch, national and local leaders threw their support behind Shinto funerals, clearing a path for the recently invented ceremonies through the ruins of Buddhist hegemony. Starting at the very top, nativists in Tokyo purged Buddhism from the public death rites of the imperial house. Overt Buddhist participation was barred from Emperor Kōmei's third-year memorial service in 1868 and Buddhist mortuary tablets were banished from the palace.[76] The Ministry of Rites also proclaimed that all Shinto priests—and, significantly, their families too—were obligated to receive Shinto funerals instead of Buddhist ones.[77] Moreover, to honor and pacify those who had fallen in battle during the Restoration, the new government immediately built a Shinto shrine to the war dead *(shōkonsha)* at a burial site for soldiers in Kyoto, despite the qualms of some nativists who thought that shrines ought not to be conjoined with gravesites because of death pollution.[78] Four years later a new shrine to dead soldiers reached completion in Tokyo. Renamed Yasukuni (meaning "pacifying the nation") in 1879, the Tokyo *shōkonsha* became the central node of a nationwide network of shrines built to revere and comfort the spirits of those who had died in the line of duty, although it, unlike the Kyoto *shōkonsha,* was not built on a burial ground.

In a few domains aggressive daimyo followed the example set by Nariaki before the Restoration and zealously expanded the campaign to replace Buddhist rites with Shinto ones. The daimyo of Tsuwano, Kamei Koremi, decreed in 1868 that all funerals in his domain must be performed according to Shinto ritual. The daimyo of Satsuma, Tosa, Naegi, and Matsumoto also ordered the populations under their control to adopt Shinto funerals amidst domain-sanctioned "destroy the buddhas, annihilate Shākyamuni" campaigns.[79] Meanwhile, on the village level, nativists from influential families submitted requests to domain authorities on behalf of themselves and their communities to shed temple affiliations and adopt either "Shinto funerals" *(shinsōsai)* or "independent funerals" *(jisōsai),* the term "independent" indicating a funeral, Shinto or not, that was performed by a mourning household without the supervision of Buddhist clerics.[80]

The groundswell of support for non-Buddhist funerals of course pleased nativists, both in the government and outside it. But undercutting the authority of temples and their priests potentially opened the door to an evil considered far worse than Buddhism: Christianity. Although nativist prospects had never looked better, enthusiasm for Shinto death rites was nevertheless tempered with caution.

Fear of the Christian menace had intensified after the shogunate signed the "unequal treaties" with America and Europe, and the Restoration government reaffirmed Tokugawa policy in no uncertain terms. "Evil religions like Christianity are strictly forbidden. Suspicious persons should be reported to the proper office. Rewards will be granted," read signboards posted throughout the country.[81] So-called "hidden Christians" in the Nagasaki area who had made contact with Catholic missionaries in the 1860s suffered intense persecution in the years immediately following the Restoration. Heads literally rolled, and those lucky enough not to be beheaded were deported to other regions of Japan.[82] Buddhist priests approved wholeheartedly of anti-Christian policies, predictably championing their own beleaguered faith as a defense against the foreign heresy. The Association of Buddhist Sects, founded in 1868, recommended that members study the "indivisibility of Imperial and Buddhist law" and the "study and refutation of Christianity."[83] Members pledged in 1869 that they would "lay down their lives for the country" to repel any Christian advance.[84]

Sympathetic to the nativist cause, but wary about providing Christians with room to maneuver, domains first checked with the ruling Council of State (Dajōkan) before approving grassroots requests from those seeking to perform Shinto/independent funerals in place of Buddhist ones. The council readily and regularly gave its approval, but it also reminded officials to remain vigilant against Christianity. Just months after the Restoration, for example, authorities in Shikoku informed Tokyo that both samurai and commoners wanted to perform the nativist death rites and asked how to proceed. The pro-Shinto council told them to approve the petitions, but warned the domain to confirm that applicants were not Christians in disguise,[85] a caveat that appeared in subsequent approvals. Because embracing Shinto, or "independent," funerals meant shedding temple affiliations, the council also instructed domains to devise new surveillance systems to track those who had left the Buddhist fold, guarding against the chance that former temple parishioners might surreptitiously turn to Christianity.[86]

Even during the initial burst of anti-Buddhist fervor, then, officials in Tokyo and elsewhere in Japan recognized that Buddhist priests and temples would not, and—for the sake of containing Christianity and maintaining social order more generally—should not, vanish overnight. In 1869 Foreign Minister Sawa Nobuyoshi (1835–1873) and his assistant, Terashima Munenori (1832–1893), prepared an "Outline of Doctrinal Regulations" (Kyōki no taii) calling for the registration of all Japanese as Shinto shrine parishioners (ujiko), a plan which, if put into effect, would have forced all the emperor's subjects to report births to specified shrines, receive proof of their affiliation, and participate in shrine worship. The plan was obviated in 1873, when the Meiji government instituted a system for registering births that circumvented Shinto priests,[87] but this short-lived blueprint is noteworthy in that it also reaffirmed the authority of Buddhist temples. One provision stipulated that parishioners were not to change temples at will and another that memorial rites were to be performed "in accordance with temple law."[88]

As the new regime fitfully consolidated its power, it also continued to recognize the role played by Buddhist priests in reporting deaths to local officials. In 1871 daimyo formally surrendered their domains to the imperial state, which turned them into centrally administered prefectures. That same year the government announced a new household registration *(koseki)* law that required Buddhist temples, as well as Shinto shrines, to report deaths and burials to local officials, who in turn would tally the figures and send them to Tokyo on an annual basis.[89] Buddhist clerics also continued to fulfill their Tokugawa function as inspectors of "strange deaths" *(henshi)*. When the drowned body of the unfortunate Mr. Fukui, resident of Tokyo's Roppongi district, was discovered soon after the new year of 1871, for example, it was a priest from his family temple, a branch of the Asakusa Honganji, who investigated the apparent suicide and reported it to the Tokyo Bureau of Daily Affairs (Jōmukyoku).[90]

The Buddhist clergy, meanwhile, fought to win back lost ground. With the old domains transformed into prefectures, former daimyo could no longer exercise arbitrary rule, and priests took advantage of this new political environment to revive disbanded temple communities, replaying the scenario that had occurred in Mito after Tokugawa Nariaki was removed from power. Once Matsumoto domain was abolished, for example, a priest who had fled from anti-Buddhist persecution, Adachi Tatsujun, returned to the area formerly under the domain's control[91] and preached to large crowds about the need to reestablish abolished temples. His efforts propelled the reconstruction of temples and the return of parishioners to their old affiliations. The once-mandated Shinto funerals fell into decline, eventually becoming a rarity.[92] Records from the area formerly controlled by Tsuwano domain also show that once the domain was abolished, villages quickly reverted to Buddhist funerals, even as former daimyo Kamei Koremi and right-hand man Fukuba Bisei promoted Shinto death rites from Tokyo.[93]

Thus as the Restorationists pursued a hoped-for Shinto future, they were forced to work with a resilient Buddhist present. They even went so far as to entrust priests of the "barbaric" faith with the job of propagating the imperial gospel. In the spring of 1872 the Council of State established the Ministry of Doctrine (Kyōbushō) to replace the Ministry of Rites (which had suffered from internal bickering and charges of incompetence) and ordered the new ministry to instill reverence for emperor, nation, and *kami* among the masses.[94] To fulfill this ideological task, the new ministry began the systematic training of so-called "doctrinal instructors" *(kyōdōshoku)*. Most of them turned out to be Buddhist priests who volunteered to become instructors out of a desire to improve relations with a hostile government, and the nativist-led ministry, figuring that Shinto ends justified Buddhist means, made a tactical decision to use them.[95]

The ministry once more adjusted its Shinto vision to a Buddhist reality when it decided to ban "independent" funerals early in the summer of 1872. Since the Restoration, the Council of State had regularly warned local officials to exercise caution when approving unofficiated funerals, for they could possibly provide cover for those adhering to Christianity and other undesirable doctrines. Now it decided to deal with the danger by prohibiting independent funerals altogether. This forced Japanese who wanted non-Buddhist funerals, even Confucian ones, to rely on Shinto priests certified by the Ministry of Doctrine, thus giving ritual support to the government's indoctrination campaign. At the same time, however, the law reaffirmed the existing relationship between Buddhist temples and their parishioners, explicitly stating that mortuary rites not handled by a Shinto priest must be entrusted to a Buddhist cleric.[96]

Designed mainly to bring non-Buddhist funerals under the control of Shinto priests, the ministry's ban on independent funerals had the unintended effect of assisting a reversion to Buddhist death rites. This was the case for one village in what is now Saitama prefecture. In 1869 the village headman, purportedly after having consulted with residents, obtained permission from his superiors to convert the entire village to Shinto funerals. He roused the villagers at six o'clock one morning with a drum, and members of 110 households quickly ripped out old gravestones and statues of the bodhisattva Jizō from the graveyard. The burial ground was then ritually purified and an ancestral shrine *(tamaya)* erected. According to a contemporary account, the appearance of the graveyard was "completely altered in an instant, as if in a dream."[97] But in 1872, within a month of the ban on independent funerals, 107 villagers signed a petition to become temple parishioners and engage in Buddhist death rites once more. The nativist record of events described the village's adoption of non-Buddhist funerals in 1869 as a heartfelt conversion to Shinto funerals *(shinsōsai),* but the petition of 1872 gave a very different picture. Submitted to the prefecture's head office, it claimed that the main reason the villagers had adopted independent funerals *(jishin sōsai,* a variant of *jisō-sai)* several years earlier was that at the time there was no priest in residence at the local temple, making it difficult to perform funerals. In light of the recent ban on independent funerals, however, villagers wanted to resume their standing as temple parishioners. The petition made no mention of Shinto funerals at all.[98]

It was also in 1872 that the governor of Gunma prefecture sent an inquiry to the Ministry of Doctrine asking how to handle a growing number of requests to switch back to Buddhist funerals within his jurisdiction. He noted that the true faith and intent of people who had asked for permission to conduct independent funerals was unclear and speculated that "one can imagine that there are those who were pressured by the authority of local officials and therefore had no choice but to apply." He thus concluded that people should be free to foreswear Shinto funerals and resume the performance of Buddhist ones.[99] The Ministry of Doctrine agreed with the governor, replying that permission should be granted based on people's wishes.

This did not mean that officials in the Ministry of Doctrine and elsewhere in the Meiji government were any less committed to undermining "foreign" Buddhism and boosting nativist Shinto. By 1872 the "destroy the buddhas, annihilate Shākyamuni" attacks had died down, but in their wake the regime undercut Buddhist authority with legal measures that made a greater long-term impact than did the traumatic, but transitory, violence. It was just weeks before banning independent funerals, in fact, that the Council of State officially lifted the Tokugawa prohibitions on marriage, the consumption of meat, and the donning of secular garb among Buddhist monks, a move that severely compromised the ability of the different sects to maintain discipline among their ranks.[100] Later in that year officials also required all monks and nuns to adopt surnames, another change in policy intended to blur if not erase the line between Buddhist clerics and ordinary Japanese.[101] Taken together, both measures destroyed the integrity of the Buddhist clergy as a special status group while contributing to the standardization of governance, which was a top priority for the nascent state.

THE CENTRALIZATION AND PURIFICATION OF SHINTO DEATH

As they tried to find the right balance between using and undermining the Buddhist establishment, officials in Tokyo continued to take proactive steps to advance the nativist cause and Shinto funerals in particular. Besides devising a network of shrines to honor and comfort the war dead, the Council of State established Shinto cemeteries in Tokyo, initially for officials and aristocrats, then for ordinary city dwellers. It further ordered that Buddhist priests allow Shinto burial rites in existing temple cemeteries throughout Japan.[102]

Nativist officials also sought to standardize Shinto funerals by bringing them under the control of a priesthood regulated not by the Yoshida or any other sacerdotal lineage, but by the government itself.[103] To that end the Council of State, encouraged by the Ministry of Doctrine, not only prohibited independent funerals in 1872, requiring those who wanted non-Buddhist funerals to rely on certified Shinto priests, it also commanded all priests to assist shrine parishioners and others who might wish to perform Shinto death rites, even if the priests had never handled such rites in the past.[104]

There was, however, a major obstacle to instituting this plan: the widespread and deeply entrenched belief among nativists and non-nativists alike that people who had come in contact with death pollution must refrain from worshipping the *kami* for weeks, months, or even an entire year. This belief features prominently, for example, in *Sōgiryaku* (A sketch of funeral rites), a Shinto funeral manual written just before the Restoration. The manual stresses that the local earth *kami* at the gravesite must be propitiated before burial takes place and the purification of the ground and offerings to the *kami* handled by someone "absolutely untainted by *kegare*." Nevertheless, once the body is placed in the earth, the spot becomes polluted, so although it is proper to erect a grave marker, it is "absurd" to follow the fashion of constructing a small shrine. The manual also instructs mourners to purify themselves with a *sakaki* branch after the burial and to wash themselves in a nearby river when coming out of mourning. Finally, it warns that contact with death pollution, regardless of one's relationship to the deceased, disqualifies one from serving the *kami* for thirty days, and scolds "miserable" priests who are asked to purify homes after funerals but do not take measures to guard against being tainted themselves.[105]

Running counter to this sentiment, nativists in the Ministry of Doctrine wanted Shinto priests to attend both to the private rites of death and to the public rites of the *kami,* which, according to the principle of "unity of rites and rule," were simultaneously the rites of state. But how was this going to be logistically possible if every time a priest performed a funeral he could not serve the *kami* for at least a month? Faced with this thorny question, officials in Tokyo came up with a bureaucratic solution: eliminate the legal recognition of *kegare,* at least the acknowledgement of *kegare* as a danger that diminished only with time.

In the summer of 1871, a year prior to the ban on independent funerals, Restorationists had, in fact, already begun to disentangle the mechanisms of state from the management of *kegare* by abolishing the legal status of the outcaste *eta* and *hinin* and registering them as ordinary Japanese *(heimin)* instead.[106] Then in the early spring of 1872 the state abolished intragovernmental regulations regarding birth *kegare,* a move that freed officials to go to work even if their wives or other female relatives had just given birth.[107] Designed to keep officials at their jobs as much as possible in an era of pressing change, this policy decision was another striking departure from the conventions of the shogunate, which had set up elaborate procedures to shield the

Tokugawa lineage and all of Edo castle from the *kegare* generated by births as well as deaths.[108]

The ground was therefore to an extent prepared when the Council of State, later in the spring of 1872, decreed that a person officiating at a funeral had to refrain from worshipping the *kami* only on the day the funeral in question took place. As long as he performed an act of purification *(harai)*, he did not have to wait for an entire month to visit a Shinto shrine, as the author of *Sōgi-ryaku* insisted, but could go the very next day. In one stroke the council dispensed with the centuries-old belief that pollution dissipated slowly over time, replacing it with a ritual technology that could eliminate pollution literally overnight. The practical result? As far as the state was concerned, Shinto priests could now conduct death rites on one day and carry out their duties to the *kami* on the next.[109] Proclaimed several weeks before it banned independent funerals, the council's decree allowed for the Ministry of Doctrine's plan to turn servants of the *kami* into officiants of funerals.

With independent funerals banned, and Shinto priests both enabled and ordered to perform funerals, nativists in the Ministry of Doctrine took another important step in implementing their plan to create a state-directed Shinto free from the Yoshida or any other lineage. In the remaining months of 1872 it began distributing its own manual for Shinto funerals, *Sōsai ryakushiki* (A summary of funeral rites),[110] with the aim of controlling these funerals not only from the outside in, but, by dictating their ritual contents, from the inside out.

Like its Tokugawa forerunners, the *Sōsai ryakushiki* blends the rites and paraphernalia of *kami* worship with Confucian teachings and protocol. After warning that families who wish to perform Shinto death rites must inform both their local district head *(kochō)* and the priest of their tutelary shrine *(tsu-busuna no jinja)*, the manual proceeds to explain the steps of a Shinto funeral, using both written descriptions and pictures. Initial procedures include covering the face of the dead with a white cloth, lighting a lamp, and setting up a table holding rice, water, salt, and other offerings. When preparing the corpse for the coffin, there is no need to bathe it; just wiping the corpse with a wash-cloth will do, according to the manual. This guideline was apparently included to preserve the dignity of the dead, as the process of bathing the corpse— aimed at least in part to scrub away death *kegare*—could be far from gentle.[111] The remainder of the book informs readers how to do everything from preparing the mortuary tablet (called *tamashiro* in contrast to the Buddhist term *ihai*) to burying the coffin, with each step incorporating one or more of the signature marks of *kami* worship: bowing, clapping, and presenting *tamagushi* (sacred *sakaki* branches with folded pieces of white paper attached). Conspicuously absent is the offering of incense, which had been identified by nativist scholars as something Buddhist and therefore "not the way of our country." [112]

In proper Confucian qua nativist fashion, the *Sōsai ryakushiki* promotes a rational, earthbound approach to mortuary rites, sidestepping any mention of a postmortem existence beyond the limits of family life and public order. Taking a page from the shogunate, the manual enjoins mourners not to waste coins by placing them in the coffin. Why consign money to the realm of the dead when it could instead be used among the living? Eschewing popular superstition, the manual also fails to include any discussion of the days popularly considered inauspicious for funerals and burials, in particular *tomobiki no hi,* one among six lucky or unlucky days recurring in a calendrical cycle. The widespread taboo surrounding *tomobiki no hi* was (and still is) based on the fact that the word *tomobiki* consists of two characters meaning "friend" and "pull." To hold a funeral on *tomobiki no hi* created the danger of pulling someone else into death, so if someone died on that day, his or her mortuary rites would often be postponed to the next one. The Justice Ministry's survey of Japanese customs, published in 1880, notes the popularity of this practice, but the Ministry of Doctrine's funeral manual, produced just eight years earlier, ignores it entirely. [113] Finally, and not surprisingly, hardly any of the manual is devoted to countering or even recognizing the danger of death pollution. It instructs the family of the deceased to install the mortuary tablet in a "pure" location and to clean the house and change the cooking fire when coming out of the initial stage of mourning, but not once does it refer directly to *kegare.*

By enabling, then ordering, Shinto priests to attend to both the rites of death and the rites of state, and by producing and distributing a funeral manual in which they barely acknowledged the existence of *kegare,* early Meiji leaders tried to Shintoize the populace and rationalize Shinto at one and the same time. Early in 1873 the council went a step further by abolishing any and all regulations designed to prevent the transmission of *kegare.* [114] In the bureaucratic consultations leading up to this announcement, the Council of State's Department of Ceremony (Shikiburyō) pointed out that after someone had died, his or her household was supposedly polluted for thirty days, requiring visitors to wear disposable sandals *(zōri)* into the house and to sit on specially placed mats. However, those in the middling classes often did not pay attention to such niceties, and after only seven days purified their *kegare* and went about their normal business. There were farmers and others, meanwhile, who did not take *kegare* into consideration even for a day, it was noted. [115]

Showing how plastic antiquity could be, the department also suggested the theory that Japanese of the distant past did not associate periods of mourning with the problem of *kegare*.[116] The touchstone used to support this conjecture was a passage in the *Nihon shoki* concerning the death of Emperor Chūai.[117] Immediately following his demise, Empress Jingū supposedly ordered a purification ceremony and constructed a "palace of worship" in which she "discharged in person the office of priest."[118] In the eyes of the Council of State this was sufficient proof that it was ritual purification, not time, that healed polluted wounds.

The Council of State did not mean to eliminate entirely the concept of mourning, only to disassociate it from *kegare* and to redefine it as a time of sorrow. The council's consultative branch (the Sa-in)[119] therefore recommended that the government fix mourning periods for survivors based on the nature of their relationships to the deceased, with the purpose of giving families time to grieve, not to guard against spreading *kegare*.[120] The Council of State announced in October 1874 that the mourning periods for samurai families henceforth applied to all Japanese, and it dissolved the system that had been used exclusively for aristocrats. In the consultations leading up to this decree, the Sa-in confirmed that the primary aim of mourning was to express grief, an aim shared by people of "all nations." To support this assertion, it cited the work of nativist scholar Ishihara Masaakira (1759–1821), who had argued decades earlier that the link between mourning and *kegare* was a fabrication of medieval times.[121] Severing this link confirmed the government's commitment to the Confucian/nativist view that mourning was a natural manifestation of filial sorrow, not a time to worry about the ritual danger posed by death.

CIVILIZATION AND ENLIGHTENMENT

Distancing itself from the folk belief in *kegare* also contributed to the official effort to prove to the European and American powers, and to the emperor's subjects, that Japan was on track to becoming a modern, progressive nation devoted to "civilization and enlightenment" *(bunmei kaika)*. From 1871 to 1873, as the Ministry of Doctrine and Council of State promoted a nativist agenda, some of the most powerful leaders in the Meiji government, led by courtier Iwakura Tomomi, traveled through America and Europe with the aim of revising the unequal treaties. In this they failed, but they returned to Japan with the conviction that their homeland could, indeed, achieve parity with the West *(seiyō),* and that the way to do this was to build a "wealthy country, strong army" *(fukoku kyōhei)* along Western lines. This aim increasingly dominated government policy in the 1870s and drove the establishment of post offices, railroads, newspapers, factories, and the many other accoutrements of the modern world. The assumption that to modernize meant to Westernize also took root in civilian circles, encouraged by Fukuzawa Yukichi (1834–1901) and other prominent intellectuals who equated "civilization and enlightenment" with not only the technologies and institutions of the West but its philosophies and customs as well.

For forward-looking nativists, the trick was to link the revival of an ancient way to the "enlightenment" sweeping Japan, and they were, in some respects, successful in doing just that. The decision to abolish the legal recognition of *kegare,* for instance, allowed Shinto priests to become officiants of funerals and at the same time rationalized the mechanisms of government, a critical step in the creation of a modern nation-state. Elites both in and outside government also viewed Shinto death rituals as inherently more "enlightened" than their Buddhist counterparts. A notice appearing in the July 1873 issue of a newsbook popular among the literate public, the *Shinbun zasshi,*[122] reflects this sentiment. As this was an age of "enlightenment," a Mr. Iino of Kumagaya prefecture recently wore "Western-style, tight-sleeved summer clothes" to his mother's funeral, it was reported. And yet the ceremony was not Shinto, but Buddhist, and took place at a Buddhist temple. Therefore, even though the funeral "could be thought to have the trappings of enlightenment, this cannot really be called enlightenment," the notice concluded.[123]

It was also in the name of "enlightenment" that the Council of State, in the summer of 1873, banned cremation.[124] Generations of Confucians and nativists had attacked the "barbaric" and "unfilial" custom on the grounds that it demonstrated disrespect for the dead. Now, under the banner of "civilization and enlightenment," they bolstered their timeworn agenda with a distinctly modern justification: the defense of public health.

CHAPTER 3

THE GREAT CREMATION DEBATE

Cremation in Japan today is an accepted fact of death. Fueled by a nationwide infrastructure of government-regulated facilities, the cremation rate is nearly 100 percent, defining, in large part, what it means to die Japanese. The practice of burning the dead has existed in Japan since prehistoric times and has been performed by a significant segment of the population since the medieval period, when it was propagated as a merit-generating Buddhist ritual. Yet despite its adoption by many communities as an act of spiritual merit, cremation was never mandated by Buddhist doctrine, and most temples and their parishioners preferred full-body burial well into the twentieth century. Not until the 1930s were more than half of the dead in Japan cremated instead of buried whole; and in some regions, such as Ibaraki prefecture, the number of cremations did not exceed the number of full-body burials until the late 1970s.[1] Although infused with Buddhist rituals such as reading sutras and offering incense, cremation as a standard practice is therefore a relatively recent phenomenon, one inseparable from the historical development of Japan as a modern nation-state.

The rationale responsible for this phenomenon crystallized in the 1870s, when the basic features of Japan's modernity were being argued into existence in the wake of the Restoration of 1868. In the middle of this turbulent decade, cremation became a subject of intense controversy. Reviled by Confucians and nativists alike, it was outlawed in the summer of 1873, making it a prominent casualty of the early Meiji campaign to eliminate "evil customs of the past." The ban was justified by the government on two grounds: first, consigning bodies to flames was disrespectful to the dead and therefore damaging to public morals; second, the foul smoke produced by burning corpses was injurious to public health. The ultimate irony of the ban, however, is that it facilitated the creation of a widely accepted logic for the act it was expressly designed to stop. Opponents of the ban agreed to the government's terms of engagement and turned them to their advantage, arguing in newspapers and in memorials submitted to the government that cremation actually contributed to the physical and moral health of the nation by producing compact, portable, and hygienic remains that could be consolidated in ancestral gravesites. Put on the defensive, the Council of State agreed to lift the prohibition in May 1875, less than two years after it was enacted, and in the following decades the rationale for cremation that was constructed in response to the government's ban fueled the spread of the practice in the decades to come, transforming a minority practice into a marker of "Japaneseness" in the modern age.

EXTINGUISHING THE MOST UNFILIAL OF ACTS

When the Council of State bluntly declared in July 1873, "Henceforth, cremation is forbidden,"[2] the outlawed practice was understood by both its supporters and detractors to be a specifically Buddhist mode of handling the dead, originating, like Buddhism itself, in India. Full-body burial was the choice for a majority of Japanese;[3] nonetheless, by the Meiji Restoration, cremation had become deeply entrenched in areas with large concentrations of Jōdo Shinshū believers, as well as in the cities of Kyoto, Osaka, and Edo, where the reduction of corpses into bones and ash allowed parishioners to build family graves in crowded urban graveyards. Although not theologically mandated by Buddhism, cremation was credited with great spiritual merit. As Yoda Hyakusen, head of the Tokyo City Council (Kaigisho), noted during a debate on the subject, "There are those who truly believe that cremation turns one into a buddha."[4]

The Restoration government was hostile toward Buddhism in any form, so the ban on cremation can be interpreted as yet one more means to undermine the "foreign" faith. It would be a mistake, however, to view cremation as just one Buddhist custom among many. To its enemies, it was the most heinous practice of all, an evil in and of itself. In bureaucratic correspondence leading up to the ban, officials singled out cremation as a particularly cruel custom "intolerable to humanity,"[5] and a few months before the ban went into effect, an anonymous author submitted a letter to the leading newspaper of the day, the *Tōkyō nichi nichi shinbun*, asserting, like Kumazawa Banzan two centuries earlier, that cremation was even more despicable than butchering a corpse with a sword. "How could a filial child, a humane person, tolerate this?" the indignant writer asked, and then suggested that the practice be abolished as part of the nation's efforts to "enlighten" the masses.[6]

Immediately after the Restoration, anti-cremation forces saw their chance to do just that. Kyoto officials petitioned the central government in 1869 to let them prohibit cremation, noting that it was a "terribly inhumane" and "truly intolerable" practice. They were told, however, that the matter had to be given more thought, since it affected the "unity of the entire realm."[7] Also in 1869 a majority of the regime's new deliberative assembly (Kōgisho), which was composed of samurai representing the different domains,[8] passed a resolution to prohibit cremation, but the Council of State failed to enact it into law.[9] With more pressing matters to attend to, Restoration leaders took no action for the next several years.

In the spring of 1873, however, developments in the government's own backyard finally prompted the Council of State to enact a nationwide ban. On May 22 the Tokyo police sent a proposal to the Justice Ministry (Shihōshō) suggesting that cremation grounds be removed from densely populated neighborhoods in the capital. Referring specifically to the "cremation temples" *(kasōdera)* of Senju, as well as to the cremation grounds at the Reiganji and Jōshinji temples, the police wrote, "when bodies are burned, the smoke spreads out in all directions and the severe stench injures people's health."[10] The police therefore suggested banning cremation at these three locations and at other places inside and immediately around the "red line" *(shubikisen)* that encircled the city's six main wards.[11] This proposal did not call for a comprehensive ban of cremation, recommending only that any new facilities for the practice—which, at the time, comprised little more than fire pits covered with roofs to keep out the rain—be built outside the city.

Relocating cremation grounds was not an entirely new idea. The cremation temples of Senju were themselves established in 1669 after Shogun Ietsuna (1641–1680), offended by the smell of burning corpses when he visited his family's tombs at the Kan'eiji temple in Ueno, ordered a halt to cremations within the precincts of temples located in the nearby Shitaya and Asakusa districts.[12]

The smell was also a factor in the decision to ban cremation in 1873. There was, nonetheless, a novel factor at play in 1873, and that was a distinctly modern concern to protect the health of the masses. This concern was increasingly shared by Meiji elites, both in and out of government, who wanted healthy bodies to man the armies, schools, and factories of the new Japan. Even before the Tokyo police made their proposal, one city resident submitted a letter to the *Tōkyō nichi nichi shinbun* complaining that the stench produced by cremation was not only offensive but also "injurious to people's health," adding that he hoped the practice would be abolished.[13]

The Tokyo police suggested that cremation grounds be removed from populated areas, but when their concern for public health collided with the centuries-old Confucian bias against cremation, events quickly took a new direction.[14] The Justice Ministry passed the police proposal on to the Council of State, and the council's General Affairs Section (Shomuka) composed a memo warning that an official relocation of the cremation grounds would translate into de facto approval of cremation on the part of the state. It therefore suggested,

> How about taking this opportunity to decisively prohibit [cremation]? Naturally, long-standing temple parishioners will be stubborn, and it is difficult for the authorities to gauge the difficulties arising from a sudden ban. So in the meantime, if it is not too inconvenient, perhaps we should solicit the opinion of the Ministry of Doctrine.[15]

On June 3 the Council of State contacted the ministry, proposing that the mere relocation of crematories be transformed into an outright prohibition, not just

A cremation in 1860s Edo. From *Sketches of Japanese Manners and Customs,* by J. M. W. Silver.

in Tokyo but throughout all Japan. Not surprisingly, nativists at the Ministry of Doctrine jumped at the chance to outlaw the "barbarian custom," as they put it, and gave their reply within twenty-four hours of receiving word from the Council of State: ban cremation.[16]

The prohibition of cremation was of course anti-Buddhist to the extent that cremation was a Buddhist practice. Those who argued against cremation from the Song period to the Meiji Restoration, whether Confucian scholars or Shinto nativists, consistently blamed the Buddhist clergy for encouraging the custom. And throughout the bureaucratic communiqués leading to the ban, Meiji officials repeatedly claimed that cremation had originated in India and had only been brought to China and Japan through the corrupting influence of Buddhism. Yet in an era when anything Buddhist was subject to condemnation but not necessarily proscription, the Meiji government sought to ban cremation for more specific reasons, isolating the act as a menace in and of itself. The argument against cremation had first developed in Song China, where the practice was identified as "the greatest possible sin" against filial devotion. This moralistic stance was imported into Japan in the Tokugawa period and, after the Meiji Restoration, was augmented by a new understanding of cremation as "injurious to people's health." This hybrid of a new concern for hygiene and a long-standing characterization of cremation as "unfilial" constituted the foundation for the ban, setting the terms for the subsequent controversy.

DEFENDING CHOICE

Determined to honor the traditions of their ancestors, there were those who openly flouted the government's ban. In an inquiry to the Home Ministry (Naimushō) dated January 13, 1874, for example, officials in Ishikawa prefecture asked how to deal with one man who, after having buried his father in accordance with the law, later exhumed and cremated him. And on April 12, 1875 (only about a month and a half before the ban was repealed), community leaders throughout Aomori prefecture were warned to keep the cremation ban firmly in mind, as there were reports of people defying the government's will.[17] But while there were those who did not comply with the ban, it was successfully enforced in many regions—especially in more easily monitored urban centers—and the resulting hardship and resentment generated one of the great debates of early Meiji.[18]

The government presumed to know what was best for the moral and physical health of the nation, but protesters argued in newspapers and petitions that it was no business of the state to determine how mourners disposed of their dead. One of the more eloquent proponents of this view was Ōuchi Seiran (1845–1918), the prominent Buddhist activist who in 1874 founded Japan's first pan-Buddhist magazine. In characterizing cremation as a practice "contrary to humanity *(ninjō),*" the Council of State presumed, in good Confucian fashion, that "humanity" was something normative to be guided from a ruling center. In his memorial to the Sa-in, Ōuchi countered that "humanity" was molded by custom and therefore prone to local variation. If, as supporters of the ban maintained, cremation was "intolerable" to those with the correct measure of "humanity," how could they explain the distress produced by the ban? In Shiga and Ishikawa prefectures, those prevented from burning the dead tried to "alleviate their feelings" by piling firewood on top of graves and lighting them on fire, wrote Ōuchi. Although he called this proxy cremation something "foolish" done in remote areas, it nevertheless showed the depth of the commitment to cremation, a phenomenon that should be understood by the government to be an expression of humanity, not a corruption of it. "Even beasts and birds are moved by death. Therefore people are moved and cry whether they bury in the ground or whether they cremate." Consequently, "why should we make the customs and views of one person standard throughout the realm?" he asked. He answered his rhetorical question by further writing,

> It is insupportable to say that districts practicing cremation do not produce any good, filial people, and that households practicing burial do not produce wicked, immoral children. Therefore, we should not argue about the reasonableness, the emotional effect, and, finally, the right and wrong, of cremation versus full-body burial.[19]

Most of the ban's opponents, like Ōuchi, framed their efforts as a defense of personal or local autonomy, calling on the government to leave the decision of whether to cremate to individual mourners and their communities.[20] The fact that there was a ban to start with, however, meant that the government was not willing to leave its hands off the minds and bodies of the masses. At the time of the prohibition the government was in the midst of its campaign to proselytize state teachings, coordinated by the Ministry of Doctrine. The new regime was also tightening its grip on the bodies of the emperor's subjects through the creation of a new household registration system and the establishment of a conscript army. It would take more than enunciating the principle of laissez-faire to undermine the ban.

Therefore the ban's opponents did not rest with the argument that, because the expression of "humanity" was a relative phenomenon, the state should allow freedom of choice. In order to gain a sympathetic ear both in and out of government circles, they became cremation boosters, and they did so by hijacking their opponents' appeals to filial piety and public health.

THE FAMILY THAT GRAVES TOGETHER STAYS TOGETHER

In February 1873 a petition was submitted to the Shūgi-in suggesting that the majority of Buddhist temples in Kyoto, Osaka, and Tokyo be abolished and their graveyards converted into economically productive land. The author of the petition reasoned that, once the spirit had left it, the body was like "the molted shell of a cicada," so it was foolish to treat the grave as if it were the eternal domicile of the dead. Nativist and Confucian officials were not averse to consolidating Buddhist temples, but destroying graveyards was another matter. In an indignant response to the petition, the Shūgi-in stressed that worship at ancestral graves was the "wellspring" of civic morality and that the fortification of people's hearts through this practice was the "lifeline of the nation's health." If the government trampled on the graves of commoners, it would not be long before the imperial tombs themselves were destroyed, it warned.[21]

Despite the expression of such sentiments, the Meiji state seriously compromised the integrity of ancestral graves when it decided to ban cremation only a few months later. In claiming that burning the dead was "unfilial" and "contrary to humanity," officials condemned the immediate act of consigning the deceased to flames. But this fixation on burning flesh did not acknowledge the end result of cremation: remains that were compact, portable, and thus easily gathered into family graves. Full-body burial required relatively large plots of land, whereas the bones and ash of many family members could be interred in one small area. The space-saving quality of cremation made it especially attractive to urban households, and by the end of Tokugawa rule many city residents had come to depend on cremation as a way to maintain family graves at crowded temple cemeteries. Furthermore, cremated remains could be transported over long distances, allowing for the retrieval of relatives who had died far from home. Supporters of cremation therefore hailed the practice as the most efficient means to consolidate deceased relatives at one site and attacked the ban as a sanctimonious measure that, in dividing families from their dead, was anything but a defense of "humanity."

Even in China, where cremation had been outlawed for centuries, the Qing government permitted the practice for cases in which someone had died far from home, thereby allowing the remains to be transported back to his or her ancestral tomb. Apparently to the Chinese, the integrity of the corporate gravesite was more important than the condition of the individual body.[22] Meiji leaders, in contrast, made no such allowances, adhering instead to the hard-line position espoused by Confucian scholar Ōtsuki Risai in the seventeenth century: "Even if [those who die far from home] turn into grass that is trampled underfoot, this is preferable to consigning them to fire."[23]

The government's rigid stance opened the ban to attack as a cold-hearted policy that exiled the deceased from distant relatives. A few months into the ban (November 1873), the Senju cremators *(onbō)* petitioned the governor of Tokyo to allow them to resume operations. In support of their case they pointed out that there were many travelers who came to Tokyo from distant places; if they died, the only way to return the remains to their families was to cremate the bodies. "It is deeply lamentable when the corpse is buried in a faraway place and becomes a ghost without any ties," they wrote, addressing Confucian/nativist sensibilities while at the same time expressing a popular fear of homeless souls.[24] In a memorial submitted to the Sa-in a year later, Shinshū leader Shimaji Mokurai (1838–1911) also mentioned that those buried far from home became "unworshipped spirits" and that, even if relatives desired to visit their distant graves, often they could not afford the cost of travel.[25] A further dimension was added to this argument when a Tokyo priest, in his memorial to the government, pointed out the benefit of transporting the cremated remains of soldiers who had perished on battlefields far from home. Appealing to a regime that had just instituted a conscript army, he stated that the cremated remains of a soldier, if brought home, would naturally be revered, and as a result "public sentiment would be harmonized."[26] Burning the dead was thereby promoted as a way to unify not only individual families but also the entire nation.

THE PROBLEM OF SPACE

Cremation was of particular importance for townspeople who could afford to maintain only small family graves in crowded temple cemeteries. They depended on the practice to keep the dead in close proximity, both to each other and to the living. In their petition to the Tokyo governor, the Senju *onbō* grumbled about the trouble caused when families accustomed to relying on cremation were suddenly forced to perform full-body burials. In one city temple with little land, they wrote, the gravestones of different households are lined up right next to each other, so when you try to bury a body, you have to dig up not only the gravestone of the mourning family but also those of neighboring plots. ... Disliking this, people rent land from other temples, but then the grave of one family is split in two and the upkeep becomes more troublesome. Furthermore, the cost of renting land and digging a hole for the grave costs several times as much as cremation, and this is terribly worrisome for the chief mourner.[27]

There were also city dwellers who buried their dead whole, whether in their own backyards or in temple graveyards large enough to accommodate full-body burial. But even before the ban went into effect, city officials were aware that a significant number of urban residents depended on the space-saving aspect of cremation to create and maintain family gravesites. When the Tokyo police submitted their initial proposal to move cremation grounds from the city center, they acknowledged that "graveyards in the city are cramped, so it is said that people often have no other choice but to cremate."[28] After the Council of State decided to outlaw cremation, it therefore instructed the authorities of the three metropolitan prefectures—Tokyo, Kyoto, and Osaka—to procure adequate space for mandated earth burial. Kyoto, which had pushed for a cremation ban four years earlier, responded that it had plenty of room at its disposal, but Osaka said it would need to condemn land in surrounding villages to supplement its six main graveyards. Tokyo, meanwhile, calculated that simply seizing empty temple land within the city's red line would provide enough gravesites to last about two hundred years. City officials added, in a blunt expression of anti-Buddhist opinion, that even more land would become available as "temple halls and pagodas naturally fall into ruin."[29]

The Council of State initially approved Tokyo's plan to appropriate temple property, seeing it as a convenient way to meet the need for more burial space, but when it learned of the proposal, the Finance Ministry (Ōkurashō) condemned the plan in a letter sent to the Council of State. Angrily noting that it was "unseemly" for decaying corpses to litter the capital, the ministry reminded the council that there were plans to build roads and other public improvements in the future and that even more "intolerable" than cremation was the prospect of having to exhume bodies and move them out of the path of development. Most important, however, prime tax-producing land would be converted into tax-free graveyards, depriving the government of a valuable source of income.[30]

Swayed by Finance Ministry arguments, the Council of State made an ironic about-face, creating a situation that, instead of alleviating the need for burial space, intensified it. The council not only reversed its earlier decision to turn temple property into graveyards, but it went so far as to inform the governor of Tokyo that it was planning to forbid *all* burials within Tokyo's red line. This regulation would not merely stem the creation of new sites for full-body burial. It would also prevent the use of preexisting graves, a policy that forced families to abandon ancestral gravesites, whether they were located in temple graveyards or plots of residential land.[31] The cremation ban thereby impinged not only on families who cremated but also on those who buried their dead whole.

The cremation ban also created difficulties for the residents of Osaka. Officials there set aside new areas for burial, but despite attempts to institute price controls, the cost of plots skyrocketed, making it impossible for the poor to buy them.[32] In July 1874 the governor of Hyōgo prefecture, Kanda Takahira, submitted an open letter to the *Tōkyō nichi nichi shinbun* asking the Council of State to lift the cremation ban because of public anger over the lack of affordable space.[33] The decision to outlaw burial within the red line made the cremation ban particularly onerous for Tokyo residents, however. As the September deadline approached, scores of temple priests and parishioners in the capital submitted memorials attacking both the impending prohibition on urban burial and the year-old ban on cremation that was ultimately responsible for it.

Tokunaga Kanmyō, priest at a branch temple of Kan'eiji in Yotsuya, noted in his August 1874 petition to the Council of State that there were "thousands of temples of the seven sects and hundreds of thousands of parishioners" within Tokyo's red line and that the approaching ban on urban burial had thrown them into confusion and grief. The parishioners at his own temple were questioning him every day, but he was not able to respond adequately, he wrote. This was because "they do not understand the reasoning of 'civilization.' Mired in old habits, they are attached to the graves of their ancestors." In drawing up the new regulations for burial in Tokyo, bureaucrats had decided to allow spouses whose mates had already been buried within the red line to join them when they themselves died.[34] But while an exception was made in deference to the conjugal bond, no allowances were made for other family ties —this despite the fact that, as Tokunaga pointed out, "families put the greatest importance on ancestors." Claiming that he desired to protect "reverence for *kami* and love of country," Tokunaga asked, "How could people not perform rites for the ancestors?" He also joined the Confucians at their own game by writing that it was only natural for children to adore their parents, so if their graves were located far away, the bond between parent and child would be strained and the ancestral rites "thrown into confusion." According to Tokunaga, the most practical way to avoid this fate was to lift the cremation ban and allow people to resume burying cremated remains, if not necessarily whole bodies, within the red line.[35]

Cremation advocates also argued that new cemeteries outside the red line would rapidly fill with dead bodies, making them insufficient to meet the growing need for grave space. Buddhist spokesman Ōuchi Seiran conjectured that the public cemeteries would reach capacity within several years, creating a situation in which "graves will have to be built on top of graves so that, finally, coffins will be exhumed and remains disturbed."[36] Despite such protests, however, the ban on burial within the red line went into effect in September 1874, and even city dwellers accustomed to earth burial were evicted from their ancestral graveyards. As a consequence, residents of Tokyo, like those of Osaka, saw prices for gravesites rapidly escalate. Only a month after the red line ban went into effect, Shimaji Mokurai noted, "Land [for graves] is being sold in the city [Tokyo], but the asking price is hard on the poor, so there are complaints on all sides."[37] The solution he offered was the same proposed by Tokunaga, Ōuchi, and others: lift the ban on cremation.

By coming to the defense of ancestral graves, particularly those in Tokyo, cremation advocates highlighted the inconsistency of a government policy ostensibly designed to promote filial devotion and "humanity." However, they also addressed the issue of grave space on a more dispassionate level, appealing to the materialistic concerns of a government bent on creating a "wealthy country and strong army" *(fukoku kyōhei)*. One cremation advocate, in a letter to the *Yūbin hōchi shinbun,*[38] attacked the wastefulness of the government ban by extrapolating its consequences far into the future: "Land in Japan is exceedingly scarce. . . . If the limited land of Japan is used for potentially limitless burial plots, after several thousand years, the majority of fields will become graveyards."[39] In another letter to the newspaper entitled "Kasō ben'e-kiron" (On the benefits of cremation), an educator at an academy in Tokyo also brought up the issue of urban development. "In these times, for the benefit of the people, the court commands roadwork, and even if there is a temple graveyard in the way, it must be removed," he observed. Since it was far easier to relocate cremated remains than whole bodies, instead of banning cremation, the government should encourage it, he wrote.[40] Cremation advocates therefore not only sought to preserve access to existing ancestral graves, but also, by taking a broader and more forward-looking perspective, argued that cremation provided the best means to maintain contact with the dead in an increasingly urban and mobile world.

FOUL SMOKE AND ROTTING CORPSES

In order to outflank their foes on the issue of "humanity," cremation proponents made the case that worship at family graves was facilitated by the reduction of corpses to bones and ash. Similarly, when they tackled the charge that crematory smoke was damaging to public health, the ban's opponents deflected attention away from the process of burning itself and on to what it produced: remains that were not only compact and portable, but "clean" as well. By arguing that rotting corpses were a far greater menace than burning ones, they successfully turned the issue of hygiene to their own advantage. Several months into the ban, for example, one Tokyo resident noted in a letter to the *Yūbin hōchi shinbun* that epidemics spread from diseased corpses, and he underscored the fact that these epidemics could filter up from the people to eventually threaten the emperor himself. Cremating diseased corpses was the proper way to manage this danger, he said, adding that it was inconsistent to view cremation as inhumane at a time when doctors were dissecting bodies for the advancement of science.[41]

This view of cremation as a measure to protect against disease was not new. By the end of the Tokugawa period it had become common practice in urban areas to cremate those who had died of contagious diseases such as tuberculosis, leprosy, and cholera.[42] However, whereas the letter to the *Yūbin hōchi shinbun* appealed to science, ordinary city dwellers burned the dead from the folk belief that the *kegare* (pollution) produced by corpses disfigured by illness was particularly dangerous. The Senju cremators admitted as much when they pleaded with the governor of Tokyo to allow them to resume operations on a limited basis. Their petition noted that people feared the transmission of diseases like leprosy and tuberculosis from afflicted corpses: "According to popular belief . . . if their corpses are burned, the origin of the disease is arrested, and one is relieved of the fear that [the illness] will be passed on to others." The representatives did not cite medical authorities, conceding, "we do not know whether rumors are true or not." Nevertheless, "it has been a custom from long ago for families with people afflicted with these diseases to burn them without fail when they die." Even though such a belief might be "baseless" and merely "superstition," it was commonly accepted as true and should therefore be honored, they wrote.[43]

The belief that fire could destroy pollution *(kegare)*, both physical and spiritual, was also accepted among educated elites. "As a rule, there is nothing more purifying for rituals in heaven and earth than fire. . . . Everyone knows that cypress wood is used in the sacred precincts of Ise to create fire for purification," stated the author of "Kasō ben'ekiron," who did not limit his advocacy of purification through fire to diseased bodies, but recommended cremation as the best method to dispose of corpses in general, since any dead body "rots and gives off a foul smell." Especially in the summer months, wrote Satake, graves "exude a rotting stench into the heat, which is carried by the wind into the atmosphere and hurts animals and spreads disease, injuring even human life." Through cremation, in contrast, one "transforms a body with five *shaku* [approximately five feet] of rotting stench into a pure cache of precious bones. . . . In this manner, cremation purifies the filthy body and it becomes a means toward worship. Who could call this disrespectful?"[44]

The supporters of the ban had no trouble calling it disrespectful, vigorously disputing the argument that cremation should be utilized as a way to dispose of the dead, diseased or not. One man from Shiga prefecture wrote to the *Tōkyō nichi nichi shinbun* saying that there was no need to cremate those who had died of infectious disease if they were buried in remote locations.[45] And the leader of the Tokyo City Council, Yoda Hyakusen, mocked the claim that cremation was a cleaner way of disposal by retorting in his debate with colleagues that if simply getting rid of the dead body were the highest priority, "then not asking whether it is [emotionally] tolerable or not, we should attach stone weights to corpses and sink them in deep ponds or in the ocean." Furthermore, cremation might prevent corpses from rotting slowly over time, but Yoda reminded his listeners that the process of burning a corpse was physically repulsive. To emphasize his point, he gave a graphic description of despicable cremators who "remove clothes and gowns and chop up bodies with an ax, burning them with bundles of wood. When the bodies fail to burn completely, they throw away [the remains], making them food for birds and beasts. Is this not extremely wretched?"[46]

Such dismissals, however, failed to stem a growing conviction among the educated public that, compared to full-body burial, cremation was the more sanitary and therefore the more "enlightened" option. This trend was encouraged by a happy coincidence for cremation advocates: at the time Japan banned cremation, medical professionals in the West were just beginning to promote the practice as a progressive method to dispose of the dead. In his defense of cremation in the *Meiroku zasshi*, the premier forum for those committed to "civilization and enlightenment," scholar Sakatani Shiroshi argued that "the rotting vapors of the dead mix with the atmosphere and mingle with the groundwater, harming the public's health"; and he supported his point by adding, "I have heard there are societies for cremation in America and that cremations are often performed there. In Europe too, there are many arguments being made [for the practice]."[47]

Sakatani's claim that Americans widely practiced cremation was mistaken, as the first cremation, at least the first cremation in an oven created especially for that purpose, would not occur there until the end of 1876.[48] He was correct, however, about the formation of societies to promote it. Cremation in the Christian world had been suppressed for centuries mainly due to the biblical doctrine of the resurrection, which taught that the dead would be raised from the earth body and soul to be judged by God. In fact, when the globe-trotting Isabella Bird mentioned Japan's cremation ban in a travelogue written three years after its repeal, she suggested, apparently unaware of its homegrown origins, that the prohibition had been ordered "in deference to European prejudices."[49] During the early 1870s, however, cremation was a cause célèbre for prominent medical professionals and social reformers in Europe and the United States. Great Britain's cremation society was formed in 1874 by the eminent surgeon Sir Henry Thompson (1820–1904), and an American counterpart was convened in New York that same year. It vigorously promoted cremation through books, articles, pamphlets, and lectures.[50]

In Europe and the United States, cremation was advocated as an up-to-date, hygienic means of disposal. Since the mid-eighteenth century, concern had been growing about overcrowding in urban graveyards, which were viewed by the medical establishment as breeding grounds for disease. "The doctors assure us that the putrid vapors that emanate from cadavers fill the air with salts and corpuscles capable of impairing health and causing fatal disease," reads one French report from 1774.[51] The initial solution devised for this problem was to move cemeteries out of city centers and into the suburbs. For example, the early 1780s witnessed the closure of all the great medieval cemeteries of Paris, which were replaced by burial grounds located out of town.[52] This trend was duplicated throughout Europe.

By the 1870s, however, doctors like Sir Henry Thompson had concluded that cremation was the long-term solution. Even if moved out of town, corpses continued to emit "poisonous exhalations" that could seep into wells and lead to the "generation of low fevers." Cremation, in contrast, was clean and efficient. It made the dead "harmless to the living."[53] The practice was further advocated from an aesthetic viewpoint. In his sermon "The Disposal of the Dead," Rev. O. B. Frothingham noted that, with cremation, "the thoughts instead of going downward into the damp, cold ground, go upwards towards the clear blue of the skies."[54]

The Western promoters of cremation faced an uphill battle against a deeply ingrained religious and cultural attachment to full-body burial. As late as 1930 Britain's cremation rate remained under 1 percent,[55] and today in the United States the majority of the dead are still buried whole.[56] In the hands of those battling the ban on cremation in Meiji Japan, however, European and American campaigns were transformed into evidence that cremation was, in fact, suitable for "civilized" nations. References to the growing acceptance of cremation in the West appeared not only in the essays written by enlightenment activists like Sakatani, but also in the petitions written by outspoken Buddhists like Shimaji Mokurai and Ōuchi Seiran, the latter noting in his memorial that "recently, foreign doctors have been arguing that buried corpses are dangerous to the living, and in Europe, treatises supporting cremation have been widespread."[57]

In fact the spread of cremation in "civilized lands" became a staple of almost all pro-cremation essays after the summer of 1874. This trend was fueled by an article appearing in the *Yūbin hōchi shinbun* that reported, in detail, the proceedings of a meeting held in London in the spring of 1874 to promote cremation. The article noted that arguments on behalf of the practice were sweeping Europe and that modern equipment for cremation was being built in Italy. Readers were then introduced to a history of cremation in different regions and times, ranging from ancient Greece to contemporary India, followed by arguments concerning its sanitary advantage over earth burial. To reinforce this point, the article also mentioned a case of workers building a railway in Quebec who contracted smallpox after digging up land where people who had died from the disease were buried. Finally, the piece introduced suggestions made by Sir Henry Thompson on how to reduce the expense and time involved in cremation through the introduction of new technology.[58]

By strategically introducing the authority of the West, the model for Japan's modernization, cremation advocates transformed what had been a local intuition about the health benefits of burning the dead into an internationally accepted fact that their opponents found difficult to deny. What made this all the more remarkable was that in Europe and America at this time the cremation movement was highly controversial, not representing at all mainstream belief and practice. Of course, the validation of cremation as a more sanitary alternative to full-body burial did not on its own dissipate the problem of crematory smoke, an issue that its advocates were still forced to address. For example, when Tokyo priest Tokunaga argued in his petition that terrible smells were released by bodies buried in shallow graves, he conceded that burning bodies also produced an unpleasant stench. He claimed, however, that cremations did not impinge much on people's lives because they were usually performed at night.[59] Other advocates did not rest with this lesser-of-two-evils defense, instead accepting that something should be done about crematory smoke. Only a few months into the ban, a Tokyo resident proposed that the problem could be alleviated by building crematories from brick and stone and furnishing them with smokestacks.[60] When the ban was lifted in May of 1875, Tokyo cremators were at the ready with plans to construct such facilities. These efforts to clean up the process of cremation set the stage for more thorough modernization in the years to come, a precondition for the acceptance of the practice throughout all Japan.

CREMATION REIGNITED

Japanese who publicly argued in favor of the ban—and they were far fewer than those who opposed it—employed the indignant language used by Toku-gawa-period Confucian scholars and their Chinese predecessors. In a letter submitted to the *Yūbin hōchi shinbun* a couple of months after the ban was implemented, an assistant Shinto priest at Tokyo's Minamimiya shrine wrote that it was "heartless" to roast a body "as if it were a small bird or eel," and then applauded the government's prohibition of the "cruel" practice, enjoin-ing his readers to obey it.[61] To its defenders, any inconvenience caused by the ban was justified by its moral purpose. In December 1873 a letter appeared in the *Tōkyō nichi nichi shinbun* claiming that during the winter months the cre-mation ban was a terrible burden on those living in the northeastern Hokuriku region, where it had been customary to cremate the dead on top of the deep winter snows and wait to bury the remains until spring. Sympathizing with the mourners who were now being forced to dig through the deep snow, its author suggested that the government show pity and lift the ban.[62] A sup-porter of the ban published a rebuttal soon after, writing that the accumula-tion of snow in his native Ushū (Dewa) was double that of Hokuriku but that the custom there had always been to bury the dead in the ground: "Even when the snow is many feet deep, it is cleared away. As few as four or five people are sufficient to dig up the earth." Deep snow, according to this writer, was no excuse to indulge in the barbaric practice of cremation.[63]

When government officials rejected petitions to lift the ban, they also denounced cremation formulaically as too "intolerable" to be defended. In response to Ōuchi Seiran's memorial, the Sa-in wrote that the arguments of cremation advocates "deviate from humanity, violate the law, and are not worth consideration." It was "unnatural" to nonchalantly put the bodies of one's parents into flames, officials stated, adding, of course, that people's natural instincts had been perverted by Buddhism. Instead of arguing with the points made about grave space and hygiene, the Sa-in dismissed them by claiming that no practical benefit could possibly outweigh the damage wrought by cremation:

> Those who argue for cremation say they worry that, since graveyards are small, if full-body burial is followed as a general rule, bodies will be exhumed and exposed. Or they say that burying a body is harmful to people's health. All these sorts of [arguments], however, derive from a rationale that is devoid of feeling. Since they only pay attention to reason, the logical conclusion of their line of argument is certainly to say that, without debating the right and wrong of cremation and burial, we should process bodies into beneficial fertilizer.[64]

Some anti-cremationists did address more directly the issues raised by their opponents. In confronting the charge that diseased corpses injured public health and should therefore be burned, they suggested the alternative of burying them in segregated graveyards. And in countering the assertion that full-body burial consumed more space than the nation could reasonably afford, they stressed that communities had been following this practice for millennia without exhausting the land, so why the sudden panic? In an August 1874 letter to the *Tōkyō nichi nichi shinbun* that began by expressing shock and dismay at Governor Kanda's open opposition to the cremation ban a month earlier, an anonymous writer from southern Kyushu cited the case of his home village, where shortage of space had never been a problem. This was due to the fact that "when people perform burials, they do not reserve one piece of land for only one body. Because it is common to bury fresh corpses in old mounds, one piece of land is sufficient for the burial of several tens of bodies."[65]

Periodic churning of the dead was not an acceptable solution, however, to those Japanese who had grown accustomed to interring cremated remains in ancestral graves. The moralistic arguments made on behalf of the ban also failed to curb public discontent, which grew as time passed. Resentment in Tokyo was particularly strong, stoked by the added prohibition on burial within the red line.

By the end of 1874 the ban's defenders had failed to gain popular support in favor of the anti-cremation policy, while their adversaries, through newspapers and petitions to government officials, had developed a compelling rationale for cremation. Proclamations that cremation was "inhumane" rang hollow in the face of arguments that burning the dead saved space, facilitated ancestor worship, and eliminated the health hazard of rotting corpses.

Badgered by the pro-cremation forces and dismayed at a lack of sufficient grave space, Tokyo officials therefore asked the Home Ministry in January 1875 to lift the ban. In doing so, they repeated the arguments of cremation advocates, noting, for instance, that even in "civilized" Western countries, cremation had begun to gain acceptance as a clean and efficient way to dispose of the dead.[66] The Home Ministry supported Tokyo's case in a letter sent to the Council of State. Despite the expansion of public graveyards in Tokyo, well-to-do families had already purchased so many plots that the city was now faced with a shortage of space, argued the ministry. It also reiterated the point that Europeans had begun to promote cremation as a hygienic measure.[67] Under pressure from both inside the government and out, the Council of State grudgingly relented. Acknowledging that the ban was extremely unpopular, the Sa-in drew up a new policy statement at the end of January that reflected the "freedom of custom" argument made by Ōuchi Seiran and other opponents of the ban: "In regard to matters such as burial, the government should not control popular opinion. One must consider the feelings and thoughts of foolish men and women and leave it to their choice. This is not a problem for governance, so the ban should be lifted." The Sa-in did lament, however, that "the people's deep commitment to cremation is not due to belief in natural law, nor out of concern for a lack of space, but actually derives from faith in Buddhism."[68]

The prohibition against cremation was officially repealed on May 23, 1875; on the same day Tokyo was informed that cremated remains could once more be interred in city graveyards.[69] The government's action was welcomed throughout Japan. Two days after the ban was abolished, Osaka's *Chōya shinbun* celebrated it in an article entitled "Kasō jinmin no jiyū to naru" (Freedom for the cremating populace). The newspaper expressed gratitude to Governor Kanda for his role in overturning the ban.[70] In Ishikawa prefecture, a Shinshū stronghold, many of those who had been barred from performing cremations took advantage of their restored freedom by exhuming the dead who had been buried whole, smashing their coffins, and cremating their remains.[71]

The decision of whether to cremate or not was once more left in the hands of "foolish men and women," but in the ban's aftermath the government still asserted ultimate jurisdiction over the bodies of its subjects—even if this meant abetting the very practice it had just been trying to extinguish. In Tokyo, for example, residents were once more allowed to bury cremated remains within the red line, but the ban on burying whole corpses remained in place, effectively *encouraging* city dwellers to practice cremation. Kyoto residents were likewise informed in September 1875 that they were to bury only cremated remains in the precincts of city temples; full-body burial was now relegated to suburban cemeteries.[72] Such restrictions on urban burial were instituted by authorities throughout Japan over the next several decades, based on the premise—firmly established during the cremation debate—that rotting corpses posed a risk to public health while cremated remains did not.[73]

Diseased bodies were considered especially dangerous, so local authorities not only encouraged cremation by banning urban burial but also mandated it during times of epidemic. In September 1877, for example, the Tokyo police ordered all bodies of cholera victims to be cremated.[74] Over the next two decades the central government gave local authorities the choice of cremating those corpses deemed contagious or quickly burying them in segregated "infectious disease graveyards" *(densenbyō bochi)*. This second option was eliminated in 1897, however, when a new law required cremation of infectious corpses throughout Japan.[75]

A practice once reviled by government officials thus became an important tool in their effort to guard public hygiene. Conversely, the public health agenda reshaped the process of cremation. When the Sa-in initially approved the proposal to abolish the cremation ban, it recommended that Tokyo and other regions establish regulations to manage crematories, taking care to keep them distant from residential areas. Alluding to the abuses of corrupt *onbō,* the Sa-in predicted, "if local officials do not manage them, past evils will resume and the poor will suffer."[76] In the months between the decision to lift the ban and its official abolition, the Home Ministry therefore began looking into the establishment of appropriate guidelines, drawing from proposals that had been put forward by cremation advocates. On June 24, a month after the ban was lifted, the ministry notified prefectural officials of the new rules, thus fulfilling the anxious prophecy voiced by the Council of State two years earlier: state-sanctioned cremation.

The Home Ministry regulations required crematories in Tokyo to be built outside the red line and those in other regions to be located in unpopulated areas with low tax revenue. Local authorities were also advised to take "suitable measures," such as constructing walls around crematories and furnishing them with smoke stacks, to reduce the adverse effect of crematory smoke on public health. Finally, the Home Ministry cautioned officials to monitor expenses and make sure that remains were not buried on crematory premises but properly interred elsewhere.[77]

Working within these guidelines, crematory operators cooperated with local authorities to build a more "civilized" form of cremation, one that would not only ameliorate evils of the past but also make the practice an increasingly attractive option for the future. Cremators in Tokyo were especially aggressive in this effort. In the month between the repeal of the ban and the announcement of the Home Ministry's new rules, they submitted requests to resume operations, and in the process transformed cremation from a parochial custom embedded in temple-parishioner relationships into a public service available to anyone who paid the necessary fee. The Senju *onbō*, for example, proposed consolidating their sect-specific facilities into a building divided into two sections, one holding three "middle-class" cremation pits and the other holding six "lower-class" pits.[78] A separate structure would also be built to accommodate solitary cremations for the elite. According to this blueprint, it was money, not sectarian affiliation, that would divide the dead from one another. Fees for cremation were fixed at standard rates of 75 sen for lower-class, 1.5 yen for middle-class, and 1.75 yen for upper-class cremations, with solitary cremations costing 5 yen.[79]

During the Tokugawa period urban cremations had commonly been performed in primitive structures called *hiya* ("fire huts"), which were usually little more than fire pits topped with roofs to keep out the rain. Consequently smoke billowed into surrounding areas. The proposed Senju crematory, however, would be a substantial building crowned with a tiled roof and a pair of smokestacks intended to disperse the stench of burning bodies. In order to further minimize the impact of smoke on people living nearby, cremations would be performed only between 8 p.m. and 10 a.m. The Senju representatives also noted that cleanliness within the building would be made a top priority and that, in times of epidemic, coffins would be tagged with the names of their occupants so as not to be confused. New rules of operation further specified that corpses were to be handled with care and the chief mourner shown due respect, while crematory attendants were to be prohibited from accepting saké and other gifts from mourning families.[80]

Dr. Tjarko Beukema, a Dutch instructor at Tokyo Medical College, investigated the new Senju facility in 1877 with a Japanese assistant and submitted a report to the governor of Tokyo in which he praised its cleanliness and efficiency. Witnessing one middle-class and two lower-class cremations—the only difference between the two classes seeming to be that the body in "middle class" was encoffined, while those in "lower class" were not—he noted that the stench "was far less offensive than we had previously imagined" and that the cremators went about their business in a very orderly and attentive manner. He concluded, "As a beneficial, sanitary method, [cremation] should be encouraged," efforts made all the while to introduce technological improvements.[81] Over the next few years, in fact, the Senju crematory built coal-burning furnaces and a new ventilation system, also installing lime-based filters to reduce the smell.[82]

The lifting of the ban stimulated efforts to modernize crematories in Osaka and Kyoto as well. In Osaka, as in other regions, Meiji economic reforms left *onbō* stripped of their feudal rights,[83] and since they lacked the necessary capital to build new crematories, big money filled the vacuum. In June 1876 Sumitomo magnate Hirose Saihei (1828–1914) helped to found the company Hachikōsha, which built crematories according to government specifications in Osaka's Nagara and Abeno cemeteries.[84] Meanwhile, in Kyoto, the Higashi and Nishi Honganji headquarters of the Shin sect's two branches reached into their deep pockets to fund the construction of that city's first modern facilities for cremation. They built a pair of crematories that opened in 1879 in Toribeno, the age-old cremation ground featured in Yoshida Kenkō's fourteenth-century *Tsurezuregusa*.[85] Designed in "Western" fashion with brick smokestacks and a ventilation system to manage the smoke, it soon became one of the "famous sites" *(meisho)* of Kyoto and was listed in an 1880 guidebook depicting the attractions of the old capital.[86]

The modernization of crematories did not sweep all of Japan at the same pace. In rural areas, where cremations were usually performed in remote fields and mountain valleys, there was little incentive to reduce or control smoke from burning corpses. Consequently, villages in certain regions continued to perform outdoor cremations well into the twentieth century.[87] Nevertheless, the new crematories of Tokyo, Osaka, and Kyoto became prominent models that were imitated throughout the nation from the 1880s on.[88] They also provided inspiration for the Western cremation movement. In 1878, for example, the English traveler Isabella Bird gained permission from the governor of Tokyo to visit the Kirigaya crematory, which, like the new crematories in Senju and elsewhere in Tokyo, had been built according to the government's recently introduced regulations. In her *Unbeaten Tracks in Japan,* she favorably noted,

> Thirteen bodies were burned the night before my visit, but there was not the slightest odour in or about the building, and the interpreter told me that, owing to the height of the chimneys, the people of the neigh-

borhood never experience the least annoyance, even while the process is going on. The simplicity of the arrangement is very remarkable, and there can be no reasonable doubt that it serves the purpose of the innocuous and complete destruction of the corpse as well as any complicated apparatus (if not better), while its cheapness places it within the reach of the class which is most heavily burdened by ordinary funeral expenses.[89]

In a footnote following this passage, Bird remarked that her visit to the Kirigaya cremation grounds was reported in the December 19 edition of the *Yomiuri shinbun,* and she noted with surprise the paper's claim that she was motivated by a desire to introduce cremation into England. Although she found the paper's reporting to be "very inaccurate," her positive impression was indeed circulated by cremation advocates in the West, appearing, for instance, in Dr. Edward J. Bermingham's 1881 polemic *The Disposal of the Dead: A Plea for Cremation.* In reviewing the state of cremation around the world, Bermingham wrote, "In Japan, where cremation has been in operation for many years, its feasibility is practically proven"; and he supported this assertion with a nearly verbatim reprise of Bird's account.[90]

Two years later German cremationists asked to see plans for the Senju facilities, now outfitted with modern ventilation systems and lime filters,[91] and in November 1884 the British government requested blueprints of the Honganji crematories.[92] England's first crematory was subsequently built in 1885 just outside London by the British Cremation Society. At a time when technology was being transferred overwhelmingly from West to East, this inversion of the usual flow was a dramatic marker of the success of Japanese cremation advocates. The new facilities were concrete evidence that an "evil custom of the past" had been transformed into a modern, "civilized" means to dispose of the dead.

Meanwhile the idea that graveyards were a health threat was accepted by widening circles of the Japanese public. In a January 1881 inquiry from Nagasaki prefecture to the Home Ministry, for example, local officials noted that, in order to block breakaway parishioners from building a new graveyard, a Shinshū temple had argued, in the new scientific fashion, that the proposed burial ground would pollute drinking water and harm the health of nearby residents. Nagasaki officials investigated the site and decided that it was far enough from houses and wells that burial there would pose no real harm. They concluded that the temple was using the issue of hygiene as a red herring, its real goal being to punish former parishioners who had converted to the Nichiren sect, the Shin sect's most antagonistic Buddhist foe. Yet the fact that the Shinshū temple legitimized its opposition by appealing to concerns over hygiene indicates the extent to which those concerns had already permeated public consciousness.[93]

In fact by the mid-1880s they had become so entrenched that one contributor to a Buddhist magazine felt obliged to remind readers that cremation was valuable not only as a public health measure but as an expression of Buddhist teachings. Writing in 1883, he first noted the extraordinary improvements that had been made in cremation technology, citing the fact that "even a country like Germany" had recently requested to see plans so it could build its own crematoria. But he regretted that the ban on cremation in Japan had been lifted not because of any consideration of its religious merit, but "solely due to its convenience for public health." He added, "Now crematories are being reconstructed, and there is a rumor that all earth burials in Shiga prefecture will be abolished and everyone forced to cremate. But this is being done only out of concern for public health. Even though there are those who preach this eloquently, one must not stop with this argument." Drawing from the writings of Chinese Buddhist monks, he asserted that cremation was an act of religious merit. Not only did cremation aid in "the meditation and knowledge of

Mourners pay final respects to the dead at a crematory in turn-of-the-twentieth-century Tokyo. From *Tōkyō fūzokushi,* by Hirade Kōjirō.

the two emptinesses (of self and phenomena)," it also reenacted the passing of Shākyamuni Buddha into nirvana. "The *manji* [reverse swastika] in one's breast consumes the wood," he concluded, emphatically asserting a Buddhist understanding of cremation as it underwent its transformation into a public health measure.[94]

When cremation was banned in 1873 as a "barbaric" Buddhist ritual, probably no Japanese could have foreseen that a mere ten years later a magazine contributor would feel compelled to remind readers of its Buddhist roots. That one did is a testament to the success of Buddhists and their allies in constructing a modern rationale for cremation that was independent of Buddhist significance. Like other interest groups in the early Meiji period, cremation advocates quickly learned how to turn state-sanctioned values and goals to their own advantage, redefining their scope in the process. Cremation boosters became standard-bearers of filial devotion and Western science, portraying the opposition as a menace to the integrity of ancestor worship and public health. After the Council of State revoked its prohibition in 1875, some continued to speak out against the practice, but their voices were muffled and soon smothered by the pro-cremation consensus that spread among policy makers and the educated elite.

CHAPTER 4

DIVESTING SHINTO FUNERALS

*A*fter rescinding the failed ban on cremation, the Meiji regime retreated from the anti-Buddhist agenda of the nativists. Leading the way was the increasingly powerful Home Ministry, whose primary mission was to build a "wealthy country, strong army" in the Western mold, not to rework the ritual lives and deaths of the emperor's subjects. In the decade following the cremation ban, it dismantled the cumbersome system of "doctrinal instructors" and mandated a separation between the public rituals of state-supported Shinto and the private rituals of individual Shinto sects. This division of Shinto into a supposedly "nonreligious" state teaching on the one hand and a cluster of sectarian "religions" on the other allowed the government to separate daily governance from otherworldly affairs while preserving at least a formal commitment to the nativist underpinnings of imperial rule. In the process, it dealt the Shinto funeral movement a blow from which it would not recover.

GETTING RELIGION

When Restorationists took power, they quickly announced the principle of the "unity of rites and rule." To many, if not all, nativists, "rites" stood for both the protocol of the imperial house and the private rituals of every Japanese, an equation that provided the foundation of both the Shinto funeral movement and the nationwide ban on cremation. As we saw in Chapters Two and Three, however, nativists ran into strong resistance, not only from those reluctant to give up the customs of their ancestors, but also from pragmatic officials who were more concerned with maintaining public order, protecting hygiene, and promoting the efficient use of land than they were with furthering an anti-Buddhist, pro-Shinto agenda.

There was yet one more obstacle to the nativist project: the recently imported idea that religion *(shūkyō)* was a distinct and ultimately private realm of human experience properly separated from the affairs of state. To win the goodwill of Western nations, Meiji officials legalized Christianity in 1873, and with the foreign faith came the idea that individuals had a right to religious beliefs and practices outside the purview of government.[1] Not surprisingly, among the first Japanese to seize on the notion were the standard bearers of "civilization and enlightenment," such as educator Mori Arinori (1847–1889), who wrote his bluntly titled "Religious Freedom of Japan" while visiting the United States in 1872.[2]

The twin concepts "religion" and "religious freedom" were also embraced by prominent Shinshū Buddhists Shimaji Mokurai and Ōuchi Seiran, who submitted petitions to the government opposing not only the ban on cremation but also the radically pro-Shinto Great Teaching Academy (Daikyō-in), the nerve center of the government's "doctrinal instruction" campaign. Buddhist clerics initially supported the school, which was located in the Zōjōji, a Tokugawa mortuary temple in Tokyo, in the hope of bolstering their standing with the new government. Nativists in the Ministry of Doctrine, however, were determined to purge the institution of Buddhist teachings and practices, and in 1873, the same year the "barbaric" custom of cremation was banned, they stripped the temple of Buddhist iconography and outfitted it with an altar dedicated to indigenous *kami*. In front of this decidedly non-Buddhist, and, significantly, non-Tokugawa, altar, all doctrinal instructors were required to wear Shinto vestments and perform Shinto ritual.[3] In response, Shimaji led a campaign to withdraw Buddhist support both for the academy and for the doctrinal instruction campaign more generally, arguing in a score of memorials to the central government that religion should not be fashioned or disseminated by the state.[4] Supporting him was Ōuchi Seiran, who in his 1874 petition to the Sa-in emphasized that Shinto rituals were "national or public in character, and so the state should itself perform rites at national shrines," but that officially supported priests should not be allowed to interfere in people's religious faith, which was private in nature. "You can try all you wish to make people have religious faith, but if the people do not have it of their own accord, all your efforts will be in vain," he warned.[5]

Shimaji, Ōuchi, and other like-minded Buddhists successfully thwarted the Ministry of Doctrine's plans. The Great Teaching Academy, starved of Buddhist support, shut its doors in May 1875, the same month, in fact, that the government formally lifted the ban on cremation. Two years later the Ministry of Doctrine itself was abolished, replaced by an Office of Temples and Shrines placed firmly under the control of the Home Ministry.[6]

Buddhist opposition to the Ministry of Doctrine and its teaching academy did not mean that the majority, or even a sizable minority, of Buddhist clerics embraced the principle of religious freedom. Even as Buddhist priests fought off attacks on their own faith, they remained hostile to Christianity and actively obstructed Shinto funerals. In August 1873, for example, Myōdō prefecture circulated a notice that scolded "wicked priests" for refusing to recognize Shinto funerals and forcing people to submit to Buddhist rites instead.[7]

In an ironic turn of events, officials in Tokyo tried to overcome such obstructionism by appropriating the concept of religious liberty themselves, instituting measures that asserted the right of people to perform funerals in accordance with their beliefs. In January 1874 leaders of the state's indoctrination campaign asked that *all* doctrinal instructors—and this included Confucian scholars, professional storytellers, Kabuki actors, and others not necessarily categorized as Buddhist or Shinto priests[8]—be allowed to perform funerals, the assumption being that loosening controls would benefit the spread of Shinto over Buddhist and, even more importantly, Christian death rites. Responding to the request, the Council of State declared that people could entrust funerals to doctrinal instructors "in accordance with their beliefs" *(shinkyū ni yotte)*. This was followed in July by an order from the Ministry of Doctrine stating that someone who wished to end a temple affiliation to convert to a new sect and adopt new funeral rituals (i.e., Shinto funeral rituals) no longer had to obtain a certificate of "parishioner severance" *(ridan)* from that temple. Conversions merely required informing local officials, who would duly note them in their registries.[9]

Recognizing that members of the same family might opt for different funeral rites, the Council of State then declared in August that local officials should record individual conversions to different faiths, not just those executed by entire households.[10] This administrative ruling represented a striking departure from Tokugawa policy, according to which a patriline *(ie)* was considered an indivisible unit bound to a particular sect. The Council of State decision, in contrast, acknowledged sectarian affiliation to be a matter of personal conscience.

Yet like the defenders of Buddhism, nativists in and out of the Meiji government ignored the principle of religious liberty when it suited them. Even as they asserted the right of an individual to convert to a different faith, they continued to rise to the defense of a state-directed Shinto that encompassed both the public rites performed by and on behalf of the state and private rites performed for individual Japanese. Take, for example, a memorial submitted to the Council of State in 1874 by a Shinto priest from northern Kyushu. The recommendations in his petition included making offerings to the *kami* in all government offices, merging the Ministry of Doctrine and the Ministry of Education (Monbushō), and, last but not least, establishing one national format for death rites, which was touted as a way to unify the populace.[11]

Another, and more prominent, nativist petitioner was the chief priest of the Ise shrines, Tanaka Yoritsune (1836–1897), who defended the "unity of rites and rule" in an 1874 memorial by arguing that Shinto in fact transcended the relativizing category of "religion." According to Tanaka, Shinto was a "national teaching" *(kokkyō)* superior to any mere religion "because religions are the theories of their founders. The National Teaching consists of the traditions of the imperial house, beginning in the age of the gods and continuing throughout history. Teaching and consolidating these traditions for the masses are inseparable from government, related as the two wheels of a cart or the wings of a bird."[12]

Yet to claim that Shinto was not a religion had a downside for those who wished to change the hearts and minds of the masses, especially for those who saw death rites as central to this mission. For this put them in the awkward position of having to downplay or disown rituals that could be categorized as "religious," and funerals, which were private affairs concerned with the fate of individual souls, were explicitly composed of such rituals.

Ōuchi Seiran made this point in his 1874 petition to the Sa-in, which, like Tanaka's memorial, asserted that Shinto did not constitute religion. This was not because Shinto was superior, but quite the opposite: Shinto was not properly a religion, according to Ōuchi, because it had failed to develop a systematic, ethical understanding of the "other realm." "How can such a creed give rise to faith beyond the realms of knowledge and experience; how can it afford solace to the souls of the dead?" he asked.[13] Thus Ōuchi concurred with Tanaka that Shinto was not a religion, but he did so not to elevate Shinto, but instead to make Shinto a matter of life to the exclusion of death. He differentiated between public "rites" and private "religion" by associating the latter with the "other realm" and barring the former from it, creating a theoretical wall that could thwart the advance of Shinto funerals.

Ōuchi had identified Shinto, a priori, as unconcerned with the "other realm," but later petitioners pointed out that in practice Shinto had taken on the appearance of religion. Maintaining that Shinto *should* be nonreligious, they attacked Shinto practices that smacked of religion, particularly those concerned with death. In their 1881 appeal to the Home Ministry, for example, the two Higashi Honganji prelates, Atsumi Keien and Suzuki Ejun, declared that the ambiguous status of Shinto ought to be resolved by proscribing Shinto funerals and anything else of a religious nature.[14] Home Minister Yamada Akiyoshi (1844–1892) was receptive to the idea, and he therefore proposed to Prime Minister Sanjō Sanetomi (1837–1891) that all shrine priests be ordered to cease proselytizing and performing funerals and be confined to state ritual instead.

Informing Yamada's decision was a rancorous dispute among nativists over the nature of the afterlife and the roles of the particular *kami* who inhabited it. Different nativist factions promoted competing visions of the beyond, solidifying into two main camps. One wished to add the *kami* Ōkuninushi, the main deity of Izumo shrine and lord of the underworld, to the official state pantheon, which consisted of Amaterasu and the so-called Three Deities of Creation. But Tanaka and his supporters opposed any challenge to the position of the sun *kami*/imperial ancestress, thereby generating a bitter theological controversy that lasted throughout the 1870s and into the 1880s.[15] Thus Yamada's decision to bar shrine priests from performing funerals was shaped as much by a desire to disentangle the state from the internal squabbling of nativists as it was a way to mollify the Buddhist establishment.

If all shrine priests were forbidden from officiating at funerals, however, who would perform Shinto death rites? Presented with this question, the government decided to divide Shinto into two parts: publicly regulated state Shinto and privately managed sectarian Shinto. The Home Ministry formalized this split in 1882 when it announced that henceforth those serving as Shinto priests at state-controlled shrines could not double as doctrinal instructors. The ministry's edict explicitly prohibited these priests from performing funerals, steering them away from the on-the-ground (and under-the-ground) evangelizing that distracted them from the duties of state ritual and served only to fuel theological strife. In an addendum to the decree the Home Ministry said that priests assigned to shrines at the prefectural rank and under could, "until further notice," continue in their capacity as doctrinal instructors *cum* funeral officiants.[16] The elite priests of national and imperial shrines were, however, cut off from the rough-and-tumble world of grassroots ministry. This was a development welcomed by some priests but deplored by others. One priest living in what is now Saitama prefecture expressed approval in his diary, but a colleague in the same region signed a memorial protesting the restriction.[17]

Middling and lower-ranking priests were free, but not obligated, to continue performing funerals. Priests could also choose to shed their state affiliation and form or join independent Shinto sects such as Kurozumikyō and Shintō Taikyō.[18] But the Home Ministry policy of forbidding high-ranking priests to perform funerals, along with a decision to prohibit the construction of new Shinto graveyards,[19] dealt a devastating blow to the Shinto funeral movement, which had largely been a top-down phenomenon orchestrated by local nativist elites and sympathetic Tokyo bureaucrats.

In the region formerly encompassed by the radically pro-Shinto Tsuwano domain, the Home Ministry decision was bemoaned by nativists trying to sustain Shinto funerals in the face of Buddhist assaults. After the abolition of Tsuwano domain in 1871,[20] most people soon reverted to Buddhist ceremonies, but much of the upper class still chose to adhere to the Shinto rites championed by Kamei Koremi and Fukuba Bisei. For example, a group of former samurai asked prefectural officials in 1876 if it could establish a "collective spirit shrine" for the worship of ancestral spirits, starting with those of the Kamei lineage.[21] The request noted that spirit shrines were being established in other prefectures so as to memorialize the dead outside of Buddhist temples. The shrine was approved through consultation with the Ministry of Doctrine, and it initially thrived, judging from an 1879 request to expand the building where it was housed.[22] But after the Home Ministry drew the line between state liturgy and private funerals, supporters of the spirit shrine found themselves on the defensive, and in 1883 one of them wrote "An Opinion Paper For Ways to Preserve the Collective Spirit Shrine" (Sōreisha hozonhō ikensho).[23] In it he lamented that Shinto priests were not sufficiently devoted to proselytizing and that the order to separate Shinto priests from their role as doctrinal instructors had precipitated "a decline in ancestral spirit shrines everywhere." He contrasted the apathy of Shinto instructors with the energy of Buddhist priests, who "bustle day and night from east to west, instructing each household in their sectarian teachings." The Shin sect was particularly successful in winning converts, he complained, and then proposed a number of administrative measures to ensure the survival of the "collective spirit shrine."[24] These included putting the management of funerals in the hands of two specially appointed ministers (known as the shrine "president" and "vice president"), since the Shinto priests who had handled funerals in the past would no longer be doing so.

In the wake of the Home Ministry's action, there were those who held out hope that the state would nevertheless continue to promote Shinto funerals, even if not through the offices of high-ranking Shinto priests. For example, in 1882 two Shinto priests from Yamanashi prefecture and one from Mie prefecture together submitted a petition to Prime Minister Sanjō to include the regulation of funerals in the constitution that was then being considered.[25] The priests argued that "the teaching of Shākyamuni" (Buddhism) had been entrenched in Japan for so long that it was no longer considered a foreign teaching, but that did not change the fact that it was still an "import," even if a very old one. It was not right to entrust funerals to a foreign teaching and thereby enable those who desired to "plunder the sacred spirit of our citizenry," stated the priests, who then took Tokyo officials to task for recognizing Buddhist funerals simply because of "needless fears" concerning the "maintenance of order." Significantly, the petitioners agreed with the policy to exclude Shinto priests from death rites, but obviously not because they thought that the state should avoid meddling in matters of faith. Instead, they interpreted the ruling as a recognition that those who "serve the deities of heaven and earth should not have contact with death pollution," invoking the belief in death pollution in spite of the Meiji government's policy to downplay its importance. The petitioners therefore recommended that a separate funeral office be set up in Tokyo, with branches in the different prefectures, to oversee the mortuary activities of doctrinal instructors disconnected from the Shinto rites of state.

Of course this never happened, since the primary aim of the Home Ministry was not to protect state ritual from death pollution but to separate the state from "religion." Death management was indeed standardized, but not according to the aims of nativists. In 1884 the ministry announced comprehensive rules to regulate burial throughout Japan, putting their execution in the hands of police in place of doctrinal instructors. That same year the ministry abolished the status of doctrinal instructor altogether, sweeping away the remains of the state's defunct proselytization campaign. The ban on independent funerals was likewise removed,[26] freeing Christian funerals from legal limbo and creating an officially sanctioned free market for death rites.[27]

At the same time the Home Ministry ordered all deaths to be certified by physicians, a policy it based on measures imposed in Tokyo in 1876 and 1880.[28] Mourners were also required to present medical death certificates to local authorities in order to procure permits for cremation or burial.[29] The ministry's policies thus created an official break between the handling of souls and the disposal of bodies, with the former entrusted to religion and the latter controlled by the state. In the process Buddhist priests were displaced once and for all from their centuries-old role of investigating and confirming deaths. This caused little consternation among the Buddhist clergy, who were relieved of a bureaucratic task even as they continued to enjoy the profits generated by funerals and memorial services. The threat from Shinto funerals was now, for the most part, behind them.

STATESMEN AND SOLDIERS

Creating a distinction between sectarian and state Shinto did not mean that the government exhibited no religious bias in the following decades. Japanese soldiers who died in imperial wars were enshrined as *kami* at Yasukuni shrine regardless of their personal beliefs, and this was in spite of the fact that the constitution promulgated in 1889 contained a provision stating that Japanese subjects would "enjoy freedom of religious belief."[30] And although they were infused with European protocol, state funerals were unmistakably Shinto in flavor. Organizers of the funeral for Iwakura Tomomi consulted English precedent in determining the number of, and intervals between, military gun salutes. Attendees were told to wear black armbands, neckties, and gloves, and to cover any adornments on their hats with black gauze, even though the conventional color for mourning in East Asia was white.[31] The Westernized funeral was officiated, however, by the influential head priest of Izumo shrine, Senge Takatomi (1845–1918), who was assisted by nativist scholar Motoori Toyokai (1834–1913). Iwakura's obsequy was replete with the by-then standard hallmarks of a Shinto funeral, including ritual bowing, clapping, and offering of *tamagushi.* Naturally the funeral for the Emperor Meiji in 1912 also proclaimed to the world that Japan's modern progress was anchored in a venerable Shinto past. The funeral featured a military band and gun salvos, and the imperial remains were taken by train for final burial in Kyoto; but like the emperors listed in the eighth-century history *Nihon shoki,* the emperor was placed in a "court of temporary interment," which became the locus of presumably ancient Shinto death rites.[32]

Determined to shield a rarified state Shinto from sectarian slings and arrows, the government held to the position that state-sponsored funerals did not constitute religion. Bureaucrats even eschewed the term "Shinto funeral" when describing these solemn events, opting instead to use the religiously neutral term *kōsōshiki* (public funeral ceremony).[33]

Some Buddhists purposefully assented to the fiction that state funerals *(kokusō)* were not necessarily Shinto funerals, hoping that one day Buddhist priests would be allowed to infiltrate them. This view was expressed in an article appearing in the March 23, 1891, issue of the Buddhist magazine *Reichikai zasshi,* which reported on the state funeral of Prime Minister Sanjō Sanetomi.[34] The article reported that there were all sorts of rumors about what constituted a state funeral. People assumed that it must be limited to a Shinto ceremony and regarded this fact as a sign of the state's hostility toward Buddhism. But this view was mistaken, the article asserted, going on to explain that a state funeral was simply an honor bestowed upon someone who had done great service to the state and that, "fundamentally, court ceremony is not fixed on Buddhist funerals or Shinto funerals." So far state funerals had been executed with Shinto rites, but since this was "an age of freedom of belief," if a chief mourner so desired, a state funeral did not have to be limited to Shinto ceremony, the article optimistically professed.

In fact Buddhist priests did intrude on the state funeral of Meiji oligarch Itō Hirobumi (1841–1909) in 1909, if in a limited fashion. The funeral was essentially Shinto, but since Itō was buried at his family temple, the Sōjōji, the priests there insisted on performing a ceremony for merit transfer *(ekō)* at the time of burial. This led to speculation in the press about the extent of Buddhist involvement in the funeral, which in turn prompted the Shinto magazine *Zenkoku shinshoku kaikaihō* to publish an editorial stressing the need to make a strict distinction between the public and private sectors.[35] Religious activities had to be rigorously excluded from state funerals, the magazine said, arguing nonetheless that "the sacredness of the state funeral" for Itō had not been compromised.[36] The editorial cited Viscount Suematsu's explanation to the press that the merit transfer was simply a courtesy, an accommodation of temple custom that did not reflect state policy or any desire for Buddhist rites on the part of the Itō family, although they were of course appreciative of the services that other temples had also performed on behalf of the former prime minister.[37]

Clearly, although Buddhist priests had been removed from bureaucratic roles and Shinto elevated to the status of a nonreligious state doctrine, the Buddhist establishment was not content to remain in a privatized realm sequestered from public affairs. Nowhere was this more evident than in the management of soldiers' deaths, which blurred, if not erased, the line that had been drawn between Buddhism and the state. Nativists may have succeeded in building a national cult of the war dead centered on Yasukuni shrine, from which Buddhist ritual was strictly excluded, but the Shinto priesthood was ambivalent about handling funerals for individual soldiers, just as it was about funerals in general. After all, the Home Ministry had forbidden priests of national and imperial shrines to officiate at any funeral, and lower-ranking priests were free from the obligation to perform death rites, a policy supported by many priests because of their continuing aversion to death pollution. In fact, when priests did conduct funerals, they did so not in their public capacity as shrine "priests" *(shinshoku* or *shinkan)* but as private Shinto "ministers" *(kyōshi).*[38]

The division within the priesthood over funerals and state policy can be ascertained from two letters submitted to consecutive issues of the Shinto magazine *Jinja kyōkai zasshi* in 1904. In the first, a priest from Iwate prefecture lamented that the Home Ministry ruling had led to a serious decline in Shinto funerals. Unable to depend on respectable priests of tutelary shrines, "chief mourners do not rely upon the sectarian Shinto instructors of meager ability, but turn to Buddhism and Christianity instead."[39] He argued that there was nothing wrong with representatives of the state becoming involved in life-cycle ceremonies, including funerals, and pointed out that, even though people said those serving the deities must not come in contact with death pollution, the Council of State had in fact ruled in 1872 that those who dealt with death had to refrain from *kami* worship only for a day.[40] This letter elicited a retort from a priest in Shiga prefecture, a farmer from a remote village who had begun serving at his local shrine a few years earlier.[41] He wrote that it was appropriate for a priest to conduct weddings, but not funerals, despite the Council of State ruling on death pollution. Refraining from shrine duties even for a day was an inconvenience, he claimed, especially in rural areas where it was difficult to enlist the help of other priests. The primary responsibility of a Shinto priest was to be a representative of state ritual, so he should have no relation to death, even if this presented an obstacle to Shinto funerals. If people wanted Shinto funerals badly enough, he wrote, they could turn to the ministers of Shinto sects.

The debate over death rites prevented the Shinto world from presenting a unified front against the Buddhist takeover of publicly sponsored military funerals. Buddhist priests claimed their turf during the Sino-Japanese War (1894–1895), when they marched off to China along with citizen-soldiers. In a letter sent in May 1895 to the family of Private Nakamura Kōsuke, an army officer expressed regrets at not being able to send any remains back to Japan. Four Shinshū priests had been sent along with the army to handle cremations, he wrote, but so many men died from disease in such a short space of time (Nakamura himself died not in battle, but from the epidemic) that they were quickly overwhelmed. One of the clerics had also died, wrote the officer, so they halted the cremations and eventually stopped sending even the hair of the dead back to their families.[42]

Buddhist priests may not have cremated Private Nakamura overseas, but they made sure to memorialize him through a grand funeral sponsored by his home village in the Tama region of Tokyo prefecture. According to records taken by the local conscription official, the funeral procession consisted of relatives, policemen, schoolchildren, government officials, and members of the Red Cross, as well as Buddhist priests from ten different temples and subtemples. Conspicuously absent from this display of civic cooperation were Shinto priests. They might have been present at the funeral as private citizens, but not in any official capacity. A diagram of the funeral service shows that it was conducted before a Buddhist image (apparently a statue of Amida Buddha) with a table for offering incense placed squarely in front of the coffin.[43] Records for the funeral of Private Iwata, another soldier from the Tama region, show that it was conducted in similar fashion.[44]

A man of Nakamura's status would normally not receive such a grand ceremony, but having died in service of the state transformed him into a local hero. During the Sino-Japanese War (and subsequent wars), towns and villages across Japan were infected with "funeral fever" as they vied with each other to sponsor splendid mortuary rites. An article in the May 10, 1895, issue of the provincial newspaper *Shinano mainichi shinbun* noted that local officials had been instructed to be thrifty, using funds to help the mourning family pay future expenses, but that these instructions were largely ignored.[45] Buddhist priests reaped the benefits of this trend, as they were drawn into the center of public memorialization. They officiated not only at individual funerals but also at group funerals for several or more soldiers. They also sponsored large-scale, collective memorial rites for the war dead, allocating to themselves a function that Shintoists had hoped to reserve for Yasukuni and its network of shrines. Buddhists worked closely with local officials in pursuing this end. For example, in July 1895 the district office of Nishi Tamagun provided the names, ranks, and addresses of eighteen dead soldiers to the head priest of Zenkōji temple in Tokyo, who requested the information for a set of memorial rites lasting several days.[46]

Buddhist priests thereby placed themselves at the highly charged juncture of celebrating service to the state and grieving personal loss—to the chagrin of Shinto ideologues. Even if a Shinto priest were involved in a military funeral, he often had to accommodate himself to Buddhist demands. The author of an article appearing in the *Jinja kyōkai zasshi* during the Russo-Japanese War (1904–1905) deplored the performance of both Buddhist military funerals and those funerals that mixed Shinto and Buddhist elements. He especially took to task those Shinto priests who agreed to participate in composite death rites, calling their involvement a "disgrace," a "cold-hearted crime toward their professional duties," and "behavior that sullies the rites of state." If a funeral were performed privately, it could be done in accordance with a family's religious beliefs, but when a public entity such as a city, town, or village sponsored rites "for our loyal dead," it should instead use "the rites particular to our nation." Like those obsequies for great statesmen, public funerals for soldiers should properly be called "state ceremony funerals" *(kokureisō),* said the angry writer, who argued, "If city, town, and village officials, as well as other volunteers, would lecture on the Imperial Way, clarify the rites, and take leadership, these sorts of disgraces would not happen."[47]

The magazine also printed a letter in the same issue relating that the head office of a certain prefecture (unspecified) had told Shinto priests to wear their ritual vestments to military funerals, which had resulted in the unseemly vision of Shinto priests attending Buddhist ceremonies in full regalia. He had also heard that priests who chose to attend in ordinary formal wear were forced to line up with members of the Red Cross rather than with other priests. Believing the prefecture to be mistaken, he communicated with the Home Ministry several times, but apparently without success.[48] In commenting on the letter, the magazine said it was indeed wrong to attend funerals in ritual garb, since a priest who went to a funeral did so in a private capacity.[49] However, there were cases where priests not only attended military funerals but also officiated, and the magazine printed a question from another reader about what they should wear in such instances. The reply was that Shinto priests did not handle funerals in their role as priests *(shinkan),* but as ministers *(kyōshi),* so they should wear the dress determined by the Shinto sect to which they belonged.[50]

Shinto priests were thus forced into the awkward position of having to shed their public affiliation with the state in order to honor the sacrifice of lives to the state. Buddhist priests, in contrast, could slide comfortably into their familiar roles as guardians of the dead, soldiers or not. This does not mean Shinto priests gave up on the effort to conduct funerals for soldiers (in their role as sectarian ministers, of course). As Japanese soldiers began dying during the military campaigns of the 1930s, Shinto priests once again tried to lay claim to them, igniting conflicts with their Buddhist counterparts. The battles over soldiers who had died in battle (or on their way to battle) dismayed those who wished to fuse the hearts and minds of the Japanese people. For example, the "spiritual mobilization" campaign launched under Prime Minister Konoe Fumimaro (1891–1945) put out a book in 1937 to spread its message of national unity, and in it stressed the importance of memorializing the war dead, "flowers of the military nation," who were transformed into "nation-protecting *kami.*"[51] The jingoistic work professed that public funerals for soldiers, like those for great statesmen, should "follow as much as possible the rites that are unique to Japan," claiming that this was only proper for heroic spirits *(eirei)* destined for enshrinement at Yasukuni.[52] Municipal officials and local notables ought to serve as ceremonial leaders for these public funerals, which were, of course, not to be considered "religious" in character.[53] But the propaganda manual admitted that, in reality, military funerals had become sites of intense bickering between Buddhist clerics and Shinto priests, who were often forced to compromise by performing Shinto and Buddhist ceremonies one after the other at the same memorial service. According to the manual, such a composite service was in danger of "losing its solemnity and integrity, so from the perspective of unifying the psychology of the masses, it is not something to be commended."[54]

Dual funerals were described as a necessary evil by a Sōtō Zen priest in his 1941 guidebook for the Buddhist clergy. Choosing a format was straightforward when funerals were held for individuals, but it was necessary to negotiate a compromise for those memorializing multiple soldiers of different faiths, he wrote.[55] If the dead belonged to different Buddhist sects, it was not too difficult for priests to agree upon shared scriptures, but communal funerals incorporating Shinto priests were more complicated. In these cases it was necessary to perform one ceremony after the other. Since Buddhist altars were completely different from Shinto ones, two separate altars had to be set up one next to the other. Or they could be erected across from each other so that attendees could face one altar for the first set of rituals and then turn around to observe the second set. The Sōtō cleric added that he had heard of Shinto priests who argued that since the war dead were worshipped at Yasukuni shrine as nation-protecting *kami,* funerals should be Shinto through and through. But these were just "clever words" to "tempt the ignorant masses," and it was the responsibility of temple priests to lead their parishioners carefully and explain that their relationship to the temple and the process of enshrinement at Yasukuni were two totally separate affairs.[56]

Shintoists sought to unite the Japanese people through uniquely Japanese worship. But their struggle with Buddhist priests created bitter divisions, starkly and ironically displayed through the ritual time and space of dual-ceremony, dual-altar military funerals. Most funerals, for soldiers and civilians alike, remained solidly Buddhist. Stripped of feudal privileges after the Meiji Restoration, Buddhist priests made sure to defend their rice-winning role as mortuary specialists. As Shinto commentators ruefully noted, preachers energetically crisscrossed the countryside, exhorting people to remain true to Buddhist practice. Lineage-conscious households were loath to part with the graves of past family members, so temples also retained parishioners by holding hostage their ancestral graves and denying burial to apostates unless, in the end, they received a temple funeral.[57]

Not all Buddhists approved of strong-arm tactics. One contributor to an 1886 issue of the Buddhist magazine *Reichikai zasshi* condemned selfish clerics who "covet prosperity" and "battle over the corpses of the dead."[58] He scolded priests for fighting with nativists and foreign preachers (Christians), saying it was a "big mistake to think that the professional role of the cleric is to inspect the dead body and conduct a funeral for it."[59] Responding to the argument that temples survived on proceeds from death rites, he retorted that clerics should instead practice the Dharma (Buddhist law) and strengthen people's morals and by doing so receive support as a matter of course. A funeral should simply be an extension of the bond forged through true faith, he said, criticizing the custom inherited from the Tokugawa period of regarding parishioners as members of patrilines and not as individual believers. Because of the proprietary attitude taken toward the patrilines attached to their temples, even when individuals converted to other faiths during their lives, clerics fought to hold onto their deaths, an evil practice "inviting public scorn."[60]

Later proponents of the so-called "new Buddhism," such as Inoue Enryō (1858–1919) and D. T. Suzuki (1870–1966), dismissed the old cosmology and ritual conventions of Japanese Buddhism in order to construct a modern, cosmopolitan religion.[61] The lay Nichirenshugi (Nichirenism) movement started by Tanaka Chigaku (1861–1939) also tried to extricate Buddhism from its age-old association with death. Tanaka went so far as to construct a Buddhist wedding ceremony,[62] and his heir, Satomi Kishio (1897–1974), emphasized that religion must be emancipated "from the grave."[63]

It was through the grave, however, that a place for Buddhism in modern Japan was ensured. Clerics sometimes found themselves battling with converts, but by and large families kept their own members in line. This was also true among those in the elite who might have been expected to reject Buddhist death rites. A notice appearing in the *Tōkyō nichi nichi shinbun* a day after the funeral of Count Yamada Akiyoshi (1844–1892) explained that this "protector of our *kokutai* (national body) who taught the Japanese classics" had received a Buddhist funeral in accordance with "the household system of his ancestors," not because he himself was a believer, but because his mother was "an adherent of the Shin sect."[64] Fukuzawa Yukichi, the great preacher of Westernization, who at one time even promoted Christianity as a means for Japan to civilize, also received a Buddhist funeral, at Zenpukuji temple in Tokyo.[65]

Family pressure to adhere to ancestral ways fortified the Buddhist establishment for the remainder of the twentieth century. In her 1986 study of Kuro-zumikyō, established in early Meiji as one of the officially recognized sects of Shinto, Helen Hardacre wrote that, especially in rural areas, "Kurozumikyō followers are in a majority of cases affiliated with a Buddhist temple, and the usual arrangement is that the temple is expected to perform all funerals and ancestral rites of the household. Even individuals who desire to have their own funeral conducted by Kurozumikyō typically encounter serious opposition from other family members if the household maintains, as most rural families do, a hereditary affiliation with a temple."[66] The same could be said of anyone trying to break ties with a family temple, whether for the sake of joining a Shinto or Christian sect, or even another Buddhist one.

Shinto funerals have survived to the present day to the extent that they too have become tradition. Certain families have now undergone several genera-tions of Shinto death rites, the imperial family being a striking case in point. But by and large, Shinto funerals are regarded as curious exceptions to a Bud-dhist rule, remainders and reminders of a convoluted history.

CHAPTER 5

GRAVE MATTERS

𝒜t the end of the Tokugawa period the communal burial ground divided into family plots was a familiar feature of the Japanese landscape. Many of these graveyards had developed in and around temple precincts, a medieval trend accelerated by the Tokugawa policy of requiring households to register as temple parishioners *(danka)*. Others were located in fields and forests held jointly by villagers. Dotted with grave markers erected on behalf of the family members interred below—whether rough stones, carved monuments, or merely wooden posts—these burial grounds were a concrete manifestation of the integrity and continuity of individual patrilines. Yet located on communal property, they were also a testament to the strength of broader temple and village affiliations.

Not all the graveyards in pre-Meiji Japan conformed to the family-plot-communal-burial-ground model, however. In many regions, especially thinly populated ones, families buried their dead around their homes, unrestricted by any shared boundaries. On the other extreme were communities of Shin-shū believers who, after performing a cremation, sent a small portion of the deceased's remains to the sect's headquarters in Kyoto (the Nishi or Higashi Honganji) and then left the rest of the bones and ash at the cremation ground without building any individual memorial. There were also villages where families erected memorial stones, but not in the same places where they disposed of their dead. In the so-called "double-grave system" *(ryōbosei)*, corpses were buried in remote, unmarked grounds while memorials were built closer to the heart of the community, usually in the precincts of village temples. Finally, even in areas where it was customary to construct family graves and memorials in communal burial grounds, a significant number of people could not afford to do so. In Edo, for example, family members were ideally buried in ancestral gravesites at the temples where they were parishioners. But many of the urban poor lacked an affiliation with any temple, government policy notwithstanding, and their corpses were unceremoniously dumped in mass graves.[1]

After the Restoration of 1868, Meiji officials embraced the model of the temple and village cemetery, implementing policies to universalize the practice of building family graves and memorials in communal burial grounds. These policies either prohibited the aforementioned alternatives or at least undermined them.

Initially government policy was tied to the anti-Buddhist, pro-Shinto agenda of nativists, reflected in the 1873 ban on cremation and efforts to establish specifically Shinto cemeteries beyond the control of Buddhist clerics. But policies with a religious thrust were intermingled from the start with concerns about hygiene and the efficient use of land. In the wake of the cremation-ban debacle, these material concerns clearly superseded the earlier drive to promote a nativist agenda, a dramatic indicator being the government's quick adoption of a pro-cremation stance in order to protect public health. From the late 1870s and on into the twentieth century, officials pursued policies that tried to diminish, not heighten, the impact of sectarian divisions on burial practice. In fact, by ordering local authorities to establish public cemeteries open to citizens of any religious persuasion, and then putting their oversight in the hands of the police, the government sought to bypass religious structures entirely, creating in the process an unmediated link between individual families and the state.

The legacy of government policy is the standard format for burial epitomized in the large-scale "soul parks" *(reien)* that now blanket the Japanese countryside. These subdivisions for the dead, where cremated remains are domiciled in orderly rows of family graves, are now so prevalent that they are considered an environmental menace.[2] However, temple graveyards from the Tokugawa period continue to thrive, and since the end of World War II most soul parks have, in fact, been established by developers and gravestone makers in partnership with Buddhist temples.[3] The double-grave system also continues in some communities, providing an object of perennial interest to Japanese folklorists and anthropologists.[4] So while officials succeeded to a great degree in standardizing burial practice, they were not able to obliterate local and sectarian differences, and, in fact, created the parameters for chronic disputes.

The government also pursued goals that were in conflict with one another, building lasting tensions into Japan's modern burial system. On the one hand, the state favored ancestral veneration as a force for social stability; on the other, it fostered an economy that required ever-increasing levels of mobility and urbanization. Marching into the future with one foot in the grave required constant negotiation and compromise in imperial Japan, as it still does today.

OF BURIAL AND BUREAUCRATS

The first official Meiji dealings with the dead were shaped by an anti-Buddhist agenda that culminated in the cremation ban, a triumph for those who wished to rid Japan of foreign customs. As we saw in Chapter Three, however, this proved to be a short-lived and ultimately pyrrhic victory. In order to overturn the ban, defenders of cremation extolled its virtues in the press and in petitions to the government, creating a modern rationale for the practice that fueled its spread once the ban was lifted. This was not the only ironic consequence of the prohibition, since it also propelled a broader secularization of state policy toward burial, a process that quickly marginalized any Shinto agenda.

Nowhere was this more evident than in the handling of the showpiece Shinto graveyards in Tokyo. The ban created a surge in demand for new grave space throughout the nation, and this was especially true in the capital, which, thanks to the intervention of the Finance Ministry, was saddled with an additional prohibition on burials in the city center. The government therefore set up alternative cemeteries in the suburbs and, in the process, appropriated the existing Shinto graveyards as public burial grounds. The management of Shinto cemeteries had originally been placed in the hands of designated shrine priests.[5] But the ban on cremation and the outlawing of burial within Tokyo's red line made it far more important for government officials to meet increased demand for gravesites than to promote a specifically Shinto agenda. Consequently, these cemeteries lost their short-lived distinctiveness as "Shinto" burial grounds and became municipal ones instead. In July 1874, after nearly a year of negotiations between the Finance Ministry, Home Ministry, Council of State, and Tokyo officials, supervision of the existing Shinto cemeteries, as well as several new public burial grounds, was entrusted to the Tokyo City Council, not to Shinto priests.[6] In a book published in September to explain regulations for the new cemeteries, no mention was made of government support for Shinto funerals. The introduction provided by Tokyo prefecture expressed the sentiment that "tombs should be built in pure earth and preserved forever,"[7] but this was a belief shared across Japan's religious spectrum, and the businesslike regulations that followed dealt exclusively with managerial concerns such as the sizes and prices of gravesites.

Even before the cremation ban, the Finance Ministry had begun grounding state policy toward burial in the secular agenda of land reform. In 1871 the government reorganized the Japanese institutional landscape on the macro level by consolidating feudal domains into prefectures directly under the control of the Meiji state. The rest of the 1870s was spent restructuring land use on the micro level, as officials replaced feudal privileges and obligations with a market-driven system of ownership and exchange. Gravesites, like other forms of land, were subject to this process of restructuring and standardization. Theoretically, burial grounds were not economically productive, so the Finance Ministry declared in its 1872 edict on procedures for conferring property deeds that "graveyards, as in the past, will be tax-free land."[8] The ministry thereby established as a general principle the widespread, though not universal, Tokugawa precedent of exempting burial grounds from taxation.[9] Asserting the tax-free status of graveyards did not mean that the ministry intended to let these sites go unregulated. Finance officials did not want to encourage the random proliferation of tax-free plots of land, and they were wary of potential abuses. In another pronouncement made that same year, they forbade the burial of human remains "at will" *(hoshiimama)* in privately owned fields.[10]

Cremation was then banned in 1873, initiating a nationwide scramble for more grave space. The Finance Ministry was alarmed at the prospect of wholesale conversions of land into tax-free graveyards, not only in Tokyo, but across Japan. It therefore prodded the Council of State to clamp down on the "indiscriminate" construction of gravesites in October 1873, just several months after the ministry had engineered the ban on burials within Tokyo's red line.[11] In its edict the Council of State informed prefectures that it was now forbidden to build or expand graveyards on any form of private land—whether fields, forests, or residential plots—without explicit government approval.[12] Such permission was intended to be the exception and not the rule, since the edict also charged local authorities with the task of establishing public "eternal graveyards" *(eikyū bochi)* in order to consolidate burials into clearly demarcated areas. Decisions about where to locate these graveyards were to be approved by the Finance Ministry. In responding to an 1874 inquiry from Myōdō prefecture, the ministry's Land Tax Reform Bureau (Chiso Kaisei Kyoku) left no doubt about the intent of the Council of State's edict. Myōdō officials noted in their communication that people in remote mountain areas had arbitrarily constructed burial grounds in scattered locations. They asked whether these plots of land were to be designated as tax-free graveyards or not. The bureau answered that preexisting burial grounds should be given tax-free status, but that in the future the prefecture ought not to allow this sort of "indiscriminate burial" to take place. Instead, it must designate "eternal grave-yards owned in common" *(eisei kyōyū no bochi),* each one assigned to one or more villages.[13]

The Home Ministry worked within the guidelines established by the Finance Ministry and Council of State to announce its own regulations in April 1874. These were designed to clarify state policy toward graveyards, with a graveyard *(bochi)* officially defined as "an area with tombs *(funbo)* clustered together that is approved and registered by the government." A burial ground with clear boundaries—whether it was used by one family or by an entire village—was considered to be a tax-free graveyard, even if located on land that had been taxed before the Restoration. In contrast, tombs "scattered in fields" did not qualify as authorized graveyards. Furthermore, while the Home Ministry accorded official status to private burial grounds that were clearly demarcated, it also curtailed their future use. Citing the Council of State's edict, the Home Ministry confirmed the ban on freely building or expanding private gravesites, requiring local governments to build communal "eternal grave-yards" in their place.[14]

Until the late 1870s local Confucian- and nativist-trained officials used the rules issued from Tokyo as a means to crack down on practices that they considered uncivilized. Of particular concern was the custom, prevalent in some regions of Japan, of burying corpses in mass graves in one location and erecting memorials in another, a practice today referred to by Japanese anthropologists and folklore scholars as the "double-grave system." Authorities in Saitama prefecture vigorously attacked the practice of burying corpses in mass, unmarked graves, comparing it, in a notice distributed throughout the prefecture in March 1874, to "tossing away the remains of dogs and cats." Writing to the Home Ministry in April 1876, officials in neighboring Tochigi prefecture criticized the custom as well, noting that it encouraged people to "forget the *true* burial grounds" [italics are mine] of their relatives. Calling this "deplorable," they then pointed out that Home Ministry regulations forbade unauthorized burial in private land but did not address the construction of stone memorials apart from human remains. In order to eliminate confusion over what was to be considered a graveyard and what was not, and to keep people from "forgetting the graveyards of their ancestors," the Tochigi letter suggested banning the construction of memorial stones outside burial grounds. Individual stones to commemorate the dead would be erected on private land only with explicit permission from authorities, ending, in effect, the double-grave system.[15]

The Home Ministry approved the Tochigi proposal.[16] In the 1880s, however, the ministry withdrew support for zealous reformers in the countryside. This change is reflected in correspondence between Shiga prefecture and the ministry in 1885. Shiga officials explained that it was customary throughout their jurisdiction to set up memorial stones in temple land and simply "dump" corpses in communal burial grounds. People referred to the memorial sites as "graveyards," but these were not graveyards in a legal sense. Shiga prefecture therefore asked the Home Ministry if it should nullify the deeds that had been granted for these groupings of memorial stones. In response the ministry said that the deeds should not be revoked, only that the designation "graveyard" should be changed to another land title based on the judgment of local authorities.[17] Significantly, there was no mention of putting an end to the double-grave system.

While the Home Ministry distanced itself from the moralistic crusades of officials determined to put a stop to the double-grave system, it nevertheless enforced its own vision of a standardized format for burial. This was particularly true in regard to its 1873 order to consolidate future burials into new communal graveyards, as Ibaraki prefecture discovered when it sent a letter to the Home Ministry in 1878 asking if six families sharing the same surname could reconstruct their privately held graveyard in a new location. The current one was susceptible to mudslides during the rainy season, so they wanted to move the graves to higher ground, and had chosen a spot in a privately owned mountain forest far away from habitation. Ibaraki officials admitted that it was difficult to sanction such a move in light of the Council of State's edict concerning burial, but they sought to allow it in this case. The ministry answered several weeks later, saying that they could not build an exclusive burial ground, but had to move graves to a communal graveyard.[18] Ibaraki sent another letter in May explaining that nearby graveyards were too small to accommodate the move. In response the ministry ordered Ibaraki officials to set up a new communal graveyard, and in November the officials informed the ministry that, after consulting with other villagers, the six families in question had agreed to establish one for use by the entire village. The proposal was then quickly approved.[19]

Over the course of the Meiji period private burial sites were rendered obsolete in one village after another, replaced with communal graveyards. The tightening of regulations sometimes led to subterfuge. For example, communal sites were established in Ichinoseki, a city in Iwate prefecture; but while residents buried bodies in them during the day, they dug up the dead and reburied them in private burial plots under the cover of night. The same held true for a village in Miyagi's Tamatsukuri county, where a communal graveyard was established in late Meiji.[20] The fact that people resorted to this kind of deception is a testament to how intrusive regulations issued from Tokyo had become by the early twentieth century.

Looking to diminish rather than accentuate religious divisions, the Home Ministry also outlawed the construction of new sectarian graveyards, whether Shinto or Buddhist. In a set of rules in 1882 the ministry announced that "communal burial graveyards" *(kyōsō bochi)* had to accept the corpse of anyone who died nearby, regardless of geographical or sectarian origin.[21] Some provincial officials were incredulous about the change in policy. Saga prefecture tested the parameters of the new rules in a June 1883 inquiry, asking if the prohibition on building sectarian graveyards really applied to Shinto cemeteries. The Home Ministry replied that it certainly did.[22] In 1884 Yamaguchi officials asked if they could set up Shinto cemeteries as a way to head off disputes between Buddhist temples and those who wanted to perform Shinto burials within their graveyards. Once more the ministry stood its ground, asserting the general principle that "all are to be buried communally without distinguishing between Shinto and Buddhism."[23] Naturally, new Buddhist graveyards were also forbidden. In 1881 the Home Ministry refused to allow the former parishioners of the Shinshū temple mentioned in Chapter Three to build their own graveyard, not because of the bogus claim that it would harm public health, but because any new cemeteries had to be built by towns or villages without regard to sectarian affiliation.[24]

The Home Ministry's effort both to standardize and secularize the administration of burial reached its fulfillment in 1884. In that year the nationwide system of doctrinal instructors was formally abolished and the prohibition on unofficiated funerals lifted.[25] The Council of State also enacted the most comprehensive rules to date for the management of graveyards and burial, and the Home Ministry announced a set of detailed guidelines to accompany them.[26] In a letter to the Sanji-in (the institutional successor to the Sa-in) concerning proposals for the new rules, the Council of State observed, "Now that Edict 19 has eliminated the doctrinal instructors, we will not be able to rely solely on the power of religion to regulate burial in the future."[27] The government would have to rely on local police forces instead, wrote the council. Accordingly,

Article Two of the new rules declared, "all graveyards and crematories are subject to police control," and stipulated that anyone wanting to rebury a body, or erect a new grave marker, had to get permission from the authorities. The rules also required that mourners obtain certificates authorizing burial or cremation and that caretakers of graveyards, including clerics, apply for licenses from local officials. In order to facilitate investigations into potential foul play, the Council of State also prohibited the burial or cremation of any body until twenty-four hours after it was pronounced dead.[28]

The Home Ministry assigned the task of certifying deaths to medical doctors. Previously there had been no uniform, nationwide standard for verifying and reporting deaths. In some cases the corpse was inspected by a doctor, but more often than not, death was confirmed by a local temple priest or even a family member. If a death were considered mundane, it might not be reported to the authorities for months, and if it were viewed as suspicious or unusual, Buddhist priests, not doctors, were usually the ones to investigate.[29] In 1880, however, the Home Ministry ordered deaths in Tokyo to be certified by medical professionals, and the 1884 guidelines instituted this policy on a national level, making permits for cremation or burial contingent on the presentation of death certificates to local officials.[30] This rule tied mourners into a bureaucratic process divorced from clerical oversight, giving the expanding institutions of the secular state new authority over the disposal of the dead.

The Home Ministry did not stop with the verification of death and burial. Out of concern for public health it ordered that graveyards be built more than sixty *ken* (about 109 yards) from residences and not located alongside highways, railroads, and rivers. It also warned local officials to make sure that graveyards did not poison drinking water. The ministry established further guidelines for the internal management of cemeteries, stating that caretakers should regularly clean the burial grounds under their oversight and that graves must be at least six *shaku* (about six feet) deep. The ministry even asserted that the government had the right to regulate what was written on tombstones. In Article Ten of its guidelines, the ministry stated that a stone did not need police approval if it displayed only the name, posthumous title, and birth and death dates of the person it memorialized. Anything else, however, had to be cleared with the authorities.[31] After all, who knew what kinds of inflammatory statements might appear on gravestones? By asserting police control at such a minute level, the Home Ministry sent a message with broader implications: no boundaries, certainly not religious ones, ought to come between the individual and the authority of the state.

FOR CUSTOM'S SAKE

The Home Ministry stuck to its plan for the future, requiring that all new cemeteries be open to any of the emperor's subjects, regardless of sectarian affiliation and place of origin. Most Japanese, however, continued to be buried in preexisting graveyards, and as part of the land tax reform of the 1870s, which converted feudal obligations into property rights throughout Japan, local officials, under orders from Tokyo, distributed deeds to confirm the ownership of these sites.

This was a difficult task, for it was not immediately obvious whose names to affix to the deeds. While it was easy enough to authorize the ownership of a burial ground used by only one family, the assignment of property rights was far more complex for what the Land Tax Reform Office (Chiso Kaisei Jimukyoku)[32] designated "graveyards owned in common by the people" (*jinmin kyōyū bochi).*[33] Who constituted "the people," after all? Authorities had a number of alternatives to choose from. In some instances, they opted to record the names of official villages on deeds, giving burial rights to anyone living— or, more to the point, dying—within them. But others interpreted the term "owned in common" *(kyōyū)* more narrowly and, accommodating local precedents, tailored property rights to distinct subgroups. As a result, graveyards were also assigned to small hamlets and temple communities instead of the administrative units of towns and villages.[34]

Because the process of assigning ownership was often arbitrary and ambiguous, it generated situations ripe for conflict,[35] and fights over temple graveyards—which pitted the autonomy of temple communities against both the religious autonomy of individuals and the material and ideological interests of government—were particularly explosive.

The legal parameters for these disputes originated in the appropriation and redistribution of shrine and temple property that began in late 1870, when the Council of State ordered the seizure of shrine and temple lands that had been free from tax under the old regime, including "red seal" *(shuin)* and "black seal" *(kokuin)* properties donated by the shogunate and individual daimyo. During the Tokugawa period, many of these lands had been worked by local farmers, who were taxed by their priestly overlords. Following the Council of State decision, bureaucrats assigned ownership of these parcels to those who cultivated them, putting forests and other property without clear title into the hands of the state. The takeover eliminated clerical enfeoffment while raising revenues for the fledgling government. Property-stripped shrines and temples were compensated with stipends, and parcels that were owned outright by priests, or fields that had been developed into productive land through their direct investment, remained under clerical control. Institutions that had not depended on the largesse of feudal authorities—that is, temples and shrines on taxable land—were allowed to keep their assets intact.[36]

In its initial order to reallocate temple lands, the Council of State exempted the ritual precincts *(keidai)* of shrines and temples and in 1871 clarified that graveyards were also free from assessment and seizure by the state.[37] Then in 1874 the government designated precincts and their graveyards to be privately held land if there were clear records of ownership and as state land if there were not.[38] Finally, in 1875 the Land Tax Reform Office ordered local officials to register even temple burial grounds located on state land as "graveyards owned in common by the people,"[39] effectively putting them in the same legal category as the graveyards of private temples. The government thereby created a formal distinction between the ownership of temple graveyards and the ownership of the temple precincts with which they were affiliated.

Clerics, parishioners, and officials responded to this confusing policy of registering temple graveyards independently of temple precincts in several ways. During the drawn-out process of land reform (the Land Tax Reform Office did not shut its doors until 1881),[40] temples on state land had the opportunity to lay claim to "graveyards owned in common by the people," and depending on the circumstances, local authorities issued deeds showing the names of parishioners, or clerics, or simply the temples. But in many cases no name was listed at all, whether because there was no adequate proof of ownership or because temples failed to assert their property rights. A history of shrine and temple land reform published by the Finance Ministry in 1954 notes that many temples did not declare ownership of property for which adequate proof was available and that a majority of them even refrained from staking out their ritual precincts as private land, leaving them registered as state land instead. The reason for this is uncertain, wrote the ministry, but it speculated that they followed instructions coming from local officials.[41] Thus the deeds for temple graveyards often lacked any designation other than "graveyard owned in common" *(kyōyū bochi)* and were entrusted to local ward or village offices, not to the temples themselves.

Officials apparently arranged this in order to undercut the ability of temple communities to exclude outsiders from their cemeteries.[42] The concern about such incidents was well founded. In 1872 the Ministry of Doctrine had ordered temples to allow Shinto burials in their graveyards, but this did not stop priests and parishioners from defending their turf against heretical incursions. Shimane prefecture contacted the Home Ministry in May 1877 to address this problem, writing that despite the separate registration of temple graveyards and precincts, the former still fell under the "jurisdiction" *(sho-katsu)* of the latter. Therefore temples regularly denied burial to nonparishioners and also stopped parishioners who had converted to Shinto funerals from either reburying ancestral remains or conducting Shinto rites at existing tombs. Shimane officials sought confirmation from the ministry that temples did not, in fact, have the right to exclude Shinto burial and memorial rites, even if the graveyards in question were located on what had always been considered temple-owned, not state-owned, land. The ministry agreed with this position.[43]

In its June 1877 reply to Shimane officials, the Home Ministry supported the policy of forcing Buddhist temples to allow Shinto burials in their graveyards, even when they owned the land outright. However, the original architect of enforced plurality, the Ministry of Doctrine, had already been abolished in January of that same year, marking the government's accelerating retreat from a blatantly Shinto agenda. This retreat was reflected in subsequent communications between the Home Ministry and prefectural officials, reversing the stance taken in response to Shimane. In October 1878, for example, Kanagawa prefecture asked the Home Ministry how to handle the assignment of deeds for "graveyards owned in common by the people" that had been hewn from temple-affiliated state land and from state land in general. Should communal ownership be limited to those who already had family plots or should deeds go to towns and villages? In its reply (delayed until July 1879), the ministry said this question should be answered case by case, with local officials taking into account the "customary practice" *(kangyō)* of each graveyard.[44] This policy was confirmed in the Home Ministry's burial regulations of 1884, which stated that graveyards were not to discriminate according to sectarian affiliation, but added that graveyards with "special customs" *(betsudan no shūkan)* were not bound by this general "common burial" principle.[45]

With this deliberately vague caveat in place, the Home Ministry wiped its hands of burial disputes, leaving them to be decided locally.[46] In effect, this was a traditionalist policy that acknowledged the power of longstanding local, and for the most part, Buddhist, practices. The authority conferred by deeds, backed by the government's "special customs" clause, provided powerful ammunition for Buddhist temples seeking to maintain control over parishioner graveyards while playing to the conservative instincts of local officials more concerned with maintaining order than with defending the rights of religious converts.

For example, an article appearing in an 1892 issue of the Buddhist magazine *Mitsugon kyōhō* reported a burial dispute in a Mie prefecture village where a local branch of the Shinto sect Maruyamakyō wanted to bury a member according to Shinto rites in one of three cemeteries in the village.[47] The resident priests of the three temples attached to them concluded, "even though today is an age of freedom of belief, burying those of a different religion goes against custom to date," so they opposed the burial, despite the fact that preparations had already been made.[48] The village office was dragged into the conflict, and the village head tried to convince the Maruyamakyō members to accept a Buddhist service. They initially refused, but supposedly after losing a theological debate with the clerics, were forced to acquiesce.[49] Following this incident the priests wrote to the prefectural office to confirm their rights over the three village graveyards. They noted that they had been granted deeds with joint signatures and that it was inappropriate for descendants to break with tradition and attempt non-Buddhist burials. The governor replied in favor of the priests.[50]

Thus room was made for the past in the present, reflecting and contributing to a broader conservatism that swept Japan beginning in the late 1880s in response to the political, economic, social, and cultural upheavals following the Restoration. The government was unwilling, nonetheless, to sacrifice its vision of the future, especially insofar as it involved Tokyo, the nation's capital. This vision led to a bitter and highly publicized clash with hundreds of Tokyo temples.

MAKING ROOM FOR THE FUTURE

In October 1887 three Shinshū priests, backed by a letter from Patriarch Ōtani Kōshō (1817–1894) himself, complained to the governor of Tokyo that many temple graveyards "owned in common" *(kyōyū)* in the city were, in fact, being treated as "common burial grounds" *(kyōsōchi)*. The priests wrote that parishioners considered temple-affiliated graveyards to be "Buddhist holy ground" *(bukkyō no reichi)* and were therefore "greatly shocked" when the graves of those adhering to alien religions appeared in them. This distress gave rise to fights and even lawsuits among the "foolish masses." Speaking also on behalf of other Buddhist sects, the Shinshū clerics asked that temple graveyards "owned in common" be clearly designated the property of parishioners and priests. The supporting letter from Ōtani noted that some deeds for graveyards displayed the names of temples on them, but in many cases they simply read "owned in common," with no other qualifiers, which led to confusion.[51] Another letter sent to the governor of Tokyo in February 1888 by one of the Shinshū clerics listed specific examples in which the Tokyo police, put in charge of burials and graveyards by the Home Ministry, had forced temples to allow Shinto and Christian burials in their graveyards.[52]

After getting clearance from the Home Ministry, the governor of Tokyo responded to the Buddhist petitions by deciding in the spring of 1888 to allow temples to prohibit "the mixing of different religions and sects" in graveyards where burial had traditionally been limited to temple parishioners.[53] The police were ordered to investigate cemeteries throughout the city to confirm which ones were affiliated with what temples and sects.[54] However, the governor drew the line when it came to putting title of the graveyards "owned in common" in the hands of temple communities. During the land-reform process the deeds for these graveyards had been deposited with ward registrars throughout Tokyo, and that is where the governor wanted them to remain, at least for the moment. In his October 1887 report to the Home Ministry, he wrote that even though it was sensible to respect religious differences, trying to resolve conflicts by making graveyards the private property *(shiyūchi)* of temples would interfere with urban renewal plans. These plans, then in the works, tentatively called for the removal of graveyards from the city center to allow for wider roads and improvement of the city's overall appearance.[55]

Tensions seem to have temporarily died down after Tokyo instituted its new sect-conscious burial policy, but the shaky boundary between graveyards "owned in common" and those open to "common burial" became a battle-front when Tokyo declared temple graveyards to be city property in 1891.[56] In 1889, the same year that its plans for urban renewal were officially announced, the city of Tokyo (Tōkyōshi) was established as an independent entity within Tokyo prefecture (Tōkyōfu) amid a reorganization of municipal governments nationwide.[57] Consequently, oversight of city graveyards devolved to the new city government from the prefectural governor in February 1891.[58] In anticipation of the administrative handover, the governor of Tokyo corresponded with the Home Ministry several times in 1889 and 1890, sending proposals to deal with the graveyards "owned in common" that were located on former temple land.[59] The governor recommended that the city annex those affecting urban renewal projects, but he also suggested privatizing the remaining burial grounds in the city's main wards and outlying districts, making them the indisputable property of the temple communities who used them. The governor's plan to appropriate some temple graveyards but to privatize others was rejected outright by the Home Ministry.[60] Clearly it had no intention of condoning the wholesale transfer of land to temple control. The central government's position was that graveyards "owned in common" within Tokyo prefecture were the legitimate property of the city of Tokyo and surrounding townships and villages.

Pursuant to the Home Ministry guidelines of 1884, the Tokyo police department issued a set of detailed burial regulations in August 1891.[61] These enunciated the responsibilities of graveyard managers *(bochi kanrisha)*, who were required to register with the police, and included fines and jail time (several days worth) for managers who did not follow proper procedures.[62] Heads of the different wards and districts then informed temple priests that by the end of October they must apply for formal designation as managers of the graveyards they tended.[63] Clerics complied with this order, but the permits that were issued recognized them as managers not of "graveyards owned in common" *(kyōyū bochi)* but of "common burial graveyards" *(kyōsō bochi).*[64] The city subsequently announced a directive at the end of November aimed at the "common burial graveyards" of "former temple precincts." Among other things it ordered temple priests to record clearly the individual graves used by parishioners and to get approval from local authorities when collecting money to pay for expenses. Temples were also forbidden to build "buddha halls" *(butsudō)* or other structures in graveyards.[65] The coup de grace to the autonomy of temple burial grounds came in the form of a prefectural order to ward and district officials impounding graveyard deeds that had been "mistakenly" issued to temples.[66]

In 1888 Tokyo had recognized the special status of temple graveyards by allowing temple communities to forbid "the mixing of different religions and sects" in them. In 1891, however, these burial grounds were suddenly stripped of their "owned in common" standing and made into "common burial graveyards," putting them in the same category as public cemeteries run directly by the city. As managers for these graveyards, temple priests were effectively turned into city functionaries. Not surprisingly, they protested this power grab, forming a cross-sectarian committee to fight the government. According to the *Yomiuri shinbun,* no fewer than 1,200 clerics signed onto the graveyard campaign.[67] In early 1892 the committee petitioned the governor of Tokyo prefecture to reinstate the "owned in common" status for temple graveyards now considered available for "common burial," but this appeal was summarily rejected. The committee was also stonewalled when it met face-to-face with Tokyo and Home Ministry bureaucrats and pressed them to justify Tokyo's seizure of temple graveyards.[68] As a result the affair landed in the Tokyo District Court, which had to weigh the competing claims to the graveyards in question.[69]

How to understand the scope of the term "owned in common" was the main issue before the court. Graveyards owned outright by temples on private land were not called into question. But Tokyo had a high proportion of temples that had been granted tax-free lands under the shogunate, and prefectural and city officials maintained that the "graveyards owned in common by the people" carved from them during the late 1870s and early 1880s were, in fact, "owned in common" by all the people of Tokyo. Therefore the governor of Tokyo was acting within his rights when he assigned them to the city of Tokyo in 1891, they argued. Temple representatives rebutted that, even if their deeds read "owned in common" and nothing more, logic dictated that burial grounds traditionally limited to parishioners fell under the jurisdiction of temples and not the city at large. The 1891 order from the governor of Tokyo merely transferred the oversight of graveyards, not their ownership, they said.

The court agreed with the temples on this last point, concluding that the 1891 order did not give the city of Tokyo the right to seize those graveyards clearly belonging to temples. Appeals from Tokyo to overturn this ruling were rejected. However, the court also decided that graveyards not explicitly assigned to temples during the land reform investigations were to be considered public property. This gave Tokyo a legitimate right to the "graveyards owned in common" whose deeds had originally been deposited with ward and district offices. Legal scholars Yoshida Hisashi and Murayama Hiroo, in their discussions of this court case, do not explain why temples failed to act more aggressively to secure their graveyards during the land reform process. But an answer to this question is suggested in an opinion paper written and published by the cross-sectarian committee on temple graveyards.[70] In this publication temple priests incongruously advertised tensions with parishioners in order to regain control over their gravesites. According to the committee, several people involved in the land-reform process told them that the ownership of temple graveyards was left unspecified to ensure that neither clerics nor parishioners would wield too much power over one another. That is, registering temple burial grounds simply as "graveyards owned in common" was an attempt to maintain a balance of power between clerics and parishioners; it was in no way intended to transfer ownership of graveyards to the city as a whole, the committee argued.[71]

The court, however, sided with Tokyo in regard to burial grounds "owned in common" without any clear title, allowing them to become "common burial graveyards" run by and, more importantly, moved by, the city. Temple priests had rightly concluded in their opinion paper that the city's "unfilial" purpose in claiming these graveyards was to ease their clearance from the path of development.[72] So throughout the 1890s and on into the twentieth century, clerics and parishioners submitted angry petitions to the Home Ministry via Tokyo prefecture to try to regain control over the "holy ground of their ancestors."[73]

By the 1890s the Meiji state had clearly retreated from its pro-Shinto agenda and, in deciding to allow temples to assert their ritual authority in the name of "special customs," had made room for a measure of communal autonomy. The fight over temple graveyards in Tokyo demonstrated, however, that this autonomy was acceptable only to the extent that it did not block the secular path of an aggressively modernizing government, albeit one that extolled the virtues of ancestor reverence.

URBANIZATION AND THE DEAD

The seizure of temple graveyards by Tokyo was representative of bureaucratic efforts in the late nineteenth and early twentieth centuries to organize urban growth, fueled by rapid industrialization and waves of immigration from the countryside. From an urban planning perspective, dead bodies were a hindrance, if not a menace. They endangered public health and occupied land that could be put to economically productive use. Therefore Tokyo's first comprehensive plan for urban renewal, announced in 1889, included the goal of "gradually" relocating burial grounds "scattered around the city," excepting those of particular historical value.[74] Officials in Tokyo and elsewhere had already begun removing graveyards to make way for roadwork and railways earlier in the 1880s,[75] but this plan articulated a long-term vision of systematically excising burial grounds from the city center.

Directing the removal of burial grounds was not an easy task, especially for a government publicly committed to preserving the institution of ancestor worship. One impediment was the financial cost of reimbursing families to move their graves. But a more recalcitrant obstacle was the general unwillingness of communities to surrender control of their ancestral gravesites, a sentiment made loud and clear during the battle over temple graveyards in Tokyo. Opposition to government measures continued into the twentieth century, as the removal of graveyards accelerated along with urban growth. In 1917, for example, the *Ōsaka asahi shinbun* reported that a new school was being constructed in an Osaka neighborhood to accommodate a rapidly rising student population. The site of the school was a 600-year-old communal cemetery, and the paper said that the removal of tombs was in progress. Older residents protested the construction of the new school, and, in an ironic attempt to turn state policy to their own end, justified their opposition on the pretext that it would be "disrespectful" to the emperor to build a school on the "polluted ground" of a former graveyard. Their reasoning was based on the fact that all schools in Japan were required to enshrine an image of the emperor along with a copy of the Imperial Rescript on Education. The protest failed, however, and construction went forward, a scenario that was repeated in cities across Japan.[76]

Graves were moved not just by public officials but also by private interests looking to make money from the cleared land. For example, the *Asahi shin-bun* reported in 1886 that a restaurateur was consolidating the graves of feudal retainers in the old Sennichi burial ground of Osaka (one of the city's famous seven graveyards), presumably to make room for commercial use.[77] Temples, too, were not averse to moving ancestral gravesites as long as they stood to profit. In 1899 a Sōtō Zen temple in Shitaya ward submitted a request to Tokyo officials to rezone part of its privately held graveyard. The temple explained that it wanted to build rental housing as a new source of income and noted that graves had already been consolidated to prepare for construction. The request, signed by the priest and four parishioner representatives, was approved.[78]

Local governments encouraged the orderly removal of graveyards, whether on the initiative of the public or the private sector, but this does not mean that they condoned careless treatment of the dead. Their utilitarianism was counterbalanced by a strong dose of respect for human remains. After all, government officials and their loved ones died too, and they were just as entwined in the practices of ancestor worship as ordinary Japanese. So even though authorities cleared graveyards from city centers, in other respects they acted according to the principle, established by the state in the 1870s, that tombs and their contents ought to be "preserved forever."

When officials condemned graveyards, for instance, they took care to find new homes for the dead and reimburse families for the cost of moving them. Utilizing the police powers granted by the 1884 Council of State and Home Ministry rules concerning burial, they also passed ordinances to monitor the activities of crematory managers and cemetery caretakers, stipulating penalties for negligence and abuse. In its 1885 set of burial rules, Osaka warned crematory managers to stand guard over bodies until they had been thoroughly burned so that none of the remains would be snatched by wild animals.[79] The

Osaka rules also required grave markers to be erected after one year's time even for those who had been buried without anyone to claim them.[80] Tokyo regulations were similar in character, obliging cemetery caretakers, most of them temple priests, to record clearly the area of plots assigned to each family and to keep graveyards tidy. Even the contents of abandoned graves *(muenbo)*[81] could not be "carelessly reburied" or the structures above them arbitrarily removed. Any exhumations required prior approval from the police.[82]

It is not clear to what extent the new police restrictions of the Meiji period were obeyed or enforced, but they were apparently intrusive enough to prompt seventeen Shinshū priests to submit a petition to the Tokyo governor in 1899 asking, along with the familiar appeal to return ownership of graveyards to temples, for the right to limit the amount of time remains could stay in independent gravesites before being consolidated. They noted that the "eternal graveyard" system imposed by the police was impractical since space would eventually run out.[83] The rules remained on the books, however, and in 1926 and 1927, led to a citywide crackdown on priests who had been illegally disinterring remains to create room for both new burials and new housing. They had apparently been taking advantage of the confusion surrounding the reconstruction of Tokyo after the great Kantō earthquake of 1923. Police efforts were approvingly recorded in newspaper articles sporting headlines such as "Arrests of Evil Priests Who Tamper with Graves."[84]

Meanwhile the burial grounds founded in the early Meiji period both filled up with the dead and were engulfed by the living. In order to put them beyond the reach of urban sprawl, planners located new cemeteries at ever-increasing distances from city neighborhoods and relied on expanding transportation networks, railways in particular, to make them accessible.

In fact, from the 1920s, city officials accentuated this growing distance between the suburbanized dead and the urbanized living by transforming graveyards into carefully landscaped parks. The model for the new generation of cemeteries was Tama cemetery, opened in the southwestern suburbs of Tokyo in 1923. It, in turn, was modeled after the park-like cemeteries used in the West since the mid-1800s.[85] It was thoughtfully planned, laid out in a geometric pattern and adorned with trees, lawns, and flowerbeds.[86]

The main force behind Tama cemetery was Inoshita Kiyoshi (1884–1973), one of a new breed of bureaucrats who sought to improve not just the infrastructures of cities, but the life- and death-styles of their inhabitants. After having researched the suburban cemeteries of the United States and Europe, Inoshita planned one for Tokyo that, like its Western counterparts, was

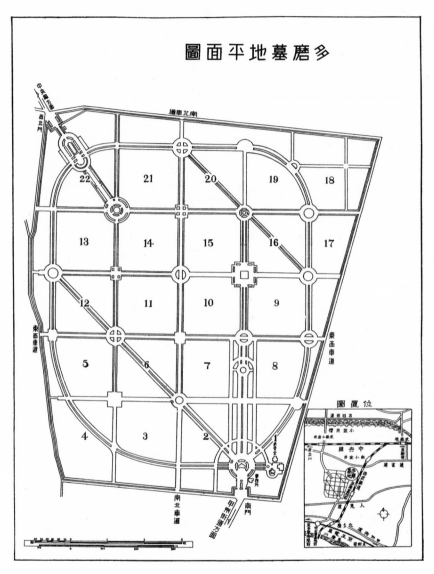

Blueprint for Tama cemetery. The smaller map shows how to get to the cemetery by train. From *Bochi keiei*, by Inoue Yasumoto.

intended to serve as an escape from the city as much as a place to visit the dead.[87] Inoshita was made chief of the Tokyo parks department in 1923, which had managed Tokyo's municipal cemeteries since its founding in 1921.[88] It was in this capacity that he oversaw the planning of another park-cemetery that opened in Tokyo's northeastern outskirts in 1935. This one was called Yabashira *reien* (soul park),[89] a title that clearly expressed a vision of the suburban cemetery as a tranquil resting place for the dead. In fact, starting from 1935 the term *reien* was applied generally to other municipal cemeteries as well.[90]

In an article appearing in a 1937 issue of *Toshi mondai,* a magazine devoted to urban planning, Inoshita expounded the virtues of what he called "garden-style" *(teienteki)* cemeteries, which are "completely different in their intent from the cemeteries [designed] merely for the disposal of human remains through burial. The object is to construct noble and tranquil communal dwelling places for the souls of the deceased, in scenic and pure garden locations. . . . Through subsequent management and care, they will retain their sacredness perpetually."[91] In a 1941 work on the management of cemeteries, another city official, Inoue Yasumoto, contrasted the "realm of happiness for entering nirvana" that was Tama cemetery (now called a *reien*) with the "shadowy realm" of a traditional graveyard. Reflecting a growing appreciation for green space, he wrote that, at Tama *reien,* family members could pray for the welfare of spirits "sleeping in natural beauty."[92] The concept of the garden-style cemetery spread rapidly in other cities in the 1920s and 1930s, as they too ran out of room in their older public burial grounds. With the garden cemetery, cities could kill two birds with one stone, meeting the need for burials while providing a respite from hectic city life. Illuminated at night by electric lighting, their cheery designs chased away the gloom of death.[93]

The desire to brighten and sanitize death carried over into the construction of crematories as well. During the first few decades of the new century, municipal governments mustered the resources to build crematories directly under their control and to buy out existing operations and upgrade them, replacing wood-burning ovens with coal, oil, and even electric-powered equipment. In Tokyo, Hakuzensha remained independent and is a formidable power to this day, but Hachikōsha was acquired by Osaka in 1907, and the Honganji crematories were ceded to Kyoto in 1931.[94] Back in 1904 Kyoto had already completed a city-managed facility on the premise that cremation was truly a "public enterprise" and therefore most appropriately supervised by bureaucrats, a conclusion reached by authorities in cities, towns, and villages across Japan, who gradually displaced the small-scale *onbō* with more efficient, large-scale crematories.[95] This trend was reinforced by tales of abuse perpetrated by unscrupulous private operators. Newspapers published chilling accounts of body parts being stolen to make medicines that were rumored to cure syphilis and other diseases. Cases where *onbō* stole gold teeth and other items from the dead were also reported in the press.[96]

In contrast, journalists enthusiastically endorsed the up-to-date facilities built and managed by city governments. A newspaper article from 1927 described a crematory in Kobe where electricity had been used since 1922, claiming that the facility exhibited "no melancholy gloom, no disagreeable smell of death."[97] Another article from 1928 reported the construction of a new crematory for four villages in Hyōgo prefecture, which, the author noted approvingly, was "stylish" *(haikara)* and did not even look like a crematory.[98] A smart-looking facility was also built in Japanese-controlled Seoul, a newspaper reported in 1929. It was surrounded by a park-like setting, and the city crematory was attached to a funeral center decorated with marble and decorative tile "like a dance hall." Here one could die "at ease," said the paper.[99]

The new furnaces used at these up-to-date facilities, which burned fossil fuels instead of wood, also made the management of death easier for survivors by compressing the time needed for cremation. Before the installation of this equipment in the 1920s and 1930s, mourners had to accompany corpses to crematories on the day of a funeral, leave them to be burned overnight, and then return the next day to retrieve the charred remains. As a precaution against the theft of body parts, gold teeth, jewelry, or articles of clothing, mourners were given keys to the individual ovens, which they had to bring back to the crematory to recover the bones and ash. Writing in his diary about the funeral for his daughter in 1911, novelist Natsume Sōseki (1867–1916) described the two trips he made to Ochiai crematory in suburban Tokyo. He noted that he received a key for the furnace on the day of the funeral but that his wife forgot it when they headed back to Ochiai the following day to collect his daughter's remains. They did not discover this until reaching the crematory. "Thinking this foolish, I was angered," Sōseki wrote, noting that it had taken forty minutes by carriage to get there. He and his wife had to send one of their sons back home to retrieve the key.[100]

The new crematories radically changed the experience of burning the dead. Since the advanced designs produced even less smoke and stench than their Meiji predecessors, rules that had once required cremations to take place overnight were lifted, and mourners could go to the crematories just once, waiting on the premises while the fast and clean-burning ovens did their work. A newspaper article from 1930 describing a new crematory about to open in Fukuoka noted approvingly that, when operational, it would burn bodies in just an hour's time, allowing mourning families to take bones home with them on the very day of the funeral.[101] Despite the fact that Hakuzensha, which was controlled by Buddhist priests, continued to control most crematories in the capital, Tokyo did decide to build one public crematory in the 1930s, the Mizue "funeral center" *(sōba)*. Describing the funeral center in a 1938 article (serialized in four issues of a weekly bulletin published by the city of Tokyo),[102] Inoshita celebrated same-day cremations. He did note, however, that it was necessary to wait a short while before the bones and ash were presented to the mourning family because showing them the "glowing red remains" fresh out of the oven would be "disconcerting."[103] Inoshita emphasized that, like grave-yards themselves, modern crematories—or, rather, "funeral centers"—should be placed in garden-like settings, creating elegant buffer zones. It was also important to set aside space for bone-collection rooms to afford families privacy for this sad task.[104] Inoshita regretted that most crematories in Japan were still "primitive" at the time he wrote his article, but what he called "aesthetic management" was indeed taking hold during the 1930s, setting the

A postcard of Tokyo's Mizue crematory in the 1940s. From *Bochi keiei,* by Inoue Yasumoto.

stage for a general trend in the postwar period to diminish as much as possible the messiness and time-consuming nature of death.

The new cremation technology provided not just aestheticized environments; for many it also changed the schedule of Buddhist rituals, since it allowed the traditional seventh-day mortuary rites to be folded into the day of the funeral itself. With remains in hand, a family could quickly return to the site where the initial funeral had been held (whether the family home or a temple) to have the seventh-day rites performed immediately. Despite the contradiction of holding a seventh-day service before seven days had passed, this option became increasingly popular over the course of the twentieth century as family members, often separated by long distances, tried to lessen the inconvenience of taking time off from work to attend multiple rituals.

As municipal officials built newfangled cemeteries and crematories, temple graveyards were themselves modernized, and in this respect too, Tokyo served as an example for the rest of the country. Even as late as 1941, according to the estimates of Inoue Yasumoto, out of the 80,000 or so people who died each year in Tokyo, 10,000 were transported back to their native villages and towns and 17,000 were buried in municipal cemeteries. But the majority, 53,000, continued to be interred in temple graveyards.[105] Longtime residents were reluctant to part with old temple burial grounds (most of them technically "common burial graveyards"), despite efforts on the part of local government to relocate them to the suburbs. These efforts had gradually reduced the amount of land devoted to temple graveyards in the fifteen main wards of the city from 326,215 *tsubo* (about 266 acres) in 1889 to 246,479 *tsubo* (about 201 acres) in 1923.[106] But after the great earthquake of that year, when graveyards, along with the rest of the city, lay in ruins, Tokyo officials saw reconstruction as an opportunity to drastically reduce urban grave space in one fell swoop. The city still encouraged the relocation of gravesites to the suburbs, but faced with continued resistance and wanting to accelerate the clearance of space-consuming graveyards, Tokyo came up with a compromise, establishing rules in 1925 that allowed temples to construct walled-in sites *one-third* the size of former graveyards to hold ossuaries *(nōkotsudō)* for cremated remains. Instead of haphazardly burying cremated remains in the earth, temples had to seal them in concrete storage spaces regimented in tight rows.[107] Many temples took advantage of this option, happy to see the neatly organized dead kept close at hand. A newspaper article from 1929 praised the construction of the modern ossuary by a temple in the Fukagawa neighborhood of Tokyo, saying it ought to last "for eternity."[108]

THE ORPHANED DEAD

History showed that no amount of planning could guarantee resting places forever. In 1930 an article published in the *Hōchi shinbun* described the derelict condition of Yanaka cemetery, originally designed to provide permanent homes for the dead, but where children now played baseball among toppled, untended gravestones.[109]

Stone was vulnerable to the elements, and especially to earthquakes, but tombs fell into ruin more often for social than for natural reasons, since they depended on unbroken patrilines for their care. Article 987 of the Meiji civil code authorized the custom of primogeniture, stating, "The ownership of the genealogical records of the house, of the utensils of house-worship, and *of the family tombs* [my italics], belongs to the special rights of succession to the headship of a house."[110] Thus the government certified the privilege of first sons, and their wives, both to maintain and occupy family tombs in perpetuity. When patrilines expired or descendents were negligent, however, graves quickly became subject to removal and destruction, whether at the hands of temple priests or urban planners, because no provision for their care was made beyond the family itself.

Even the graves of the once great were vulnerable. In Tokyo, for example, a preservation society affiliated with the Home Ministry tried to save the gravesites of famous Tokugawa-period retainers, artists, literary figures, and other notables, but as one newspaper article pointed out in 1927, temple priests and the police often had little sense of history, consigning these graves and their markers to gradual decay, distant suburbs, or worse. The article singled out for special condemnation a recent case in which a foreigner had purchased the gravestones of several famous *shōgi* (Japanese chess) masters from a temple graveyard being moved from the path of an electric railway.[111] In the first issue of the magazine *Sōtai* (Clearing moss), founded in 1932 to catalogue historical gravesites and advocate their preservation, one contributor (a baron) lamented that the remains and markers of great figures from the past were not being adequately preserved, calling gravestones "objects of deep feeling."[112]

Tokyo's parks chief, Inoshita Kiyoshi, advocated the protection of graves and their contents in the magazine's next issue, but he also noted the difficulty of keeping bodily remains and gravestones intact at their original locations. In many cases financing and logistics forced the decision to protect the remains but abandon the stones.[113] Of course city officials also saw their new municipal cemeteries fill with increasing numbers of "buddhas without bonds" *(muenbotoke),* orphaned by the inevitable disintegration of family lineages. They therefore had to develop systems to try to track down surviving relatives and, if none could be found, consolidate the remains into special *muen* tombs, making the hapless buddhas into wards of the state.[114]

In *Fumetsu no funbo* (The eternal tomb), published in 1932, Hosono Ungai lamented the proliferation of abandoned graves throughout Japan and assembled a rogue's gallery of newspaper clippings to demonstrate the abuse they suffered.[115] Tombs were regularly abandoned, he said, because care was entrusted to individual families and not to local governments. He therefore proposed taking the concept of the municipal graveyard one step further by building enormous "eternal tombs," finding inspiration in the communal tombs that had been established by several rural communities.[116] Urban ossuaries in the form of massive domes, modeled after Sri Lankan stupas, would serve as civic centers, house gymnasiums, and support beacons to guide sea and air traffic.[117] No one would become a "buddha without bonds" because "all the white bones of people would be buried together in one grave equally, without distinctions."[118] Worship would not be limited to any one set of remains, but would extend to all Japanese, making these monstrosities concrete symbols of the "adamantine, indestructible strength of all the people."[119] According to Hosono's eccentric vision, these eternal tombs would be built according to a standard format throughout Japan, forming a nationwide network. He also proposed building tombs just for foreigners, characterizing this segregation as a courtesy that would signal to the world that Japan was indeed a nation of "gentlemen."[120]

Hosono's totalitarian vision was not realized, not only because of the logistics involved, but also because it was completely antithetical to the traditions of patriline-anchored ancestor reverence. Even if a stone-topped tomb were destined for obsolescence, the point of building it was to establish or enhance the imagined continuity of an individual family, not the "imagined community" of the entire nation.[121] During the Tokugawa period, it had become increasingly popular to erect gravestones; and after the Restoration, families jockeying for position in a postfeudal world erected stones on an unprecedented scale, a trend reinforced by the memorialization of dead soldiers just after the Russo-Japanese War (1904–1905). The "tombstone fad," as folklorist Yanagita Kunio (1875–1962) called it, spurred people to erect "bigger and more magnificent stones than the next person" up into the Taishō (1912–1926) and Shōwa periods (1926–1989).[122] An article in a 1927 issue of the *Kokumin shinbun* noted that Tama *reien* was rapidly filling with "grandiose" stones, the detritus of "unhealthy competition,"[123] while in 1928 the *Ōsaka asahi shinbun*

Sample illustrations of the "eternal tombs" proposed by Hosono. The one on top supports a lighthouse. Written on the tomb below are the characters for *kyōson,* meaning "coexistence." From *Fumetsu no funbō,* by Hosono Ungai.

complained about the trend among the "nouveau riche" to build great tombs among the moss-covered graves of daimyo on Mt. Kōya.[124]

⌐Of course, not all families had the resources to build splendid monuments, but they did what they could, spreading the practice of erecting some sort of memorial through descending levels of society. These increasingly took the form of stones reading "the grave of the 'x' patriline" ('x' *ie no haka*), which covered cement-lined cubicles holding cremated remains.[125] The double-grave system and communal tombs persist in some communities, but the *"ie no haka"* format is today standard across Japan, taken for granted in urban and rural areas alike. As Yanagita noted, "Many Japanese are so accustomed to the forest of monuments in modern cemeteries that they unconsciously believe the practice to have come down from ancient times and therefore to be quite proper."[126] These forests of stone attest to sought-for stability in a rapidly changing world. As Hosono predicted, however, even the most up-to-date and well tended of these forests are now regularly thinned, as family lineages expire and there is no one left to care for the weathered slabs. Meanwhile, "soul parks" run by public and private interests eat up ever-expanding areas of the Japanese countryside.

One of the requisite features of a modern state is domination of national space. The Meiji regime and its successors in Tokyo standardized the admin-istration of Japan to bring its physical and social landscape under centralized control and, in the process, indelibly shaped the way modern Japanese dispose of and memorialize their dead. Motivated by economic and health consider-ations, state policy empowered local officials to end burials in private plots of land, move gravesites from urban centers, and advance cremation.

But while officials made the modern burial system, they did not make it exactly as they pleased. Time and again they encountered resistance to their homogenizing, secularizing impulses, especially from temple communities loath to give up their autonomy. Just as the state invaded space once under clerical control—by seizing temple lands, for instance, to create public ceme-teries in early Meiji—so too did clerics and their parishioners force govern-ment officials to accommodate their wishes, as reflected in the 1925 compro-mise allowing temples in Tokyo after the earthquake to build ossuaries in the city instead of moving their dead to the suburbs. In fact the wishes of individ-uals and communities are what compelled officials throughout the twentieth century to found and approve new cemeteries, spaces designed to honor rela-tionships that were subject to, yet always took precedence over, the state⌐

CHAPTER 6

DYING IN STYLE

The Japanese funeral, at its core, is structured by a logic of social exchange between the living and the dead and among the living themselves. It is a truism that death rites in all times and places reflect the social orders that produce them, and that they provide opportunities for survivors to reaffirm or challenge those orders or to seek higher status within them. Certain rules of conduct are established to manage these emotionally charged and socially delicate events, ranging from the seating of family and guests to the format of condolences. Funerals are therefore a natural favorite for anthropologists the world over who are seeking to interpret the structure and workings of a particular society. Yet it is also true that some societies make more of death rites than others. In Japan a funeral is not just an implicit, but also an explicit, means to accumulate and spend social capital. A highly articulated piece of machinery, the Japanese funeral builds relationships as much as it reflects them, spinning off sizeable profits for those who service it.[1]

The funeral industry has been growing hand in hand with Japan's middle class since the Meiji period, when social-climbing families eagerly adopted the material trappings and social protocol once limited to the privileged few, using them to seek their place in a post-Tokugawa world. In urban areas especially, the appropriation of elite practices entailed sponsoring lavish funeral processions supplied and coordinated by undertakers known as *sōgiya* ("funeral shops") or *sōgisha* ("funeral companies"). This conspicuous consumption drew fire from critics, who condemned it for being not only wasteful but also insincere, evidence that mourners were more preoccupied with appearances than with grief. Even those who shared this viewpoint, however, found it difficult if not impossible to reject social convention when faced with the deaths of their own relatives, neighbors, colleagues, and friends.

After the Meiji period, street traffic brought processions to a halt, but this did not mean an end to mortuary splendor, which was moved to the fixed spaces of homes and temples. There, undertakers built sumptuous altars to anchor precisely choreographed memorial services that featured eulogies, sutra-chanting, and incense offerings. Even as they maintained their role as ritual performers, Buddhist priests lost their status as ritual managers, because the overall format of these ceremonies was devised and controlled by undertakers, whose first concern was to allow busy condolence callers to pay their respects as efficiently as possible. Undertakers also took on labor that had once been performed by neighbors and relatives, a professionalization of ritual that indicated not simply a breakdown of old community ties, but also a strong desire among Japanese to adapt the relationship-building function of funerals to a world where social bonds were increasingly forged at school, the workplace, and other institutional settings disconnected from residence and kin. Out of the dialectic between profit-seeking businessmen and relationship-building families was born a twentieth-century funeral service that reached its maturity in major Japanese cities by the end of the 1930s and spread to the countryside in the decades that followed, constituting a genuinely national way of death.

UNDERTAKING THE MIDDLE CLASS

The Meiji Restoration ushered in several decades of radical political and social change. With the dismantling of the Tokugawa hierarchy (which entailed the abolition of the samurai class on one end of the social scale and the outcaste categories of *eta* and *hinin* on the other), a spirit of mobility and new opportunity suffused the nation, summed up in the popular slogan *risshin shusse,* "rising in the world" or "making one's fortune." As families jockeyed for position in a society freed of former restraints, the lineage-building function of funerals, which had already grown in importance over the course of the Tokugawa period, became all the more pronounced, generating a golden age of funerary excess. In the early years of Meiji, local officials tried to check this trend with a combination of edicts and exhortations.[2] But as Japan headed toward the twentieth century, ritual micromanagement by government fell out of favor, a trend accelerated by the popular rights movement *(jiyū minken undō)* of the late 1870s and punctuated by the abolition of the doctrinal instruction campaign in 1884. In 1898 a critic of lavish funerals would note, "in today's world, it is difficult to make regulations just for funerals; if you want a law to correct this [spending on funerals], worries will probably arise about interfering with people's freedom."[3]

Acting on their freedom, ambitious families sponsored mortuary rites that displayed their wealth and strengthened communal ties. Resources were expended at each stage of the funeral, from the wake to the burial. The most conspicuous consumption, however, was achieved through elaborate funeral processions, and it was this expenditure that fueled the growth of a modern funeral industry. On the crudest level, a procession served to convey a corpse to a temple, cremation ground, or graveyard, where it became the object of obsequies (consisting mainly of sutra-chanting and offerings of incense and food) and then final disposal. The practical function of transport is reflected in the unadorned term commonly used to refer to rustic funeral processions, *nobeokuri,* which means, simply, "sending to the fields." Their public visibility, however, also made processions carefully staged displays that asserted the status of families within the wider community. A smoothly executed procession was particularly important for the successor of a household, who, by taking the role of chief mourner *(moshu* or *seshu),* ensured his legitimacy in the eyes of those both inside and outside his patriline.[4] In most regions it was the chief mourner who carried the mortuary tablet *(ihai)* on which was inscribed the name of the dead. Consequently, in households where the right to succession was unclear, fights over who would carry the tablet sometimes broke out before the start of the procession, as the Justice Ministry mentioned in its 1880 survey of Japanese customs.[5]

The procession was therefore not just a physical necessity, a means to get from one point to another, but also a powerful social statement. This is why the editors and backers of the newspaper *Kōchi shinbun* used the format of the funeral procession as a way to protest government policy in 1882. On July 14 of that year the government shut down the paper for criticizing state actions and agitating for the expansion of popular freedoms. In response, supporters of the paper mourned its death by sponsoring a funeral two days later, walking in a long cortège that culminated in a cremation complete with sutra-chanting. Journalists and company stockholders marched in formal *kamishimo* dress. The paper's former editor carried the incense burner, the current editor bore the mortuary tablet wrapped in a sheet of newspaper, and deliverymen shouldered the coffin. The spirit of the *Kōchi shinbun* was memorialized on a flag that displayed the Buddhist epithets "all things are impermanent" and "joy in nirvana," while another banner listed the names of 2,727 supporters. Witnesses were estimated to be in the "several tens of thousands."[6]

Enormous crowds also turned out for the real funeral of Mitsubishi conglomerate founder Iwasaki Yatarō (1834–1885), who died in Tokyo in 1885. According to contemporary reports, there were 30,000 members of the funeral cortège, which required the labor of an estimated 70,000 footmen. If true, that would mean approximately one-tenth of the entire population of Tokyo participated directly in the procession.[7] Osaka was awed by spectacular funerals of its own. The procession for Godai Tomoatsu (1835–1885), a prominent businessman and founder of the Osaka Chamber of Commerce who died in the same year as Iwasaki, stretched for ten kilometers through city streets. Apparently the flowers carried at the head of the cortège reached Abeno cemetery, where Godai was buried, before the litter carrying his coffin had even left the gates of his house.[8]

The funeral processions for Iwasaki and Godai were particularly grand, but they were only different in scope, not in kind, from the death celebrations that marched through the cities of Meiji Japan on any given day. These displays of capitalist wealth—or at least middle- and upper-class comfort—were referred to not as *nobeokuri,* but as *sōretsu,* literally "funerary parades." They were a regular occurrence in Tokyo, Osaka, and other urban areas, and exhibited a sort of "joie de mort" for the crowds who flocked to watch them pass. By the start of the twentieth century, certain standards had been established for the structure and content of these processions that mourning families could meet, exceed, or in most cases, probably, fail to reach. In his 1901 book on customs and daily life in Tokyo, Hirade Kōjirō observed that the quality of a funeral cortège naturally depended on the financial standing of the mourning family, so it was difficult to give a uniform portrait, but he nevertheless described what could be expected of a "middle-class" *(chūryū)* procession:

> A guide is placed up front to lead the way and is followed by tall lanterns, live flowers, artificial flowers, and birds to be released.[9] Then comes the junior priest *(mukaesō),* succeeded by those holding the incense burner and mortuary tablet. Carrying the mortuary tablet is usually the job of the chief mourner, or sometimes a close blood relative. . . . Next comes the coffin. The coffin is flanked on either side by companions who walk beside the palanquin [which holds the coffin]. If the deceased is a male, these will be men, and if a female, women. . . . Following the coffin are the immediate family, relatives, and then general attendees.

Hirade added that the well-to-do placed a banner in front of the coffin proclaiming the name of its occupant and hired musicians to play reed pipes and drums.[10] Dragon heads, canopies, and red umbrellas were listed as further accessories in a 1905 etiquette manual written by Shirai Mitsuo.[11] Both Shirai's manual and Hirade's book on customs dealt specifically with Tokyo, but the processions that wound their way through Osaka, Nagoya, and other cities were similar in makeup, incorporating the flowers, banners, lanterns, birds, and other items mentioned above.

Processions were a feast for the stomach as well as the eyes, for it was de rigueur for the mourning family to hand out sweets[12] during the course of the funeral march or at its end. In 1876 an article in the newspaper *Chōya shinbun* lamented the existence of this "terribly barbaric practice" in "enlightened Tokyo," describing how people would think nothing of going to a funeral to grab treats and then head off for flower-viewing *(hanami)*.[13] Not surprisingly, the prospect of free food attracted beggars, and another *Chōya shinbun* article, this one written in 1880, described them as a menace for the temples of the Yanaka area, where many processions reached their end. The article reported that funerals drew not only the neighboring poor but also *"kowameshi* beggars" from all directions. Ruffians would forcibly snatch seven or eight helpings each, and temples had to rely on patrolmen to manage the rowdy crowds.[14] This phenomenon continued over the course of the Meiji period, with one writer in 1898 describing the beggars as "ants" who "trail the funeral

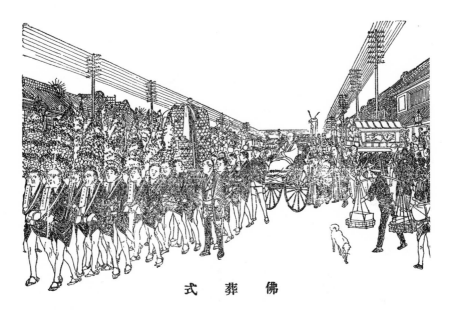

A Buddhist funeral procession in Tokyo. From *Tōkyō fūzokushi,* by Hirade Kōjirō.

to its end." If not enough food were on hand to satisfy everyone, they would "hurl abusive language to humiliate the mourners," he observed.[15]

Putting together a procession that would not humiliate its sponsors was a complicated affair, one entrusted to a class of funeral professionals that gelled during the Meiji period. The eighteenth-century satire of Sōshichi attests to the existence of businessmen who outfitted funerals in the Tokugawa era.[16] These were generally palanquin suppliers *(koshiya),* as was the case for the fictional Sōshichi, or coffin makers *(kanya).* Although there were businesses that supplied funerals, however, a specialized funeral profession that marketed itself as such would not arise until the 1880s. In fact it appears that the term *sōgisha,* today used widely alongside *sōgiya* to designate a full-service undertaker, made its debut in 1886. The *Chōya shinbun* reported in January of that year that Tōkyō Sōgisha had been founded in Kanda's Kamakurachō "to provide all funeral implements for both Shinto and Buddhist funerals, meeting the need for inexpensive rentals."[17]

Coordinating the labor of footmen *(ninsoku),* in addition to leasing equipment, was key to the survival and success of Meiji-period undertakers. This was certainly the case for what is now Nagoya's most esteemed funeral company, Ichiyanagi Sōgu Sōhonten, founded in 1877 by Ichiyanagi Ikusaburō, a twenty-three-year-old carpenter from a village not far from Nagoya. According to the company history, Ikusaburō was a skilled craftsman, and he started his business by making and selling coffins, mortuary tablets, and urns to hold cremated remains. But what launched him into the ranks of the nouveau riche —he apparently relished wearing *kamishimo* and riding in palanquins to visit Nagoya dignitaries—was his ability to muster large numbers of footmen for the processions that featured his handiwork.[18]

The management of footmen was also responsible for the success of Kagotomo, Osaka's leading funeral company until World War II. Kagotomo descended from a business that provided footmen for daimyo processions in Edo and Osaka during the Tokugawa period. After the Restoration, it closed shop in Tokyo, but parlayed its experience to coordinate funeral pageantry in Osaka.[19] There was no shortage of labor for it to draw upon, since thousands of servants who had previously worked for daimyo were left unemployed by the Restoration and poured into Osaka and other cities looking for work.[20] Incorporating into funeral marches the acrobatic stunts that they had used to enliven daimyo processions, these talented footmen conspicuously bridged the feudal past and the capitalist present.[21]

Undertakers did not passively respond to consumer demand, but shaped a product that in turn spurred more demand. Some were particularly aggressive in selling their labor and wares. An article appearing in an 1894 issue of the *Tōkyō asahi shinbun* recounted an incident that was reportedly part of a general trend among undertakers to seek out deaths and prey upon survivors. In this particular case, an undertaker showed up uninvited to the gate of a house in Tokyo, bringing along a palanquin, four white lanterns, two dragon heads, a tub for bathing the dead, and a sack of star anise *(shikimi)*.[22] The gatekeeper apparently had to chase them off.[23] Novelist Shiga Naoya (1883–1971), writing in 1912, described how a young boy working for an undertaker wandered around neighborhoods looking for clients. The boy showed up at Shiga's house "within fifteen minutes" of his grandfather's death, offering the undertaker's services.[24]

Undertakers were also not shy about hanging up large signs to advertise themselves, provoking criticism from social reformers alarmed that an event as weighty as a funeral had apparently become just another commodity in the marketplace. One critic, Noguchi Katsuichi, indignantly complained in an 1898 issue of the magazine *Fūzoku gahō* that the area where many of Tokyo's undertakers were concentrated (a section of Kanda) was filled with ostentatious signs that flaunted the funeral professionals' "insolent pride." He criticized the undertakers for "competing for prosperity just as in any other business," claiming that their signs gave the impression of "rejoicing in people's grief" and displayed "shallowness of human feeling."[25]

Over the 1890s undertakers donned the mantle of "reform" *(kairyō)*, a buzzword popular among Japan's "civilizing" middle class, in order to counter their reputation for being heartless profiteers. As one foreign observer noted, "*'Kairyō'* [reform] is the order of the day in Japan; and in Tōkyō and other large cities there are *Sōgi Kairyō Kaisha* [funeral reform companies], which among other things aim at uniformity, and strive to provide dresses and other articles necessary on such occasions, all of the latest and most convenient style."[26] Accordingly, when Tokyo crematory operator Hakuzensha expanded into the undertaking business in 1896, its advertisements marketed *kairyō sōsaigu* (reformed funeral equipment), and proposed a mortuary middle path that avoided the extremes of spectacular luxury on the one hand and the rejection of ceremony on the other. The company claimed to be participating in reform while "relying on set standards," adding that it would rent and sell funeral goods for a modest profit and provide implements free of charge to those who could not afford them.[27] Of course, despite such charitable claims, Hakuzensha, like any other business, was committed to the bottom line. According to Shirai's 1905 funeral manual, Hakuzensha quickly positioned itself as one of the two most popular undertakers for the rich of Tokyo (the other being Tōkyō Sōgisha);[28] and several decades later it came under the scrutiny of the police for corrupt business practices.[29]

Once established, successful undertakers jealously guarded their territory against intruders. In Tokyo, Hakuzensha managed to expand from cremation into undertaking, but in Osaka, Kagotomo thwarted a similar effort by the crematory operator Hachikōsha. Founded in 1875 to build Osaka's first modern crematories, Hachikōsha was a major stockholding company backed by capital from Sumitomo. When it decided to set up a subsidiary in 1887 to provide complete funeral services, it posed a significant threat to existing undertakers, the most prominent being Kagotomo. Figuring that the best defense was a good offense, Kagotomo approached the Nishi and Higashi Honganji with a plan to build their own crematory in Osaka. The powerful Honganji temples had already built impressive modern facilities in Kyoto, so they agreed to the proposal and sought permission from Osaka prefecture to break ground. The new crematory would have undercut Hachikōsha's primary business, so Hachikōsha suggested a trade-off: if the plan to build the new crematory were scuttled, it would dismantle its undertaking subsidiary. All parties agreed, and the status quo was maintained.[30]

Kagotomo further consolidated its position by helping to found the Osaka Funeral Equipment Rental Industry Association (Ōsaka Sōgu Kashimonogyō Kumiai), which began with 48 members in 1891 and grew to 124 members by 1914. It proved its value in 1907, when it came to the defense of undertakers in Osaka by opposing a newly instituted palanquin tax. Led by Kagotomo head Suzuki Yūtarō, the association submitted a petition to the prefectural government asserting that the tax placed an unfair burden on funeral providers, who relied on palanquins to transport the dead. Why not tax wheeled vehicles? They did more damage to the roads, the petition argued. After Suzuki and another association representative paid several visits to the prefectural office, the tax was finally lifted.[31] Groups of undertakers in Tokyo also formed cartels to protect their interests.[32]

By the end of the Meiji period, urban undertakers and their suppliers had consolidated themselves into an autonomous industry that was firmly entrenched and prepared to defend its interests. When he published his etiquette manual in 1905, Shirai Mitsuo presumed that the items necessary for a funeral procession would be bought or rented from undertakers and suggested that even though a mourning family could gather together a team of footmen on its own, it was best to entrust this task to knowledgeable professionals.[33] The extent to which urban dwellers had come to rely on undertakers is reflected in the wonderment expressed by Shirai regarding homemade country funerals. Families in rural areas relied on carpenters to build coffins, but all other necessary items were made on the spot by fellow villagers, he wrote, calling the fact that they could do such things as assemble live and artificial flowers without the assistance of an undertaker "quite admirable."[34]

In the city, in contrast, even relatively poor families called upon undertakers for their services, renting items that the rich might buy outright.[35] The ability to lease equipment and footmen from professionals encouraged the diffusion of funeral pageantry through descending levels of urban society. As Hirade Kōjirō pointed out in his book on Tokyo customs, "with the rental of *koshi* [see below], mourning clothes, artificial flowers, cages of birds for release, and so on, it is easy to make a funeral grand."[36] Hirade highlighted the spread of funerary extravagance since the Restoration by remarking on the increased popularity of *koshi* versus *kago* to carry coffins. Both were "palanquins," but these two vehicles differed significantly in form and function. A *koshi* was a bier consisting of what appeared to be a miniature shrine carried on top of two parallel poles. A *kago* was a compartment that hung underneath a single pole. A *koshi* indicated higher status than a *kago* not only because it was more elaborate in construction but also because it necessitated employing more footmen. A *kago* required only two men to carry it, while depending on its size, a *koshi* required four, eight, ten, or even more porters.[37] In addition, *koshi* were used to carry high-quality horizontal coffins *(nekan)*, the best being double-layered, while *kago* were used to transport the less expensive upright coffins *(zakan)*.[38] The very poor, meanwhile, squeezed the dead into what amounted to crude barrels *(hayaoke)*, merely lashing them to poles for transport on the shoulders of relatives or friends. According to Hirade, at the start of the Meiji period, many in the middle class and above still used *kago*, but "now it has come to pass that even those in the lower classes use *koshi*,"[39] indicating a general shift from upright coffins to horizontal ones. Those who continued to use upright coffins at the turn of the century frequently eschewed *kago* in favor of ad hoc *koshi* that were devised by placing coffins on top of litters *(rendai)* and concealing them with canopies.[40]

Through the intercession of undertakers, the standards for what was considered a respectable procession had therefore risen considerably by the end of the Meiji period, not only in major metropolitan areas like Tokyo and Osaka, but in provincial cities as well. In his short story "Sōretsu" (The funeral parade), written in 1906, Ishikawa Takuboku (1886–1912) described an "unusually wretched" procession in Morioka. In front was a pair of lanterns, followed by a pair of artificial lotus flowers and a crude coffin carried on a pole by two men. Afterward came a group of six mourners, who appeared to be "ashamed" at participating in such a pathetic cortège.[41] Because lower-class families "feared the public if they did not have a splendid funeral," their funerals often took place early in the morning or at night, unlike the upper-class counterparts that began in the early afternoon.[42] Novelist and critic Uchida Roan (1868–1929) recalled the modest obsequies he witnessed while living at a temple in Tokyo, writing, "These kinds of small funerals were generally done just at daybreak or at sunset, when you gradually lost sight of people's faces.

葬具

つ　龍頭附の天蓋
そ　龍放鳥籠
れ　造花
た　龍頭附の六角燈籠
よ　榊（神葬式）
か　龍頭附の高張挑燈
わ　龍頭附の幡
を　屋根附の六角燈籠
る　位牌
ぬ　香爐臺
ち　花附の立棺
り　御靈（死者の寫眞、遺髪、位牌等を納む）
と　立棺
へ　立棺を載せたる駕籠
ほ　輿（神葬式）
に　寝棺を載せたる轝臺（佛葬式）
は　寝棺を載せたる轝臺（基督教式）
ろ　立棺
い　桶棺（早桶）

Items in a funeral procession. In the center is a black *kago,* with two types of *koshi* directly underneath. To the left of the *kago* is a litter covered with a canopy. From *Tōkyō fūzokushi,* by Hirade Kōjirō.

There were also cases where [mourners] came stealthily after it had gone completely dark."[43]

The pressure to keep up appearances was roundly criticized by proponents of customs reform *(fūzoku kairyō)* in the 1890s and on into the early twentieth century. Sounding like the provincial officials who had tried to restrain expenditures just after the Restoration, these social critics underscored the financial burden that funerals, along with weddings and other ceremonies, imposed on families. One critic, Toi Masataka, in his 1891 work *Nihon fūzoku kairyōron* (On the reform of Japanese customs), argued that "poor people are distressed by funerals. . . . If someone dies, people are more troubled by financing the funeral expenses than they are grieved by the misfortune."[44] In 1898 another social reformer, Noguchi Katsuichi, observed that the assets of even a relatively well-off family would vanish if it had to provide funerals for two parents in the same year, plunging it into "dire straits."[45] He emphasized that the expenditure of resources as a way to comfort the deceased in fact achieved the opposite: "Who is there who does not wish for the prosperity of descendants? One does not only wish for this while alive; even after death, there is no one who wishes for [their descendants'] hardship. How can a spirit rest in heaven when a family falls into decline because of one or two funerals?"[46] Another article in *Fūzoku gahō* that same year focused on the practice of giving away sweets during and at the end of processions, a custom that fueled a vicious cycle of expectation and expenditure. Because there were those who gave generously, beggars regularly flocked to funerals, making it necessary for mourners of even modest means to give away large numbers of treats. "If the mourner is not particularly rich, isn't this extremely troublesome?" the author observed.[47]

According to these critics, funerary excess was a threat not just to finances but also to the dignity and sincerity of "the most important event in one's life."[48] Indulging in "empty formalities and useless ceremonies"[49] distracted people from the true significance of funeral rites. Boastful displays did not arise from a "filial heart,"[50] but from the fear of being shamed in public. "The situation is so bad that people judge the propriety of the chief mourner according to the quantity of artificial flowers," Toi lamented. He was also distressed by the "riotous drinking and eating" that occurred at wakes *(tsuya)*. A wake was initiated by a series of solemn acts that included washing and ordaining the dead, arranging the corpse in a coffin, and setting up a small stand holding incense and food offerings. But once these religious duties were performed, it was common for relatives, friends, and neighbors to throw a party that lasted far into the night, a phenomenon that persists to this day. Instead of consoling parents, children, and siblings of the deceased, guests "vainly luxuriate in

food and drink," becoming intoxicated and starting fights, Toi wrote.[51] Noguchi also rebuked mourners for getting drunk and "telling jokes" in front of the
corpse.[52]

Critics were dismayed as well by the casual attitude shown by those who
marched in funeral processions, many of whom told jokes and smoked
tobacco en route.[53] Particularly distressing was the fact that mourners had
incorporated horse-drawn carriages and rickshaws—emblems of the fast-
paced, modern age—into their marches. Yamashita Jūmin noted that in the
case of a funeral in his own family, relatives did not walk, as they properly
should have, but "haughtily" used horse-drawn carriages.[54] Even Hirade, who
generally described the customs of Tokyoites in a nonjudgmental fashion,
struck a tone of Confucian piety and censure when he characterized the Meiji
trend to ride in carriages and rickshaws as "a loss of propriety."[55]

Those who lamented the current state of funerals invoked an idealized past
when mourning was sincere and ostentation eschewed. In modern times the
poor conducted funerals at night out of embarrassment, but in ancient Japan
it was considered only proper to march under the cover of darkness, claimed
Yamashita, citing the example of Emperor Saga (786–842), who requested a
nighttime funeral before he died. Nighttime funerals were also mentioned in
the *Tale of Genji,* and it was clear that the lanterns currently used in processions were relics from a time when it was commonplace to march in the dark,
he wrote. He therefore called for a return to the "old ways" by holding funerals at night.[56] Reformers eulogized not only the nocturnal funerals of ancient
times, but also the comparatively subdued processions of the more recent
Tokugawa past, a past that had already become an object of nostalgia in a society firmly directed toward the future. Noguchi, for example, seems to have
taken Tokugawa regulations at face value, writing with approval that the different classes stayed within the norms "appropriate to one's position" under
the old regime.[57] According to his mythic rendering of the past, the modesty of
Tokugawa funerals was rooted not in government regulation, but in a genuine
and widely shared ethos that equated virtue with thrift. Although the shogunate's repeated admonitions would seem to be an indication to the contrary,
Noguchi made the sweeping generalization that "thrift was considered a
beautiful virtue and luxury recognized as wicked. Even if a man were proud,
he would be modest in his outward display. Even if there were treasures on the
inside, it was considered normal to show cotton rags to the outside."[58]

As social critics railed against profligate funerals, members of the educated
elite distinguished themselves by conspicuously rejecting the material trappings of wealth and prestige, thus proving to one another their modern "good

taste." Commenting on the recent movement to abolish "empty formalities" *(kyorei),* Shirai's etiquette manual (1905) mentioned the appearance of obituaries in newspapers that explicitly declined gifts of flowers for processions.[59] These sorts of death announcements made their debut in the 1890s, one of the earliest examples being that for Wada Yoshirō (1840–1892), an English teacher affiliated with Fukuzawa Yukichi's Keiō Gijuku (the precursor of Keiō University). The obituary for Wada, which appeared on January 16, 1892, in the *Jiji, Yomiuri,* and *Yūbin hōchi* newspapers, announced that a Buddhist funeral would be held at Sōjōji temple in Tokyo but that "live flowers, artificial flowers, and all other items" would be declined. The obituary was signed by seven of his friends, the leader being Fukuzawa, the great don of "civilization and enlightenment" *(bunmei kaika).*[60] A similar obituary was published in August of the same year for Fujita Mokichi (1852–1892), a journalist turned politician also affiliated with Keiō; and when Fukuzawa died in 1901, his sons placed an obituary in several newspapers informing readers, "in accordance with our late father's testament, we will strictly decline live flowers, artificial flowers, *kōden,* and all other gifts."[61]

During the last two decades of the Meiji period, the movement to refuse gifts and simplify funerals spread from the coterie of liberal intellectuals surrounding Fukuzawa into the professional and upper classes at large. In 1893, out of the 129 obituaries published that year in the *Tōkyō nichi nichi shinbun,* 14 of them, or approximately 11 percent, rejected offerings. The rejection rate climbed over the following years, reaching 34 percent in 1900, when 62 out of the 182 obituaries appearing in the *Tōkyō nichi nichi shinbun* refused gifts, and peaking in 1904, at slightly over 43 percent (83 out of 192 obituaries).[62]

The trend to eschew luxury did not arise from a democratic impulse. Originating not from Japanese in the lower classes, who were busy trying to appropriate the pageantry of the rich, this movement developed among the upper reaches of society. Noguchi preached that it was the responsibility of the rich to cut funeral expenses, for "if the rich go first, others will follow."[63] But the rich did so by placing relatively costly obituaries in newspapers, an act that did more to assert their status as public figures than anything else. By rejecting gifts in newspapers with large circulations, mourning families not only demonstrated snobbish good taste but also indicated they were so highly placed that if they did *not* do this, an unwieldy number of gifts would be foisted on them. In a world where, thanks to undertakers, funeral pageantry was being eagerly consumed and therefore cheapened by the masses, to reject this pageantry was the ultimate assertion of status. It was a way of not having your cake and eating it too.

Furthermore, just because mourners publicized their intent to refuse gifts does not mean people refrained from sending them. When Iwasaki Yanosuke (1851–1908), the younger brother of Mitsubishi founder Iwasaki Yatarō (the man whose funeral employed 70,000 footmen in 1885) died, his obituary soberly asked readers not to present offerings. But according to an account in the *Tōkyō nichi nichi shinbun*, various notables donated flowers anyway. Over sixty sets of live and artificial flowers were arranged outside the temple where the procession reached its end.[64] The 1896 obituary for Itō Hirobumi's father also declined all gifts, including incense money, but this apparently did little to stop donors eager to pay tribute. A month after the funeral, Itō's family was obliged to publish another notice saying that the incense money they received in spite of their request would be distributed to the Japanese Red Cross, an orphanage, and a hospital. Their donations totaled 1,500 yen, what was then an enormous sum of money.[65]

While money might be diverted toward charitable ends, the inertia of *giri*—the term for social obligation regularly invoked, often with much grumbling, by Japanese both then and now—guaranteed that funerals would continue to be important venues for conspicuous consumption. When Noguchi promoted funerary restraint in the late 1890s, he acknowledged the power of "the *giri* of the world," writing that those who recognized the "evil" of mortuary waste were nevertheless reluctant to act alone. Because few families were willing to undergo the ceremonial version of unilateral disarmament, it was necessary to construct a public, communal path of reform, he argued.[66] The elite built such a path through newspaper obituaries, attempting to replace old-fashioned social entanglements with an imagined community of the "enlightened." But this path was a privileged one that the lower classes could not travel, and most in the upper classes chose not to follow it either. Although the portion of obituaries rejecting offerings in the *Tōkyō nichi nichi shinbun* climbed from the 1890s into the following decade, it never exceeded 50 percent. After all, for immigrants to Tokyo like Wada and Fukuzawa, it was perhaps not too difficult to reject convention. But for the established Edokko (children of Edo), who were embedded in intricate social and business networks, it was no easy matter to opt out of a system built up over generations, and the same held true for their counterparts living and dying in Osaka, Nagoya, and the rest of Japan.

Even if an individual decided to risk simplifying his or her own funeral, there was no guarantee that the survivors would be of like mind, a point made clear by Uchida Roan: "We can control the way we die. If we do not want to die of sickness, we can slit our necks or take poison. But even if we write wills, the funerals are not performed by ourselves, so it happens that they do not go according to what we had imagined." In fact, cases in which the will was respected were extremely rare, he observed, for "the purpose of the funeral is less to benefit the dead than it is to comfort the survivors . . . even if people say they will not have a funeral nor a farewell ceremony nor a gravestone, there will still be big funerals for them."[67] The events surrounding the 1903 funeral of another literary figure, Ozaki Kōyō (1867–1903), attest to this simple truth. Before Ozaki died, he asked that his remains be carried in a *kago* as opposed to a higher-class *koshi*, thus following the trend to reject luxury. But because he was born in Edo, he had relatives on the scene, and they balked at the prospect of a "shabby" *kago* funeral and pushed for him to be carried on a *koshi* in a horizontal coffin instead. According to the reminiscence of Emi Suiin (1869–1934), the relatives backed down, but only after they were berated by an old childhood friend who took control of the funeral arrangements.[68]

Ozaki had opted to simplify his funeral, but his was still an impressive cortège, filling the streets with its fair share of artificial flowers and crowds of marchers and onlookers. In most respects it differed little from the processions that marched regularly across turn-of-the-century urban Japan. Yet these processions, which indiscriminately turned bystanders into witnesses, would soon be marching into oblivion. And the reason was mundane: street traffic.

As roads became increasingly clogged, they were perceived less as communal stages where life—and death—played out, and more as thoroughfares to get from one private space (whether a business or a home) to another. In 1903, the year of Ozaki's funeral and the same year that Tokyo's and Osaka's first electric streetcars went into service, prominent socialist Sakai Toshihiko (1870–1933) called for the abolition of funeral parades in *Yorozu chōhō*. At the start of his article he listed three reasons for his opposition to them: "one, they severely obstruct the roads; two, they are a nuisance for funeral goers; and three, they give rise to extremely wasteful expenses." He wrote that he did not need to justify these points "because anyone who has sponsored a funeral, or attended one, or happened to run into one, must think the same"; but he continued to express his opinion nevertheless, emphasizing that "society should not allow traffic to be obstructed for empty ostentation." Articulating the modern (and particularly middle-class) sentiment that the business of one individual should not impinge uninvited on another's, he asked, "Should not people be extremely diffident about blocking traffic for the public at large for the private affairs of their own households?"[69]

Over the last years of Meiji and especially during the Taishō period (1912–1926), street congestion increased dramatically, making funeral processions all the more impractical for both participants and the wider public. The rapid proliferation of streetcars had an especially strong impact because electric cars ran on strict timetables and did not have the flexibility to stop for every cortège that might cross their predetermined paths. The *Miyako shinbun* reported in 1913 that streetcars came to a halt for the funeral procession of the last Tokugawa shogun, but this was the exception that proved the rule.[70] New modes of transportation not only undermined processions from the outside, but sapped their vitality from the inside as well. Another *Miyako shinbun* article from 1913 noted that participants in funeral processions were frequently lured onto trains and rickshaws that reached temples, graveyards, or crematories well ahead of the processions themselves. This had a hollowing effect, making processions "lonely" *(sabishii),* the newspaper observed.[71] Another factor contributing to the demise of processions was the policy of removing crematories and burial grounds from city centers, testing the stamina of marchers by lengthening the distances they had to travel.

When Sakai called for the end of funeral processions in 1903, funeral processions were still alive and well; and while the etiquette manual written in 1905 mentioned the trend to reject offerings, it still took for granted that the heart of any funeral was its procession. A few years later, however, obituaries began appearing that attempted not only to simplify processions but to end them altogether. One of the earliest was placed in the *Tōkyō nichi nichi shinbun* on July 19, 1909, to announce the death and funeral of Kunitomo Shigeaki (1861–1909), a prominent journalist. Infused with the spirit of restraint promoted by Sakai and other social reformers, the obituary announced that the funeral would be held at 7:00 in the evening. The procession would be "abolished," it said, and asked those attending the memorial service to proceed straight to the Tokyo temple where it would be held.[72]

As streets became clogged with traffic, newspapers rapidly filled with obituaries like this one. In 1913 an article in the *Miyako shinbun* reported on the striking trend to announce the abolition of processions and appoint a specific time and place for the funeral ceremony.[73] In fact 40 percent of obituaries published that year in the *Tōkyō nichi nichi shinbun,* 41 out of 102, announced the abolition of the procession. In 1916 the percentage of obituaries explicitly eschewing processions reached 51 percent (90 out of 175 notices), and in 1918, peaked at 61 percent (184 out of 303 notices). The 1920s then witnessed a sharp fall-off in such obituaries. In 1921 the annual rate had dropped to 22 percent (94 out of 427 notices), and in 1926, to just over one percent (12 out of 671 notices). The reason for this plunge is not that processions suddenly geared up again, but that in the space of the decade they had declined in frequency to the point that mourners no longer felt obliged to announce that they would not be sponsoring them.[74] By the late 1930s funeral processions had become a rarity in the big cities. In 1938 a contributor to the Osaka magazine *Kamigata* noted that it was difficult to find footmen for a procession. With the advent of the motorized hearse in the 1910s, many footmen had changed employment, he said, adding that processions currently occurred only in cases where a graveyard was conveniently close, or if someone wished to have an especially lavish funeral.[75] Sōtō monk Mogi Mumon, in his 1941 funeral manual, remarked that hearses were becoming popular even in the countryside and predicted, "in the near future, the written characters for *kago* will vanish from the funeral ceremony."[76]

MAKING RITUAL WORK IN A COMMODIFIED WORLD

The elite's rejection of flowers and other accessories had done little to diminish funerary decadence, but the abolition of processions seemed to stab at the very heart of the beast. In 1914 the *Yomiuri shinbun* hailed the demise of funeral cortèges as an "excellent development," observing that, as a consequence, "unsightly" spectacles would "naturally come to an end."[77] The collapse of processions had a painful impact on those in the funeral industry, many of whom, footmen in particular, lost their livelihoods. In celebrating the abolition of processions *qua* simplification of funerals, the *Miyako shinbun* unsympathetically conjectured in 1913 that it would deal a significant blow to the earnings of undertakers, flower shops, and confectioners.[78]

A natural response among these businesses was to resist the trend that threatened them with obsolescence. Kagotomo's Suzuki Yūtarō, the leader of Osaka's funeral industry, tried to fight back with a pamphlet addressed to the city's well-to-do in 1914. Opposing the reformists who associated frugality with sincerity and dignity, Suzuki argued that funerary surfeit was the natural expression of filial sentiment. Adopting the Confucian language of his opponents, he professed that to abolish funeral processions was to "lose the way of humanity," and launching into hyperbole, he warned that if this trend spread, corpses would some day be "abandoned in mountain valleys." He chastised middle- and upper-class households for replacing daytime processions with nighttime funerals, reminding his audience that in the past such secretive funerals had been reserved for criminals, suicides, and the poor.

Suzuki distributed 2,000 of his pamphlets, appealing to the rich and powerful of Osaka, but he elicited no response.[79] Too many forces were at work to finish off the lavish funeral processions on which Kagotomo and other undertakers had come to depend. Suzuki himself awoke to this new reality, and just one year after distributing his self-righteous and self-serving pamphlets, he switched to a "if you can't beat them, join them" strategy. Even if processions were headed to extinction, death was not, and growing urban populations still needed to purchase coffins and other items for funerals. They also required hearses, so Suzuki suggested at a 1915 meeting of the Osaka Funeral Equipment Rental Industry Association that undertakers band together and take full advantage of these new contraptions. Most of the association members took a conservative stance and opposed the move, but Suzuki forged ahead on his own, setting up a partnership with an Osaka auto shop.[80]

When processions came to an end, undertakers like Kagotomo not only adapted to their predicament by providing hearses but also by shaping and propagating a new format for funerals called the *kokubetsushiki,* or "farewell ceremony." The term seems to have been coined in 1901 to describe the "eccentric" funeral of Nakae Chōmin (1847–1901),[81] a famous champion of popular rights and translator of Rousseau into Japanese. Chōmin was renowned for bucking the status quo, and he lived up to his reputation in his last testament, which asked that there be absolutely no religious ceremony, whether Buddhist, Shinto, or Christian, at the time of his death. He instructed his family to donate his corpse to doctors for dissection and take it straight to a crematory for burning.[82] Chōmin thus represented a radical extreme of the movement to simplify funerals, a position shared by a small cadre of other staunch materialists from the late 1890s onward. In 1894, for example, the death notice for Fukuda Keigyō declared that there would be no funeral because Fukuda had not believed in the existence of a soul that "returned to the *kami* or buddhas after death." His will asked that he be cremated and that no grave be constructed.[83] Not surprisingly, this public declaration of unbelief generated consternation among Buddhist clerics. An editorial in a sectarian magazine the following year condemned it, admitting that while it was necessary to "make a clean sweep of decadent customs," it was also important to reinvigorate Buddhist funerals.[84] From the late 1890s a small number of obituaries, like Chōmin's, also began announcing that the corpse of the deceased would be provided to medical schools and hospitals for dissection, although they did not necessarily reject religious ceremony.[85]

Chōmin's will demanded as utilitarian a disposal as possible, combining dissection with a complete rejection of any ritual. But according to an article in the *Yomiuri shinbun,* his family felt that taking the remains straight to the crematory would "present an inconvenience" to condolence callers.[86] So although they respected his basic intent, they devised a "farewell ceremony" as a way for people to pay their last respects before the dissection. The ceremony took place at Aoyama cemetery, which had originally been founded as a space where Shinto funerals and burials could take place free of Buddhist interference. It now provided an opportunity to reject any form of religion, Shinto included. The memorial service that "did without any religion" was the object of intense public interest, and newspapers gave detailed descriptions. The *Asahi shinbun* explained that the coffin was put in a carriage that left his home at nine in the morning, arriving at Aoyama cemetery at ten. At the service was a host of journalists and politicians, some of whom delivered eulogies before the coffin and the gathered crowd of approximately 1,000. Even though the *Hōchi shinbun* called Chōmin's farewell ceremony an "eccentric funeral shocking to his generation,"[87] Shirai's rather conservative etiquette manual printed the speech delivered by Ōishi Masami (1855–1935) as part of its section on how to deliver effective eulogies.[88]

The farewell ceremony was adopted by other iconoclasts over the next several decades. There were those who continued to insist on bare-bones disposal, but the new ritual format provided a way to dispense with religious rites while still allowing for friends, family, and associates to honor the dead. It was for this reason that law professor and former Meirokusha member Katō Hiroyuki (1836–1916) asked for a farewell ceremony, also held at Aoyama cemetery, in his will. An *Asahi shinbun* article mentioned that Katō specifically chose this sort of service because he did not believe in any religion.[89]

Yet what would turn this act of secular rebellion into standard practice, to the point that the word *kokubetsushiki* has today become virtually interchangeable with *sōgi* to refer to funerals, was not its antireligious spirit, but instead its practical function of replacing the hassle of a funeral procession with a ceremony circumscribed by a fixed time and place. The time frame for a procession was always unclear because it was impossible to judge how long it might take to get the cortège moving, let alone how long it would take to fight through clogged city streets. In an age that did not live by the clock, this was merely inconvenient, but in a capitalist world where time equaled money and where increasing numbers of those coming to a funeral lived outside the deceased's neighborhood, such uncertainty was fatal, so to speak.

The farewell ceremony, in contrast to the procession, drew attendees (whether by obituary, postcard, telegram, or telephone) to a predetermined location. It disciplined the experience of going to a funeral so that condolence callers could contribute their *kōden* (incense money), pay their respects, and return to work in a reasonably short amount of time. During the 1920s, therefore, the term *kokubetsushiki* appeared in an increasing number of obituaries, a trend that coincided with the rapid decline in street processions. Of the death notices published in the *Tōkyō nichi nichi shinbun* in 1918, only 13 out of 303, or slightly over 4 percent, referred to *kokubetsushiki*. But for 1920 that percentage climbed to nearly 21 percent, reaching approximately 68 percent in 1926, the first year of the Shōwa period (1926–1989).[90] This does not mean that urban Japanese were suddenly abandoning religion in droves. As the farewell ceremony increased in popularity, the initially secular format was colonized by religious professionals, mainly Buddhist priests. For example, of the 102 death notices published in the *Tōkyō asahi shinbun* from July through September in 1920, 32 of them, or about one-third, used the term *kokubetsushiki;* and of these 32, nine mentioned that the service would be Buddhist, while six were Shinto and two were Christian.[91]

The highlight of farewell ceremonies for Chōmin, Katō, and other secular thinkers was the reading of eulogies. When the ceremonies were appropriated by those who wanted to dispense with processions but not with Buddhism, however, the centerpiece became the offering of incense by each attendee, accompanied by sutra-chanting.[92] Lighting incense for the dead, both at the wake and at the funeral, had roots reaching back centuries, making it a deeply ingrained habit among most Japanese. "If one goes to a funeral and does not offer incense, there is the feeling that somehow something is missing,"[93] noted Mogi Mumon in 1941. In his pan-Buddhist manual, the Sōtō Zen cleric astutely observed that the offering of incense, along with other material practices, made it unlikely that Buddhist priests would be banished from funerals anytime soon. Writing that funerals were "the concrete manifestation of belief," he emphasized that they were, nonetheless, not dependent on a consistency of belief in everyday life. Even if people ordinarily do not seem to have "the least bit of faith," when it comes to the death of a loved one, "without doubt, they at least feel a sincere desire to make the funeral *rippa*"[94]—that is, "complete," or "splendid."

After all, most of the sutras chanted by gorgeously clad priests had always been incomprehensible to listeners. A comedic sketch *(rakugo)* from 1890 that poked fun at funerals and the priests who performed them referred to the sound of a monk reciting sutras as *kuchakucha,* onomatopoeia that can be roughly translated as "blah, blah, blah." The comedian irreverently speculated about the communication supposedly occurring between a monk and Amida Buddha, humorously translating the nonsensical chanting into ordinary language. At one point the monk tells Amida, "This buddha [the deceased] has today entered your registry, but he wants to go to paradise, so I request a few minutes of your good offices." Amida, addressed by the inappropriately diminutive "Ami-chan," answers, "Hmph, OK."[95] This sketch was intended to draw laughs of recognition from members of an audience who could not follow what was being said at the funerals they attended and sponsored. Incomprehension was not necessarily a problem, because, as Mogi observed, it was less the desire to understand Buddhist teachings than to make funerals splendid that motivated mourners. Although the old cosmology and belief system of Buddhism might be challenged and severely undermined by Shinto, Christianity, and, most important, modern science, its rich iconography and practices, ranging from reading sutras to offering incense, would continue to provide a resource for mourners who wanted to *do* something for the dead while, of course, impressing the living.

Uchida Roan made the same point in the early 1920s as he reflected on the way he handled the death of his daughter. This critic of conventional funerals found that when his own daughter died, he could not reject ritual altogether. He wrote that he did entertain the notion of following the example of others who had dispensed with tradition, one of these having gone so far as to have his ashes tossed in a river, but that he could not go through with it. "In the end, I had the degenerate bonze *(namagusai bōzu)* from my family temple read sutras and I distributed *manjū*." Why? Obviously not because he had great respect for the clergy, but because in the face of a situation out of his control, he felt he had to *do* something. He interpreted his motivation poetically: "Knowing that it is useless, to do what is useless is the beauty of human feeling *(ninjō)*." He added that people who showed contempt for such feeling had experienced only "half-baked enlightenment" *(namazen)*. What Uchida left out of this account was the social pressure he may have experienced to host a conventional funeral, but it does provide an intimate look at the personal motivation twentieth-century Japanese might have felt when opting for the tried but not necessarily true.[96]

What makes Uchida's reflection modern is not necessarily its skepticism regarding the efficacy of ritual. After all, who knows what mourners centuries earlier really believed? With fewer alternative worldviews to compete with Buddhist cosmology, the odds were certainly higher that many took Buddhist teachings at face value, but they, just like their modern descendants, would have been befuddled by priestly chants. It is also clear that what helped Buddhist funerals take hold in the medieval period was not just faith in an afterlife but also the desire to build lasting lineages propelled by lavish funerary displays. Nevertheless the situation in which Uchida found himself was far different from that of his ancestors, especially those who had lived in the relatively recent past of the Tokugawa regime. Because Buddhism had been disestablished by the early Meiji state, Uchida and others of his generation were not legally bound to their family temples and clerics were no longer responsible for the bureaucratic processing of death. Twentieth-century Japanese therefore had a choice as to what to do, and choosing Buddhism, or "tradition," was based on a perception of religious ritual as something modular, something that could be utilized or not. As it turns out, most Japanese made this choice, whether for the reason given by Uchida, or as an expression of true belief, or out of a simple unwillingness to break with social convention.

Initially the farewell ceremony was regarded as something distinct from the funeral proper. It was therefore not uncommon to have the former in one location and the latter in another. Even when held back-to-back in the same place, they were frequently treated as separate ceremonies, with a pause scheduled between them. Now shorn of the procession, the funeral was limited to family and friends and consisted of the familiar process of reading sutras and offering incense before the coffin of the deceased. The farewell ceremony followed so that other acquaintances could pay their respects.[97] Yet because the farewell ceremony absorbed the central elements of the traditional funeral—chanting sutras and offering incense—the boundaries between them increasingly blurred. During the early 1930s, when the term *kokubetsushiki* became commonplace in urban Japan, the two ceremonies were often melded. A 1932 funeral guide published by a Buddhist association explains, "generally, it is sufficient to follow the procedures for a funeral for a farewell ceremony,"[98] and in describing the recent proliferation of the latter, states that the new ceremonial format is distinguished primarily by the fact that it dispenses with the funeral procession and entails the use of motorized hearses, making it "extremely convenient."[99] In his 1941 guidebook Mogi characterized the farewell ceremony as a simplification of the traditional funeral. "Fundamentally, there is no difference," he wrote.[100]

The farewell ceremony was not passively filled with Buddhist content; instead, it significantly changed the environment and experience of that content. Significantly, although some urban farewell ceremonies took place in temples, the majority took place in private homes.[101] In the days when the procession was the highlight of a funeral, the temple ceremony was important insofar as it was a midpoint, a stopover between the deceased's home and the final destination of the crematory or graveyard, or an endpoint in itself if the graveyard were located in the temple grounds. In either case, holding a ceremony at the temple was important to the degree that it was an extension of the cortège. It is understandable, then, that with the replacement of processions by farewell ceremonies, many mourners opted to host funeral rites in their homes and not at temples. Accelerating the move to domestic funerals in urban areas was the fact that burials were being banned in increasing numbers of temple graveyards (due to their location in crowded neighborhoods), while the graveyards themselves were being moved out of city centers to make room for development. This left city residents with even less of an incentive to sponsor rites at temples. Consequently, although Mogi was optimistic in 1941 about the continued employment of Buddhist priests, he despaired that many temple halls, whose main purpose was to accommodate funerals, faced the danger of falling into disuse and obsolescence.[102]

The domestication of the farewell ceremonies changed the disposition of priests and altered the overall character of funerals, turning them into time-saving machines that processed incense-offering condolence callers as quickly as possible. Mogi's manual describes the format of the farewell ceremony as follows. In the foyer, or just inside the gate, is a reception table where attendees can deposit their *kōden* and business cards. After the family offers incense, the attendees do the same. This act, as described in the 1932 funeral manual, entails approaching the encoffined deceased, bowing, adding several pinches of incense to the incense burner, then retreating by a few steps to bow once more.[103] The attendees crowd in to do this one by one, as the priests chant sutras and prayers close to the coffin, following the procedures necessary to lead the dead to buddhahood. Because stepping up into a Japanese home means taking off one's shoes, some families, in order to move guests along as efficiently as possible, set up a second incense burner for them to use just outside the house. Other families lay a white cloth on top of the tatami mats so that mourners can step into the house without removing their shoes, thereby accommodating the funeral attendees who come in Western clothes. In its description of the farewell ceremony format, the 1941 handbook also tells clerics not to position themselves in the central space before the coffin, as they might at a temple service, but to position themselves on either side, leaving an open space between those offering incense and the coffin. The manual also notes that, since a home is far more cramped than a temple, they should refrain from banging loudly on bells and drums. Finally, clerics are advised that, even though farewell ceremonies generally last an hour, sometimes they are extended ten or twenty minutes, in which case priests are to continue sitting beside the coffin in a dignified posture.

Mogi portrayed fellow clerics as actors on a stage who had better play their roles without interrupting the overall flow of events. They were elements of the urban farewell ceremony, not its producers or directors. The latter were instead the undertakers, who drew on their experience choreographing processions to supply and manage the new procession-less ceremonies. "In the countryside, the authority figure in the mourning house is the priest, but in the city, the undertaker manages everything. [The undertaker] arranges the decorations without neglecting a single thing," observed Mogi. The 1932 manual also urges readers to entrust funerals to undertakers, who are thoroughly knowledgeable about the implements used by the different sects of Shinto, Christianity, and Buddhism: "If you retain an undertaker, you will be sent qualified helpers. Because [undertakers] will handle everything, if you entrust these matters to them, nothing will be omitted in the preparations."[104] Thus undertakers had evolved from mere suppliers of ritual to become ritual specialists in their own right, displacing the authority of clerics in the process. Contributing to this phenomenon was the fact that twentieth-century priests were not as thoroughly trained in religious ceremony as their forebears. Mogi stated that this was his reason for writing his guidebook; he explained the decline, in part, as a consequence of compulsory education mandated by the state. Young acolytes had once memorized ritual procedures and chants through constant repetition, but now they were kept too busy by their secular studies to devote much time to their religious training, he lamented.[105]

Undertakers, meanwhile, arranged funerals on a daily basis, giving them a level of expertise and influence that was hard to resist. An incident in the history of Nagoya's Ichiyanagi Sōgu Sōhonten attests to this power. In 1930 the head of Ichiyanagi convinced a chief mourner whose father had died to adopt the up-to-date farewell ceremony format. According to the account in Ichiyanagi's company history, the chief mourner, like the head of Ichiyanagi himself, was an adopted child, so he agreed to the new ceremony as a way to make himself stand out and thereby bolster his right to succession. The other relatives protested, as did a high-level monk from Kyoto brought to Nagoya for the funeral. Supposedly the monk dismissed the farewell ceremony as a "foreign way of doing things" and ordered the mourning family and Ichiyanagi not to perform it. It is not clear exactly what about the ceremony so offended him, but regardless, Ichiyanagi ignored him, pressing on with the arrangements. The company history claims that the farewell ceremony, Ichiyanagi's first, favorably impressed those who attended.[106]

Through the intervention of undertakers, a ceremony that had once been a vehicle for secularism was turned into a refuge for religious spectacle. When demand for processions waned, so did the need for such paraphernalia as caged birds, dragon-headed banners, canopies, and lanterns carried aloft on long poles. However, undertakers were able to adapt other items, including flowers, incense burners and, of course, the coffin itself, to the new ritual space of the farewell ceremony. In fact the freezing of a mobile format into a stationary one created the opportunity to arrange old items in inventive ways as well as to introduce entirely new ones.

The funeral altar *(saidan)* that undertakers set up for the farewell ceremony became, quite literally, the platform for this innovation. During the age of the procession, decorations for the temple ceremony consisted of the flowers and other items paraded through the streets and then arranged ad hoc at the temple. For the duration of the service the bier was propped up on supports athwart the permanent temple altar; the only other thing that was required was a modest stand, similar to the one used during the wake, on which to rest incense burners, offerings of food and water, and the mortuary tablet. As farewell ceremonies caught on, however, so did increasingly elaborate, multilevel funeral altars. Whereas Shirai's etiquette manual of 1905 lists the contents of a Buddhist funeral procession in colorful detail, it includes no discussion of a funeral altar, noting only the price of a *tsukue* (a low table) that could have been used either at a wake or at a temple ceremony.[107] The 1932 guidebook, in contrast, puts the altar front and center. In fact, different classes of funerals are indexed according to its size. Thus the "three-tier" funeral, whose main feature consists of three platforms stacked on top of one another and covered with a white cloth, costs about 138.5 yen to furnish, while the "two-tier" funeral, requiring only two platforms, costs 82.8 yen. Equipment for the lowly "one-tier" funeral is priced at only 36.5 yen. The "three-tier" funeral features the mortuary tablet, vessels to hold water and tea, an incense burner, a flower stand, a lamp *(andon)*, a pair of standing lanterns *(bonbori)*, a pair of candlesticks, a pair of stands to hold offerings, plates of dumplings *(dango)*, two sets of artificial flowers, and two sets of white lotus flowers (also artificial). For the "procession," all that is required is a hearse and one laborer. The one-tier funeral, while also including a hearse, is minimally adorned with just the spirit tablet, standing lamps, and a pair of white lotus flowers. The manual notes that the items and prices listed above differ of course from one undertaker to the next, but that they do give at least a rough idea of what funeral equipment might cost.[108]

During the 1930s the funeral altar was a magnet for innovative display, incorporating new items such as miniature shrines to hold mortuary tablets *(ihaidō)*[109] or photographs of the deceased, the latter growing in both popularity and size to overshadow the more venerable mortuary tablets.[110] It also featured the bier as a decorative element, the vehicle-turned-embellishment perched behind and above the ascending levels of the altar.[111] This explains why the funeral records for the Kiyomizu family of Kitaku, Tokyo, show that a bier was rented for a funeral in 1932 even though the coffin was actually transported in a hearse.[112] In the decades following World War II, the bier as ornament, or *kazarikoshi,* developed into a stylized appendage of the altar called the *kankakushi,* or "coffin disguise," since its function was to hide the coffin from view.[113] Because the *kankakushi* did not actually have to transport anything, craftsmen hired by undertakers and wholesalers of funeral equipment were free to play with their design, transforming the bier into mini-shrines complete with gates, multiple roofs, pillars, and even tiny pine trees.[114]

The splendor of processions was transferred not only onto funeral altars but also onto the motorized hearses that helped drive funeral processions to extinction. The first motorized hearses were Western in design. It is hard to say exactly when and where these vehicles were first used in Japan, but they appeared on the streets of major cities in the mid- to late 1910s. One Englishman, who returned to England from Japan in 1915,[115] was disappointed by their debut in Tokyo: "Instead of the graceful bier of fresh white wood in which, for generations, the Japanese has been wont to be borne to his 'long home' by white-clad attendants, now, too frequently, one meets a hideous hearse—motor driven, horrible in its black paint and tawdry gilding, an apparition which introduces from the West a note of needlessly depressing symbolism, foreign in every sense to the Japanese taste touching the trappings of death."[116] The first hearses used by Kagotomo in Osaka and Ichiyanagi in Nagoya were also Western imports, arabesque in style and sporting floral wreaths, just as they might in America and Europe.

By the mid-1920s, however, craftsmen in Osaka had begun producing "shrine-style" hearses *(miyagata reikyūsha)* more in keeping with "Japanese taste." As the bier was absorbed into the modern funeral altar, it was, at the same time, grafted onto the chassis of the modern hearse. In this case too, the bier's stylization generated ornate embellishments drawn willy-nilly from centuries-old motifs, making the Japanese hearse no less "tawdry" than its Western counterpart. Osaka's shrine-style hearses quickly became popular: Kagotomo exported them to Tokyo, Nagoya, Kyoto, Kobe, and other cities, varying their styles to meet local tastes. Soon enough they were being built beyond Osaka and were employing artisans in several different regions of Japan. In Kanezawa, for example, an undertaker named Etsumura Tomokichi initially imported shrine-style hearses from Osaka, but in the early 1930s he designed one that was built locally. An article in a 1932 issue of the regional newspaper *Hōkoku shinbun* described the features of the hearse, noting that its roof incorporated designs found on the tile work of the famous shrine to Tokugawa

Ieyasu at Nikkō. It also sported a loudspeaker that could be used to play music or address funeral goers.

The designers of shrine-style hearses portrayed themselves as defenders of tradition. In a 1935 brochure Etsumura emphasized that the "peerless craftsmanship of this hearse is not the result of the research and experience of just one person's efforts, but relies upon the native predilections of this region. . . ." It was no accident that the hearse was adorned with the renowned gold leaf manufactured in the area since ancient times, declared the pamphlet.[117] Modernists detested the shrine-style hearse as aesthetic sacrilege. Vivid exemplars of traditionalist pastiche, triumphs of form over function, they were an affront to the sensibilities of architects like Maekawa Kunio (1905–1986), who studied under Le Corbusier (1887–1965) in Paris. Japanese were "spellbound" by the gold-gabled funeral cars, he lamented. Another disciple of modernism, Taniguchi Kichirō (1904–1979), wrote in a 1941 essay that to draw upon "so-called traditional artistic tastes" and "create a random hodgepodge of engi-

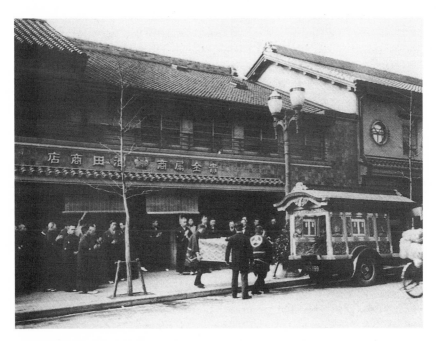

The staff of Ichiyanagi place a coffin in a shrine-style hearse. Photo taken in Nagoya, 1935. From *Ichiyanagi Sōgu Sōhonten sōgyō hyakunenshi,* edited by Ōno Kazufusa.

neering and art" was "laughable."[118] A German architect residing in Japan in the 1930s condemned the shrine-style hearses as kitsch,[119] and when modernist architects denounced the early Shōwa trend to crown buildings with temple-style roofs, they regularly invoked the unflattering comparison of the *sōgi jidōsha* (funeral automobile).[120] Yet what was kitsch for the few was splendor for the many. In the mid-1930s a charitable society that been established in 1919 to provide the poor with funerals convinced its benefactors to buy several shrine-style hearses because many of their clients, "laboring miserably in life," desired to ride these showy vehicles in death.[121] In 1941 Mogi called the hearses "majestic and beautiful,"[122] and popular demand for these "vehicles of tradition" fueled their production down to the end of the twentieth century.

During the 1920s and 1930s undertakers not only adjusted to the end of funeral processions by transferring pomp to altars and automobiles, they also consolidated their position by taking over tasks once performed by relatives and neighbors. When one of the daughters of novelist Natsume Sōseki died in 1911, an undertaker provided for the wake a stand with incense, flowers, star anise *(shikimi),* and dumplings *(dango).* All other arrangements were handled by the remaining children, according to Sōseki's diary. One son was sent off with death certificate in hand to procure a cremation permit from the local government office. Another son was dispatched to a temple to negotiate payments for the funeral and for subsequent memorial services. The surviving daughters sewed the shroud.[123] In the decades that followed, however, such tasks were increasingly entrusted to undertakers, especially in urban areas, where the fast pace of life and disintegration of community ties gave professionals an opening.[124] To illustrate: the 1932 funeral manual lists the shroud as one of the items to be purchased from an undertaker—no matter what the class of funeral.[125] And according to Mori Fusa, a woman born in 1906 who grew up in Tokyo, in the years before World War II some families chose to forego bathing the corpse themselves, letting the undertaker wipe the face with a wet cloth instead.[126]

The vocal criticism of funerary waste did not disappear when funeral processions were replaced by farewell ceremonies. In a 1917 issue of *Shufu no tomo,* a magazine aimed at housewives, prominent socialist and Waseda University professor Abe Isoo (1865–1949) authored an article entitled "The Funeral for My Father that Eliminated Empty Formalities and Waste" (Kyorei to jōhi o hai shita chichi no sōgi). Abe kept his father's funeral limited to the family and close relatives and led the farewell ceremony himself, without the help of a cleric. After he and his sister reminisced out loud about their father, each person approached the coffin for a final parting. The coffin was then dispatched to a crematory. Although simple, the ceremony was sincere, claimed Abe, a quality that truly makes the dead happy. He noted that people usually attempted to "far exceed their position *(mibun),*" creating debt that could take as many as three years to eliminate. He therefore encouraged housewives—guardians of the privatized, domestic sphere in which goods were consumed and ritual was produced—to follow his family's example.

While advocating reform, Abe's account also reveals how difficult it could be to extricate oneself from convention. He might have been able to do without a cleric, but not without an undertaker, who was involved in preparing the funeral. From Abe's description it is not clear what the undertaker did, but at the very least he would have provided the coffin. Abe also could not give up the custom of receiving *kōden* from attendees and showing thanks by sending return gifts. Ideally he would have eliminated this *giri*-laden practice, "but one cannot unreasonably refuse the kindness of relatives and friends who put store in old customs. So, respectfully, I received them." Instead of giving impersonal return gifts like tea or *manjū,* Abe "gave a lot of thought" and presented memorial handkerchiefs that he had printed with a sample of his father's handwriting.[127]

During the first few decades of the twentieth century, and especially during the Pacific War, government officials on the national and local level also took up the banner of frugality. The Boshin Imperial Rescript of 1908 expressed the state's position in terms that were crystal clear. Japanese were enjoined to be "frugal in the management of their households . . . to abide by simplicity and avoid ostentation, and to inure themselves to arduous toil without yielding to any degree of indulgence."[128] Through a series of national campaigns launched by the Home Ministry, officials worked with customs reform groups to spread the gospel of thrift, one of the main goals of bureaucrats being to direct funds into state-managed postal savings accounts. Unlike their Tokugawa and early Meiji predecessors, these representatives of the state were not free to enact sumptuary laws, so they instead relied on their powers of persuasion to convince citizens not to waste money for things such as drinking, sumptuous weddings, and, of course, lavish funerals.[129]

The campaigns apparently did help to boost the national savings rate, but they seemed to make little impact on funerals. American missionary William Erskine wrote in 1925 that funerals still impelled survivors to "do their utmost according to their means, and even beyond their means."[130] Public admonishments did not seem to do much to restrain expenditures in the Watanabe family, a prominent lineage that had made its fortune producing and selling saké back when Tokyo was Edo. In 1912, four years after the Boshin Imperial

Rescript was issued, the Watanabes sponsored rites for a dead child in which they spent over 108 yen just for treats *(kashi)* on the day of the funeral and over 53 yen for *manjū* (1,330 of them) to be sent as return presents.[131] The money spent on confectionaries alone totaled more than what Professor Abe would spend on the entirety of his father's funeral in 1917.[132] For a funeral in 1927, now called a farewell ceremony, the Watanabes spent 143.5 yen on coupons exchangeable for sweets and paid 283 yen to Mitsukoshi for textiles and clothing.[133] In 1933 they also decided to donate an extra 100 yen to their temple in order to elevate the posthumous name of the family member who had died in 1927. At the time of her funeral she had already been given the prestigious title of *ingō,* but the set of characters at the end of her posthumous name, *shinnyo,* was subsequently elevated to *daishi.*[134] It was apparently more important to the Watanabes to invest 100 yen in the status of the dead than in a postal savings account.

Of course, while families like the Watanabes spent enormous sums on funerals, those in poverty could barely scrape one together. Charities were set up to assist with the poor, but their activities were limited, and there were still plenty of people left without resources. On July 25, 1930, the *Ōsaka asahi shinbun* published an article describing the activities of a young Buddhist priest in Osaka who had organized a relief organization with three hearses to provide funerals to the indigent.[135] But on September 2 the same newspaper reported that the corpse of a man had been dropped off in a baby buggy outside the Gifu city office the previous day. A police investigation revealed the deceased was a laborer originally from Kyushu who had worked at a local garbage incinerator. Two friends were with him when he was suddenly seized with pain. They put him in the buggy to bring him to a doctor, but he died en route, so they instead brought him to the city office because they did not have the money to pay for a funeral.[136] Another article from 1930, this one published December 4 in the *Tōkyō nichi nichi shinbun,* reported the case of a local official in Kameidochō, Tokyo, who happened upon a "miserable-looking woman" carrying a three-year-old girl on her back, hauling a cart, and crying. When asked what was the matter, the thirty-five-year-old woman explained that her husband had died several days earlier, but because she had no means to deal with the corpse, she had rented a cart from a shop, wrapped her dead husband in a futon, and set out to bury him in a thicket outside the city. The official subsequently found a donor to pay for cremating the body.[137] Finally, whereas the intellectual elite donated their bodies to science as an act of noblesse oblige, impoverished families were often forced to sell the bodies of their "pitiful buddhas" *(hotokesama)* to university hospitals. A 1930 issue of the *Tōkyō nichi nichi shinbun* highlighted this trend when it called for the socialization of crematories, which, in Tokyo, remained in the iron grip of Hakuzensha.[138]

While the poor struggled to dispose of their dead and the urban elite spent freely on *manjū* and inflated posthumous names, government efforts against funerary excess did seem to make an impact in some places. Writing in the 1930s, anthropologist John Embree noted that, in the village he studied, "Formerly funerals were very expensive as the afflicted family was expected to give a sumptuous banquet, and relatives to give lavish gifts of colored cloth for the graveyard. Of late, economy measures, partly inaugurated by the village office, have reduced the expense and also some of the color and importance of funerals in buraku [hamlet] life."[139] Helping to keep costs down in this and other rural communities was the fact that the villagers constructed funeral implements, including coffins, without the help of an undertaker.[140]

In the cities, however, the indispensable undertakers colluded to keep prices and profits high. This was accomplished through the business associations that formed in the Meiji period and expanded in the 1920s and 1930s. In 1929 police in Tokyo investigated the funeral industry and discovered that "most of the 547 undertakers in the capital do not compete," a situation that guaranteed obscenely high profits during a time of general economic distress.[141]

Continuing a pattern established in the 1890s, some businesses tried to distance themselves from the popular image of the rapacious undertaker who profits from others' misfortune. A 1917 newspaper advertisement for the Tokyo undertaker Nihon Tenrei assured customers that it did not cooperate with other undertakers in fixing prices. An advertisement in 1918 also publicized the fact that the company would provide a detailed breakdown of all its charges,[142] parting with the convention of what is popularly referred to as "*donburi kanjō*," *donburi* being a bowl of rice with food heaped on top and *kanjō* meaning "tally" or "bill." The practice, which has remained widespread in the funeral industry down to the present day, entails lumping all costs under one price so that clients have no idea how much profit is really being made from the package being sold to them.[143]

The policy of financial disclosure was also embraced by Kōekisha, a funeral shop founded in Osaka in 1932 and now the largest funeral provider in Japan. Its name translates into "Company to Benefit the Public Good," a title that gives the impression of a social service rather than a corporation. The company, which from its inception marketed an up-to-date image of economy and efficiency, was the brainchild of a vice president in the sales department of Mitsukoshi department store. He originally wanted to set up a modern funeral service right in the store, but this unorthodox suggestion was rejected by other managers.[144] So he turned to friends already in the funeral business, and together they set up a stockholding corporation, the largest investors coming from families with experience as conventional undertakers.[145] Managers instituted policies to build public confidence in the new company, such as strictly prohibiting its employees (who numbered over fifty by 1934) from accepting tips from mourners. Their uniforms also bespoke military discipline. Instead of wearing the old-fashioned *happi* coats and straw sandals common among undertakers, the Kōekisha employees wore dark, Western-style suits with their respective ranks in the company indicated by stripes on their lapels.[146]

It was in this most modern of guises that Kōekisha packaged and sold traditional funeral ceremonies. Competing on the basis of price, the company came up with the slogan "Funerals from ten yen and up," advertising it on buses around Osaka.[147] The "ten-yen funeral" would never provide the profits necessary to power corporate growth, but it did contribute to a virtuous image. Naturally the big money lay in funerals for the rich. Its catalogue for 1938 displayed ten ranks for Buddhist funerals, the cheapest being a very reasonable 50 yen and the most expensive 2,000 yen.[148]

Kōekisha, along with Ichiyanagi and other major funeral providers, especially benefited from the trend that started in the 1930s of sponsoring company funerals *(shasō)* for presidents and high-level executives. The company funerals, most or all of which were paid for by the company and not the mourning family, both reflected and contributed to the replacement of old community affiliations and loyalties with the bonds of corporate capitalism. Executives succeeding their newly dead superiors recapitulated an age-old pattern by using the company funeral as an opportunity to bolster their legitimacy. Dipping into company coffers, they sponsored stupendous affairs that recalled the lavish processions of the Meiji period. They also began erecting monuments on Mt. Kōya in the manner of Tokugawa-period daimyo.[149] One of the earliest company funerals managed by Kōekisha was that for the president of insurance provider Nihon Seimei, who died in 1936. Held at a large temple, the funeral accommodated over 5,000 guests who listened to 27 company officials deliver eulogies. Alongside the road leading up to the site of the ceremony were arranged hundreds of floral displays and bunches of star anise branches donated by the Osaka elite. Kōekisha was also entrusted with the company funerals for such major clients as Marubeni and Tōyōbo.[150] Ichiyanagi, meanwhile, became the favored funeral provider for Toyota.[151]

There were, then, a number of factors working in favor of undertakers in the midst of early-twentieth-century thrift campaigns. The first and foremost was the one with the oldest pedigree: the pressure to live up to social obligations. Others of more recent vintage included the professionalization of tasks once handled by relatives and neighbors, the displacement of clerics by undertakers as ritual specialists, and the invention of equipment (such as funeral altars and shrine-style hearses) that met the twin demands for new ceremonial formats and the trappings of tradition. Some undertakers also benefited from collusive business practices, but others succeeded by publicly rejecting those practices. The result was, by the mid-1930s, a dynamic funeral industry that not only responded to demand for showy funerals but also had become an engine stimulating demand. A product of Japan's major cities, undertakers had even begun to spread into the countryside,[152] where Yanagita Kunio and other Japanese folklorists busily recorded death rites and other local customs threatened by the advance of a national consumer culture fashioned by the urban middle class.[153] One observer writing in 1938 flatly predicted that the "beautiful custom" *(bifū)* of villagers working together to produce funerals was headed toward extinction.[154] What he probably could not have predicted was that Japan's imperial order was headed the same way.

WARTIME AND POSTWAR DEVELOPMENTS

As Japan prosecuted its war in China and the Pacific, state exhortations to economize took on a salience backed by legal force. In 1939 the wartime government instituted centralized rationing systems for resources ranging from rice to oil. In 1940 the different political parties were merged, and along with a "new order" *(shin taisei)* for the state came a "lifestyle new order" *(seikatsu shin taisei)* for the citizenry propagated by the Spiritual Mobilization Board (Seidō Rijikai). In an article published in the August 22, 1940, edition of the *Tōkyō asahi shinbun,* the head of the board admonished citizens for not fully refraining from throwing parties and feasts. He noted that the government already had banned the sale of luxury goods, limited restaurant hours, and curtailed the use of automobiles, but had not focused enough attention on reducing spending at weddings, funerals, and other ceremonies. Now the government would concentrate on reducing these expenses by working with neighborhood associations *(tonari gumi)* and organizations of housewives *(fujin dantai).*[155] On the same day the newspaper printed specific government orders regarding funerals, which included making obituaries short, refraining from feasting at wakes, keeping *kōden* to a minimal amount, and eliminating offerings such as flowers.[156] Government directives apparently did not fall on deaf ears. According to Mori Fusa, her neighborhood association in Tokyo duly instructed people to forego "flashy" *(hade)* funerals, and families generally fell into line. Of course, faced with worsening shortages, wartime Japanese did not have much choice but to economize, Mori added.[157]

The state also consolidated the funeral profession. In 1940 enterprises that rented hearses in Japan's six largest cities were amalgamated into centralized companies, and smaller business associations were linked into overarching organizations such as the Tōkyōto Sōsaigyō Tōsei Kumiai (Metropolitan Tokyo Funeral Industry Regulatory Association).[158] In Osaka, Kōekisha merged with four other undertakers and helped establish a volunteer corps to memorialize the remains of soldiers returned from the battlefield, and later, during bombing raids toward the end of the war, to handle civilian casualties.[159] Ichiyanagi, meanwhile, was closed by the government in 1943.[160] Conditions severely worsened in the last several years of the war, as resources dwindled and increasing numbers of Japanese were killed in air raids. Mori Fusa recalled that when her husband died in June of 1945, she had to bring her own wood to the crematory to burn his corpse.

Japan remained in desperate straits for the first few years after surrender. As a consequence, Ichiyanagi did not reopen its doors for business until 1949. And even after economic recovery began in the 1950s, established undertakers had to face yet another thrift crusade, this one launched by the cabinet of socialist Katayama Tetsu in 1947 and dubbed the New Life *(shin seikatsu)* movement.[161] This government-sponsored effort spawned a number of savings and customs reform campaigns that were enthusiastically received and executed by civic groups, particularly women's associations, during the years of postwar reconstruction. Like their prewar predecessors, these campaigns exhorted families to improve their household economies by eliminating waste.

In the spirit of the times, businessmen across Japan established *gojokai* (mutual aid societies) that provided both weddings and funerals at modest rates. The first one was founded in 1948 by an undertaker in Yokosuka.[162] He distinguished his venture not only by managing *both* weddings and funerals but also by initiating a long-term payment plan to reduce the financial burden on struggling families. In recruiting "members" who paid installments each month in the anticipation of one day needing to throw a wedding or funeral, the mutual aid societies resembled the communal funeral funds established during the Tokugawa period by neighborhood groups and religious associations.[163] This credit-building business strategy with a communitarian gloss was highly successful, and other societies of a similar nature quickly sprouted throughout the nation, some incorporating the words "New Life" into their names.[164]

The old-line undertakers were appalled by the rapid growth of the mutual aid societies. They were also threatened by the agricultural and consumer cooperatives *(nōkyō* and *seikyō)* that had the audacity to enter the funeral business as well. In order to protect their turf, undertakers banded together in 1956 to found the Zen Nihon Sōsai Kyōdō Kumiai Rengōkai (All Japan Union of Funeral Ceremony Cooperative Associations), Japan's first nationwide funeral association. Holding its first convention in the sanctified halls of the Tsukiji Honganji temple in Tokyo, the Zensōren (as this association is commonly known) defined itself as the defender of the "beautiful customs" *(bifū)* handed down from Japan's past. Its official statement warned that the New Life movement could lead to the "destruction of funerary culture" *(sōsai bunka no hakai)* in its zeal to reduce waste, and it attacked the inexperienced "outsiders" who were primarily responsible for this destruction.[165] As Japan's economy rapidly expanded in the years that followed, however, the distinction between traditional undertakers and their competitors blurred. In response to consumer demand, mutual aid societies provided increasingly gorgeous funerals and undertakers struck deals with banks to provide their own payment plans to customers.

Both the undertakers and the mutual aid societies, along with Buddhist temples, also built modernized funeral halls in the 1970s and 1980s. The residential building boom of the 1960s had produced apartments and houses too small to host funerals, so in an about-face from the prewar trend of domestication, increasing numbers of Japanese chose to host funerals outside their homes, either turning to the newly constructed funeral halls or to the capacious temples that Sōtō priest Mogi Mumon had once worried would fall into ruin. Altars grew into the space made available, reaching as many as five or six levels and sprouting flanks of flowerbeds along the way. They expanded to the point that, when constructed in temple halls, the temple's permanent altar was completely blocked from view. For some funerals, especially Christian or nonreligious ones, row upon row of tightly regimented chrysanthemums became the main body of the altar, from the midst of which sprang a large photo of the deceased and little else.[166]

In most cases, however, Buddhist architecture and iconography continued to provide the inspiration for sumptuous postwar altars. Businesses throughout Japan mined the nation's rich legacy of religious material culture. One of the more influential was Nissō, a manufacturer of funeral equipment founded in 1952 and the first to market its products through catalogues to undertakers throughout the nation.[167] Today its altar friezes are replete with Buddhist motifs, including enlightened sages, lotuses, and dragons. Its candelabra are held aloft by guardian deities *(niō)* or the bodhisattvas Kannon and Jizō, the number and variety of light sources on funeral altars having multiplied with the introduction of electricity.[168]

The spread of the funeral industry into rural areas accelerated during the postwar decades, as these areas were either suburbanized or denuded of the young people needed to execute a funeral. Professionals took over tasks formerly reserved for family and friends in villages, just as they had those in prewar cities. They became carriers for a commodified funerary culture, which, along with the spread of cremation, drove many local customs into obsolescence. The procession-less *kokubetsushiki* is now a rural as well as urban phenomenon, and the necessary altars, coffins, hearses and other items are provided by national wholesalers.

Yet individuals, communities, and even undertakers did not passively capitulate to the marketing of commodified ritual. To this day, neighborhood leaders frequently control the pace and manner in which commercialized formats are absorbed into local practice. Yamada Shin'ya stresses this point in his 1995 study of changing funeral rites in Wakayama prefecture.[169] Focusing on several neighborhoods in a provincial town, he notes that significant ritual changes had swept through these communities since the late 1960s, but that respected "experts" *(chishikijin)* within each area made sure that these were adopted by families in a uniform manner.[170] Thus changes within one neighborhood—for example, moving a grave-cleaning ceremony that used to be done the day after a funeral to the day of the funeral instead—occurred not gradually, but rapidly, as area residents collectively embraced the new timetable all at once.[171] Similarly, tasks once performed by residents were transferred to an undertaker (beginning in 1961), but the undertaker was himself an integral member of the community, making him beholden to, and in fact an enforcer of, local customs.[172] In urban areas too, most funeral shops are small-scale operations that engage in the same neighborhood relationship-building that is crucial to other mom-and-pop businesses, turning them into local filters for, as much as purveyors of, mass-produced tradition.

Indeed, building relationships is the raison d'être of undertakers, whether they are tiny outfits serving families in a residential community, or, like Kōekisha, giants staging massive corporate funerals for the business community. It is telling that Japanese consumer cooperatives appeal directly to the sentiment that commercial funeral providers should be tied into an ongoing relationship with mourners and not be limited to one commodified moment. For example, in a promotional video made in 1997, the Tokyo Co-op touts the introduction of a new service, the "Co-op prime ceremony." Known mainly for its supermarkets, the Tokyo Co-op claims that its entrance into the funeral business will allow it to care for members throughout the entire life cycle. Just as the cooperative ensures quality in life, so it plans to ensure quality in death, explains the video. To emphasize that its "total service" will extend to the grave, the co-op stresses that, instead of conventional black-and-white bunting, its dead members will be surrounded by the consumer group's trademark green that followed them through life. Finally, when the video introduces the twenty-four-hour telephone number for funeral services, it states that the co-op's goal is "to work on people's relationships with one another."[173]

Of course, what links the members of the Tokyo Co-op is the fact that they are consumers who benefit from the coordinated purchasing decisions of a professional staff. The cooperative does not manage funerals directly, but instead cuts deals with established undertakers, using its collective bargaining power to ensure high-quality services for its members. The co-op's video glosses this reality with a mythology of warmhearted mutual aid. One can cite this recourse to mythology as proof that long-term communal relationships have dissolved in modern Japan. Yet this myth also reveals an entrenched cultural logic of social exchange that continues to determine the structure of Japanese funerals. Hikaru Suzuki stresses this point in her ethnography of a funeral company in Kyushu, "Moon Rise," which attracts customers by doing the following: "marketing Mutual-Aid Cooperative membership; establishing contracts with Elders' Clubs *(rōjinkai)* and other institutions; and holding festivals as a means of advertisement."[174]

According to the logic of social exchange, guests should not be mere audience members, but instead active participants in a process that comforts and honors the deceased. Most of the physical work involved in a funeral, from encoffining the body to setting up ritual equipment, is now done by commercial funeral providers, but efforts have been made to perpetuate elements of logistical and ritual work that can be performed by family and guests. Thus friends, neighbors, and business associates close to the mourning family are entrusted with making arrangements for the wake as well as the funeral, to which they and other guests bring *kōden*. All attendees then provide ritual support by offering incense to the dead. Although there do not appear to be strongly held beliefs about the precise nature and structure of the afterlife, a phenomenon recognized by Mogi Mumon in 1941 and encountered by a number of ethnographers after the war,[175] there does exist a compulsion to give as much support to the deceased as possible through offerings of incense.

A funeral ceremony in Japan, or anywhere for that matter, must not only incorporate participants but also differentiate them. This is accomplished to an extent through the order in which people offer incense. There are, however, more blatant ways by which family and acquaintances are distinguished from one another. For example, only relatives and friends place flowers in the coffin before it is transported to the crematory. This ritual was developed in the 1970s, according to the veteran employees of several undertakers with whom I spoke.[176] Its antecedent is the centuries-old practice of placing bags of leaves or tea in the coffin to keep the body from shifting in transit. The flowers do not serve this practical function, but they do allow for a stylized form of labor that clearly demarcates an inner and outer circle of acquaintances. An even smaller group of participants accompanies the body to the crematory once the funeral has ended; and after the bones are retrieved from the furnace, a further distinction is made between those who help lift bones into the urn and those who watch instead. At one cremation I attended, family members hesitated to approach the cart where the bones were displayed, but the undertaker urged them forward to perform their filial duty.

In sum, while undertakers have increasingly taken control of funerary behavior and have used this control to market expensive altars and other paraphernalia, they have also made sure to protect, even if only on a superficial level, the ritual labor of relatives and guests. The funeral industry thrives not because people want to discard customs of the past, but because they want to use practices, both old and new, to establish social connections lasting well into a collective future and a personal hereafter.

Epilogue

The Japanese Way of Death and Its Critics

Death in Japan today is handled through a format that is national in scope. There are local variations, to be sure,[1] but these fit within a framework of death management that is recognizable throughout the country, whether in small-town Kyushu or downtown Tokyo. The individual elements of this framework evolved at different times and for different reasons. Centuries ago Buddhist priests developed religious practices, including reading sutras and offering incense, that still feature prominently in most Japanese funerals. Measures to guard against death pollution have also long been shared by communities across the archipelago.

It was not until Japan's transformation into a nation-state, however, that a standard scheme for handling the deceased fell into place. Although it initially threw its support behind the Shinto funeral movement, within less than a decade the Meiji government abandoned its ill-fated effort to manipulate private ritual, choosing instead to acknowledge (to a self-serving extent) a separation between religion and the state. In the process it bureaucratized the management of physical remains. Detached from religious ritual, this management fell under the regulatory control of the Home Ministry, which ordered all deaths to be certified by doctors and reported to local officials. The ministry also established national guidelines for cremation, burial, and the use of graveyards. Government policies were adjusted to local realities, but combined with the forces of urbanization and the desires of a growing middle class, they engendered a standard method of cremation and burial that has made the sight of "soul parks" filled with family graves and their cremated remains a familiar one across Japan.

After it pulled out of the Shinto funeral movement, the state had little impact on the conduct of funerary rites that preceded and surrounded disposal of the dead, despite its support for thrift campaigns. Rather, it was the ascendant middle class, together with undertakers, who determined the format and conduct of modern funerals. Initially customers turned to undertakers to supply and coordinate lavish funeral processions, but as these became impractical due to street traffic, the funeral professionals created fixed (and private) ritual environments to replace them. During the 1920s and 1930s they also solidified their position by taking on responsibilities once delegated to family members and neighbors. It was, in fact, the ability of undertakers to help families cope with the dissolution of old social networks and plot the creation of new ones that fueled the development of a funeral industry that now markets a culture of ritual consumption nationwide. Because mourners do not want to risk slighting their guests and because guests feel most comfortable playing by clearly defined rules, bookstores are today filled with etiquette manuals training the ritually out-of-shape how to prepare for the marathon that is a Japanese funeral. Ultimately, however, it is only with the assistance of professionals that contemporary Japanese can bridge the gap between cultural expectations and the ritual knowledge needed to fulfill them.

Itami Jūzō's popular 1987 satire *The Funeral (Osōshiki)* exploits this gap to comic yet poignant effect. It is fitting that the protagonists of this film are an actress, Chizuko, and her actor husband, both of whom are thrust onto a stage of tradition not of their own making. Following the death of Chizuko's father, *The Funeral* is filled with scenes that humorously depict the bewilderment of Japanese faced with the task of properly performing rituals that they know they need to get right but of which they are largely ignorant. Before the wake, for example, Chizuko and her husband watch an etiquette video featuring a middle-aged woman properly dressed in kimono who tells viewers what to say and do at funerals. Fast-forwarding from the section designed for attendees to that for the mourning family, they repeat her formalized greetings with baffled looks on their faces.

In the film as in real life, it is primarily the undertaker who serves as the family's guide to the world of tradition that they have purchased. At the hospital he assigns jobs to family members for dressing the corpse, jumping in to help the fumbling mourners when necessary. This scene portrays a twofold dynamic that characterizes most funerals today: the commercialization of tasks that were once accomplished at home, coupled with an earnest if awkward effort to make family members feel that they are participants, that they are performing ritual labor on behalf of the dead. Playing a role familiar to many funeral professionals in contemporary Japan, where increased mobility means that people often live and die far from their original family temples, the undertaker in *The Funeral* also provides an introduction to a Buddhist priest whom the family has never met. When asked how much money should be given to the priest as an offering *(ofuse),* the undertaker enhances the sacred character of the product being sold by saying that such matters are "not fixed" and depend upon one's "heart" *(kokoro).* The anxious family members are not satisfied with this answer, however. How are they supposed to know what to pay someone with whom they have had no previous contact? Pressed further, he finally says, "How about 200,000 yen?" The priest arrives the next day in nothing less than a Rolls Royce, demonstrating the commonly held (and centuries-old) view of Buddhist priests as profiteers. The film also satirizes the clinical nature of modern cremation: the man who operates the local crematory matter-of-factly explains to the family how he adjusts the temperature of the oven depending on the size and age of the body inside. At every stage of the funeral, then, the family is forced to rely on professionals who have no personal connection to the dead.

In her ethnographic study of Japan's funeral industry, Hikaru Suzuki regards "consumers and producers as possessing equal suasion" and concludes that commercial services became the norm during the twentieth century "because people found value and meaning" in them.[2] Indeed, at the end of *The Funeral* the choked-up widow thanks friends and family for their help in making a *rippa* (complete/splendid) funeral. She admits regretting not being in the hospital room when her husband died, but, she adds, thanks to everyone's efforts, her husband is now a "buddha" *(hotoke).* The actor-participants have accomplished their mission: the mutual production of a benevolent spirit who ties together the living.

In the eyes of critics, however, producers of funerals wield far more power than consumers and do not hesitate to take advantage of them. Since the late 1980s a steady stream of newspaper articles, televised news segments, and books has exposed the seamy business practices of Japanese undertakers, casting them in a light far harsher than the amusing glow of Itami's satire. To give just one example, an undertaker turned critic published *Shitai wa shōhin!! warui sōgiya* (The corpse is a commodity!! Wicked undertakers) in 1992. Displaying the same indignation vented by customs reformers a century earlier, he mercilessly revealed dirty secrets of the trade. Among them is the system of paying off nurses and doctors at hospitals to gain access to the freshly dead and bereaved. Another is the practice of charging mourners according to fixed prices that disguise the true breakdown of costs involved in a funeral. The book emphasizes the insensitivity of money-hungry undertakers with sub-headings that include "The Target Commodity is the Corpse of a Small to Mid-sized Company President" and "A Child's Funeral is Rather Savory."[3]

Other books, such as *Anata no sōshiki, anata no ohaka* (Your funeral, your grave),[4] encourage readers to create personalized ceremonies that do not reject undertakers, but instead make use of them. Breaking with convention might include, for instance, hiring a chamber group to play classical music instead of Buddhist priests to chant sutras. The movement to "do it your own way"[5] —a phenomenon witnessed throughout the (post-) industrialized world— poses a challenge to the funeral industry, but like the shift from funeral processions to farewell ceremonies nearly a century earlier, it is one that forward-looking undertakers can turn to their advantage. After all, they can just as well provide classical musicians as they can Buddhist priests, and in fact many have begun marketing individualized "nonreligious" *(mushūkyō)* funerals in their company literature.

The popular reassessment of death rites in recent years extends to the grave, once again the focus of debates that call into question the boundaries negotiated between individuals, families, religious communities, and the state. Prominent among those challenging the current burial system is legal scholar Mori Kenji, author of *Haka to sōsō no genzai: Sōsen saishi kara sōsō no jiyū e* (Graves and funerals today: From ancestor worship to funereal freedom), who criticizes the postwar government for shirking what he sees as its duty to guarantee each citizen a secure resting place. The current civil code, like its Meiji predecessor, still places responsibility for the upkeep of tombs in the hands of individual families, ensuring that graves continue to go abandoned in large numbers.[6] Inspired in part by Hosono Ungai's *Fumetsu no funbo,* Mori argues that the state should abandon this vestige of patrilineal control and instead establish stringent new rules for the maintenance of graves that are oriented toward protecting the rights of the deceased, not descendants.[7]

This call for increased regulation runs counter to the interests of Buddhist temples, who generally want to keep state interference to a minimum. The dismantling of state Shinto after World War II strengthened the hand of religious organizations seeking to assert their independence from government control. In this new environment Buddhist temples not only regained control of graveyards that had been seized during the Meiji period, they also won the right to construct new ones. As a consequence, observes Mori, officials in Tokyo neglected to push local governments to meet the need for new grave space. Instead, they relinquished responsibility to Buddhist temples, who, in the name of "religious freedom," teamed up with gravestone makers and real estate agents to build suburban, for-profit "soul parks" dedicated not to parishioners but to anyone willing to pay huge sums of money for the privilege of being buried in them.[8]

Mori appeals to the state to provide for the welfare of the dead. Other critics seek change not through government but around it. Members of the Sōsō no Jiyū o Susumerukai (Society for the Promotion of Funereal Freedom) argue that Japanese should escape the grave altogether and opt instead for the scattering of cremated remains *(sankotsu),* which their society promotes as more environmentally friendly than building graveyards. Unlike Mori, they reject the regulatory power of the state, arguing that Japanese should be free to scatter remains where they please, whether on land or at sea. In addition to making an environmental argument, supporters of scattering stress that the practice frees women from patriarchal graves.[9]

Yet among those women who challenge convention—and their numbers are on the rise—very few choose the option of scattering. Most unmarried women, as well as married women seeking what amounts to posthumous divorce, do not want to leave society altogether when they die. Instead, they want to choose the particular society they wish to keep. Thus many decide to be buried with their natal families instead of their families of marriage. Japan has also seen an increase in recent years in the construction of shared graves for those either excluded from, or opting out of, the family system. A particularly famous example is a tomb established in 1990 at a temple in Kyoto for the Onna no Iwabuminokai (Society of the Gravestone for Women), a group composed of elderly women who had not been able to marry when they were young primarily because so many men had been killed during the war. Periodic festivals and memorial services held at the tomb bring together these women while they are still alive, helping them to form the social networks that they wish for in death.[10]

Care for the society's tomb is entrusted to Buddhist priests, demonstrating that challenging one convention often entails supporting another. Indeed, the profusion of literature promoting or discussing alternative death rites disguises the fact that the vast majority of Japanese continue to opt for the familiar rather than the new. Even those who want to break free from established patterns often find, like their ancestors, that they cannot. In *Ima sōgi, ohaka ga kawaru* (Funerals and graves today are changing), author Inoue Haruo relates the story of a woman whose husband died of cancer in the hospital. He had repeatedly pleaded with his wife to take him home, but there was no way to care for him there. He died in the hospital against his wishes. Because he was "very independent-minded" while alive, the husband had also told his wife how he wanted to be memorialized. He did not want the usual funeral, since he hated sutra reading, he said. Instead, he asked for a simple ceremony with pleasant music. Yet in this respect too, the will of the dead was frustrated because the wife had to consider the convenience of the survivors. It was especially important to think of their son's business relations, she explained, so the social pressure compelled her to go ahead with a standard Japanese funeral.[11]

What does the future hold for death rites in Japan? History shows that one thing is certain: whatever the changes, the dead will remain at the mercy of the living, and so too will the living remain hostage to the dead.

Notes

INTRODUCTION

1. During the spring and summer of 1997, I accompanied the staff of two Tokyo-based undertakers, Sugimoto K. K. and Ceremony Miyazaki, to a total of twelve funerals. What follows is a description of one funeral managed by Ceremony Miyazaki. In order to preserve the privacy of mourning family members, I have not included their last name.

2. This chant is known as the *nembutsu,* also written as *nenbutsu.*

3. See Chapter One, pp. 24–25, for a more detailed discussion of the cosmology that determines these intervals.

4. Jessica Mitford coined this phrase in the 1960s and used it in the title of a best-seller that scathingly criticized the profiteering of the American funeral industry. Here I use the term in a neutral sense to describe the total sum of practices and institutions that constitute the ritual management of death in modern Japan. Mitford's exposé was revised and reissued in 2000 (*The American Way of Death Revisited* [New York: Vintage Books, 2000]). Simon and Schuster published the original *The American Way of Death* in 1963.

5. A translation of this record appears in David Lu, *Japan: A Documentary History,* vol. 1 (Armonk, New York: M. E. Sharpe, 1997), pp. 11–14.

6. The earliest histories of Japan tell us that Buddhism officially entered the country in 552, when the ruler of the Korean kingdom of Paekche sent a Buddhist statue to the imperial court. It is likely, however, that immigrants from the continent had already transferred some form of Buddhism to Japan. *Nihongi: Chronicles of Japan from the Earliest Times to A.D. 697,* vol. 2, trans. W. G. Aston (Rutland, VT: Charles E. Tuttle, 1972), p. 65.

7. European historian Eric Hobsbawm devised this phrase in the early 1980s; see Eric J. Hobsbawm and Terence O. Ranger, eds., *The Invention of Tradition* (Cambridge:

Cambridge University Press, 1983). To see how this historical approach has been applied to the study of Japanese history by a variety of scholars, refer to Stephen Vlastos, ed., *Mirror of Modernity: Invented Traditions of Modern Japan* (Berkeley: University of California Press, 1998).

8. Carol Gluck, "Meiji for Our Time," in *New Directions in the Study of Meiji Japan,* eds. Helen Hardacre and Adam L. Kern (New York: Brill, 1997), p. 20.

9. Marilyn Ivy, *Discourses of the Vanishing: Modernity, Phantasm, Japan* (Chicago: University of Chicago Press, 1995). The study of death practices constitutes just one among many "discourses of the vanishing," a phrase used by Ivy to refer to various manifestations of modern nostalgia.

10. Geoffrey Gorer, *Death, Grief, and Mourning* (New York: Doubleday, 1965), appendix.

11. Inada Tsutomu and Ōta Tenrei, *Sōshiki muyōron* (Tokyo: Sōshiki o Kaikakusurukai, 1968).

12. Haga Noboru, *Sōgi no rekishi,* rev. ed. (Tokyo: Yūzankaku Shuppan, 1991), foreword, p. 1.

13. Ibid., p. 299.

14. Philippe Ariès, *L'Homme devant la Mort* (Paris: Éditions du Seuil, 1977), p. 554. For an English translation of this work, see Philippe Ariès, *The Hour of Our Death,* trans. Helen Weaver (New York: Alfred A. Knopf, 1981).

15. Ariès, *L'Homme devant la Mort,* p. 553.

16. Inoue Shōichi, *Reikyūsha no tanjō* (Tokyo: Asahi Shuppansha, 1990), pp. 183–187.

17. Stephen Prothero, *Purified by Fire: A History of Cremation in America* (Berkeley: University of California Press, 2001), p. 11.

18. See, for example, the following: Mark Rowe, "Stickers for Nails: The Ongoing Transformation of Roles, Rites, and Symbols in Japanese Funerals," *Japanese Journal of Religious Studies* 27, 3–4 (Fall 2000): 353–378; Hikaru Suzuki, *The Price of Death: The Funeral Industry in Contemporary Japan* (Stanford: Stanford University Press, 2000); Yamada Shin'ya, "Sōsei no bunka to chiiki shakai," *Nihon minzokugaku* 203 (August 1995): 23–59.

19. To illustrate: in his study comparing burial preferences in a city (Leicester) and a rural community (Fensham) in England in the early 1990s, Peter Jupp reported that in both locations, of those who opted for cremation, half chose to scatter the ashes rather than inter them; Jupp, "Cremation or Burial? Contemporary Choice in City and Village," in *The Sociology of Death,* ed. David Clark (Oxford: Blackwell Publishers, The Sociological Review, 1993), pp. 174–175.

20. Philippe Ariès, "The Reversal of Death: Changes in Attitudes Toward Death in Western Societies," trans. Valerie M. Stannard, in *Death in America,* ed. David E. Stannard (Philadelphia: University of Pennsylvania Press, 1975), pp. 153–155.

21. The *ihai,* what Hozumi chooses to translate as "memorial tablet," may also be written in English as "mortuary tablet." I use the latter translation throughout this

book because the tablet not only memorializes the dead but also serves as the focal point for rituals designed to comfort and assist the dead; Hozumi Nobushige, *Ancestor Worship and Japanese Law,* 6th edition (Tokyo: Hokuseido Press, 1940), p. 3.

22. There have appeared recently several English-language studies that closely analyze both the internal and external workings of the Buddhist clergy in Tokugawa society. See, for example, Helen Baroni, *Obaku Zen: The Emergence of the Third Sect of Zen in Tokugawa Japan* (Honolulu: University of Hawai'i Press, 2000); Helen Hardacre, *Religion and Society in Nineteenth-century Japan: A Study of the Southern Kantō Region, Using Late Edo and Early Meiji Gazetteers* (Ann Arbor, MI: Center for Japanese Studies, University of Michigan, 2002); Nam-lin Hur, *Prayer and Play in Late Tokugawa Japan* (Cambridge, MA: Harvard University Press, 2000); Richard Jaffe, *Neither Monk nor Layman: Clerical Marriage in Modern Japanese Buddhism* (Princeton: Princeton University Press, 2001); Alexander Vesey, "The Buddhist Clergy and Village Society in Early Modern Japan" (Ph.D. dissertation, Princeton University, 2003); and Duncan Williams, *The Other Side of Zen: A Social History of Sōtō Zen Buddhism in Tokugawa Japan* (Princeton: Princeton University Press, 2005). The most influential Japanese scholar writing on the economic, social, and political aspects of Tokugawa Buddhism over the last several decades is Tamamuro Fumio. For an analysis of his work, see Barbara Ambros and Duncan Williams, "Local Religion in Tokugawa History," *Japanese Journal of Religious Studies* 28, 3–4 (2001): 209–225.

23. There is a large corpus of studies on *kokugaku,* rendered into English by H. D. Harootunian as "nativism" in his seminal work *Things Seen and Unseen: Discourse and Ideology in Tokugawa Nativism* (Chicago: The University of Chicago Press, 1988). Also translated as "national learning" or "national studies," *kokugaku* has been the object of several book-length studies in English; see Susan Burns, *Before the Nation: Kokugaku and the Imagining of Community in Early Modern Japan* (Durham, NC: Duke University Press, 2003); Peter Nosco, *Remembering Paradise: Nativism and Nostalgia in Eighteenth-Century Japan* (Cambridge, MA: Council on East Asian Studies, Harvard University, 1990); and Anne Walthall, *The Weak Body of a Useless Woman: Matsuo Taseko and the Meiji Restoration* (Chicago: University of Chicago Press, 1998).

24. English-language scholarship on these combinatory systems of worship is collected in *Buddhas and Kami in Japan: Honji Suijaku as a Combinatory Paradigm,* eds. Mark Teeuwen and Fabio Rambelli (London: Routledge-Curzon Press, 2003).

25. For in-depth examinations of government policies toward Buddhism and Shinto in the Meiji period, see Helen Hardacre, *Shintō and the State, 1868–1988* (Princeton: Princeton University Press, 1989); Richard Jaffe, *Neither Monk nor Layman;* James Ketelaar, *Of Heretics and Martyrs in Meiji Japan: Buddhism and its Persecution* (Princeton: Princeton University Press, 1990); and Sarah Thal, *Rearranging the Landscape of the Gods: The Politics of a Pilgrimage Site in Japan* (Chicago: University of Chicago Press, 2005).

26. The most important of these was the "Harris Treaty," signed in 1858 and known by the name of the U.S. diplomat, Townsend Harris, who negotiated its terms with the

shogunate. Among other things, it stipulated the opening of several Japanese ports to U.S. trade, restricted the ability of the shogunate to set tariffs, and required that Americans committing crimes in Japan be tried and punished according to U.S., not Japanese, law.

27. Carol Gluck analyzes the dynamics of this dialogue between the *kan* and the *min* in *Japan's Modern Myths: Ideology in the Late Meiji Period* (Princeton: Princeton University Press, 1985).

28. For a detailed study of the birth and growth of Japan's modern press, see James L. Huffman, *Creating a Public: People and Press in Meiji Japan* (Honolulu: University of Hawai'i Press, 1997). Several of the "great debates" covered in the early Meiji press, including the battle over cremation, are presented by Makihara Norio in *Meiji shichinen no daironsō* (Tokyo: Nihon Keizai Hyōronsha, 1990).

29. My analysis supports Mary Berry's argument that the public sphere in both Tokugawa and Imperial Japan should be understood primarily "not as the space where popular sovereignty was claimed but where leadership was scrutinized and disciplined by criticism"; Berry, "Public Life in Authoritarian Japan," *Daedalus* 127, 3 (Summer 1988): 138.

30. This backlash is the subject of Kenneth B. Pyle's "Meiji Conservatism," in *The Cambridge History of Japan,* vol. 5, *The Nineteenth Century,* ed. Marius B. Jansen (Cambridge: Cambridge University Press, 1989).

31. Translation from Lu, *Japan,* vol. 2, p. 344.

32. David Cannadine, "War and Death, Grief and Mourning in Modern Britain," in *Mirrors of Mortality,* ed. Joachim Whaley, p. 242. In *Bereavement and Consolation,* Harold Bolitho introduces readers to three "thanatologues" written in the Tokugawa period and encourages them to sympathize with the grieving authors. He admits, however, that these accounts were the exception rather than the rule in a society where written displays of emotion were frowned upon. "The people of Tokugawa Japan may have been shattered by frequent bereavements, but they were not about to admit it in their writings," he notes; Bolitho, *Bereavement and Consolation: Testimonies from Tokugawa Japan* (New Haven: Yale University Press, 2003). Even when examining a time and place rich in confessional literature, such as Victorian England, making the connection between emotions and rituals is still "an extraordinarily difficult, if not impossible task," as Patricia Jalland discovered while writing *Death and the Victorian Family.* This "experiential history" aims at reconstructing and interpreting the "innermost lives" of fifty-five upper-class Victorian families. Fortunately for Jalland, her subjects produced an abundance of letters, diaries, and deathbed memorials out of an evangelical concern to probe and make manifest internal responses to death. One might assume that funerals loom large in these reflections, but Jalland discovered just the opposite. Illustrating that there is no easy correspondence between the expression of feelings and the performance of ritual, she writes, "It is difficult to evaluate mourners' responses to funerals, and to assess their therapeutic value or spiritual significance, because family comments on funerals in letters and diaries were surprisingly few and brief, in sharp

contrast to the lengthy accounts of dying and the deathbed." Jalland, *Death and the Victorian Family* (New York: Oxford University Press, 1996), pp. 2, 217.

CHAPTER I   OF BUDDHAS AND ANCESTORS

1. That Japanese religion "is less a matter of belief than it is of activity, ritual, and custom" is, for example, the central premise of Ian Reader and George Tanabe's survey of religious practice in end-of-the-twentieth-century Japan, *Practically Religious: Worldly Benefits and the Common Religion of Japan* (Honolulu: University of Hawai'i Press, 1998), p. 7.

2. Of those surveyed, 554 chose to respond to the question concerning their religious belief. Kotani Midori, *Senzo saishi no genjō to ohaka no kongo* (Tokyo: Raifu Dezainu Kenkyūjo, 1997), pp. 26–27.

3. The questions concerning grave visits and rituals at the family altar elicited answers from 565 respondents; ibid., p. 14.

4. This is Prince Siddhartha (ca. 563–483 B.C.E.), the so-called "historical" buddha, who preached the foundational teachings of Buddhism in northern India.

5. *Nihongi*, vol. 2, p. 65.

6. The word *kami* can be loosely translated into English as "deity(ies)." *Kami* include the creator gods of Japanese mythology, forces of nature, and awe-inspiring humans. The worship of these deities is designated by the term Shinto, meaning "the way of the *kami*."

7. See Joan R. Piggot, *The Emergence of Japanese Kingship* (Stanford: Stanford University Press, 1997), for a detailed study of this long and complex process.

8. Kuroda Toshio, "Shinto in the History of Japanese Religion," *The Journal of Japanese Studies* 7, 1 (Winter 1981): 1–21.

9. Today commonly referred to as *obon*. In Chinese, *yü-lan-p'en.*

10. It is referred to obliquely in the *Nihon shoki* record of events for 606 C.E. The text notes that this was the first year that temple festivals were held on the "15th day of the 7th month," the time that had been established for *urabon* in China. The *Nihon shoki* makes a more explicit reference to the festival's celebration in 657 C.E.; *Nihongi*, vol. 2, pp. 134 and 251.

11. Haga Noboru, *Sōgi no rekishi*, p. 122.

12. *The Analects*, trans. D. C. Lau (New York: Penguin Books, 1979), p. 63.

13. *The Book of Filial Duty*, trans. Ivan Chēn (London: John Murray, 1908).

14. Stephen F. Teiser, *The Ghost Festival in Medieval China* (Princeton: Princeton University Press, 1988), p. 197.

15. Known in Japanese as the *rokudō.*

16. In Chinese, Mu-lien; in Japanese, Mokuren.

17. Interring the bones of the dead after allowing the body to decompose—usually below ground, not above, as was the case in ancient Japan—is a practice still followed in some parts of the world, including Greece and southeastern China; see Loring M.

Danforth, *The Death Rituals of Rural Greece* (Princeton: Princeton University Press, 1982) and James L. Watson, "Of Flesh and Bones: The Management of Death Pollution in Cantonese Society," in *Death and the Regeneration of Life,* eds. Maurice Bloch and Jonathan Parry (Cambridge: Cambridge University Press, 1982), pp. 155–186.

18. Gary L. Ebersole, *Ritual Poetry and the Politics of Death in Early Japan* (Princeton: Princeton University Press, 1989), p. 127.

19. *Nihongi,* vol. 2, pp. 380–381.

20. Ibid., pp. 376–379.

21. Ebersole, *Ritual Poetry,* p. 168. Ebersole cites information found in the eighth-century poetry collection the *Man'yōshū.*

22. Tamamuro Taijō, *Sōshiki Bukkyō,* 11th ed. (Tokyo: Daihōrinkaku, 1993), p. 155.

23. Ibid., p. 156.

24. Ibid., p. 160.

25. A bodhisattva is a being on the path to becoming a buddha. According to Buddhist teaching, just as there are many buddhas, there are also many bodhisattvas, who use their powers to save the less enlightened. Jizō, along with Kannon, is popularly worshipped in Japan.

26. Tamamuro, *Sōshiki Bukkyō,* p. 171.

27. There are many Buddhist paradises, each with a different buddha in residence. In China and Japan, however, the "Pure Land" *(jōdo)* generally refers to that of Amida Buddha. The popularization of faith in Amida from the Heian period forward was based on the "original vow" *(hongan)* made by Amida when he was still a bodhisattva seeking buddhahood: "If after I have attained buddhahood, sentient beings in the ten directions who have sincere mind, serene faith, and a desire to be born in my country, should not be born there even with ten *nenbutsu* recitations [i.e., praising the name of a Buddha, in this case Amida Buddha], may I not attain perfect enlightenment— excepted are those who have committed the five deadly sins and abused the true law." Hisao Inagaki, *A Dictionary of Japanese Buddhist Terms* (Union City, CA: Heian International, 1988), p. 109.

28. Tamamuro, *Sōshiki Bukkyō,* pp. 197–199.

29. "The funeral of Emperor Goichijō (d. 1036), for example, involved rites performed at seven different temples, ranging from esoteric fire invocation ceremonies *(goma)* to simple chanting of the Buddha's name *(nenbutsu).* Records of the discussions held by the government ministers directing the funeral reveal that earlier precedents— not doctrinal consistency or personal religious inclinations—largely determined the selection, order, and sites of the rituals." William M. Bodiford, *Sōtō Zen in Medieval Japan* (Honolulu: University of Hawai'i Press, 1993), pp. 185–186.

30. Kakehata Minoru, "Chūgoku shūdai no sōfuku seido," in *Kazoku to shisha saishi,* pp. 9–15. For a discussion of Chinese funeral rites and their textual origins, see James L. Watson, "The Structure of Chinese Funerary Rites: Elementary Forms, Ritual Sequences, and the Primacy of Performance"; and Evelyn S. Rawski, "A Historian's Approach to Chinese Death Ritual," in *Death Ritual In Late Imperial and Modern*

China, eds. James L. Watson and Evelyn S. Rawski (Berkeley: University of California Press, 1988), pp. 3–34.

31. For example, regent Hōjō Tokimune was ordained by the Chinese monk Wu-hsüeh Tsu-hsüan just before he died in 1284, earning him a full-fledged Zen funeral. After Yoshihito (1361–1416), the son of Emperor Sukō and the grandfather of Emperor Gohanazono, died, "his head was shaved, his body was washed and dressed in Buddhist robes." Groups of monks chanted scriptures for several days, and the rites culminated in a cremation on the fourth day after Yoshihito's death. Bodiford, *Sōtō Zen,* pp. 193–194.

32. Ibid., pp. 194–196.

33. Ibid., pp. 196–204. See also Tamamuro, *Sōshiki Bukkyō,* pp. 129–130.

34. The ceremony developed for the Jōdo Shinshū (True Pure Land) sect differed somewhat from the others in that the sect did not require its clerics, and therefore its dead, to take the precepts. However, it created functional analogues that made Shinshū funerals very similar to those of the other Buddhist schools. For example, instead of bestowing *kaimyō,* which after all were ordination names, the school invented posthumous *hōmyō,* or "dharma names," indicating only that the dead who received them were believers. To learn more about ritual procedures for the Shinshū and other Buddhist sects, see Fujii Masao, ed., *Sōgi daijiten* (Tokyo: Kamakura Shinsho, 1995).

35. *Kojiki,* trans. Donald L. Philippi (Tokyo: Tokyo University Press, 1968), pp. 57–70.

36. Unfortunately we have no information about the ritual makeup of those funerals.

37. Akashi Kazunori, "Kodai no sōrei to fukukasei," in *Kazoku to shisha saishi,* ed. Kōmoto Mitsugi (Tokyo: Waseda Daigaku Shuppanbu, 1997), p. 42; and Hayashi Yukiko, "Edo bakufu fukukirei no bukki no igi to tokushitsu," in *Kazoku to shisha saishi,* p. 77.

38. Janet Goodwin, *Alms and Vagabonds: Buddhist Temples and Popular Patronage in Medieval Japan* (Honolulu: University of Hawaiʻi Press, 1994), p. 124.

39. Takemi Momoko, "'Menstruation Sutra' Belief in Japan," trans. W. Michael Kelsey, *Japanese Journal of Religious Studies* 10, 2–3 (1983): 229–246.

40. "In Shingon Buddhism, of which the Ninnaji was a center, great significance is given to A, the first letter of the Sanskrit alphabet, the beginning of things, and it is believed that all afflictions can be ended by contemplating this letter." Donald Keene, ed., *Anthology of Japanese Literature* (Rutland, VT: Charles E. Tuttle, 1988), pp. 202–203. Several stories in the *Shasekishū,* a collection of homilies compiled by Buddhist priest Mujū Ichien (1226–1312), also justified breaking the taboos surrounding death pollution as an act of mercy. In one tale a monk was traveling on pilgrimage to the shrine of a powerful *kami* when he happened upon several crying children. Asked what was wrong, one of them answered that their mother had died and that the father was nowhere to be found. "The neighbors wish to have nothing to do with such nasty, unpleasant business," leaving no one to handle the burial, the child explained. The

monk took pity on the children. He carried the corpse to a nearby field, recited prayers, and buried it. As he was about to turn back home, having decided that he could not resume the pilgrimage in his polluted state, he was briefly paralyzed and feared that he was being punished for his behavior. When he turned in the direction of the shrine, however, he was able to move without any difficulty, so he decided to proceed. As he approached the sacred precincts, he once more grew apprehensive and "recited sutras and spells as homage to the gods." The ending of the story proves the monk had been right to bury the corpse, however, for an attendant possessed by the shrine's *kami* approached the fearful monk and welcomed him, saying, "I certainly do not abhor what you have done. On the contrary, I respect compassion." Robert E. Morrell, *Sand and Pebbles (Shasekishū): The Tales of Mujū Ichien, A Voice for Pluralism in Kamakura Buddhism* (Albany, NY: State University of New York Press, 1985), pp. 81–82.

41. *Shoku Nihongi,* Aoki Kazuo et al., eds. Book 1, *Shin Nihon koten bungaku taikei,* vol. 12, ed. Satake Akihiro (Tokyo: Iwanami Shoten, 1989), pp. 23–27, 75.

42. Cremated remains have been found at more than forty excavated sites dating from the Jōmon (c. 11,000–400 B.C.E.) and Yayoi (400 B.C.E.–250 C.E.) periods. A number of poems from the *Man'yōshū* also appear to refer to cremation practices predating the death of Dōshō. See Shintani Takanori, "Kasō to dosō," in *Minshū seikatsu no Nihonshi: ka,* ed. Hayashiya Tatsusaburō (Tokyo: Dōmeisha, 1996), pp. 232–235. See also Saitō Tadashi, *Higashi Ajia sō, bosei no kenkyū* (Tokyo: Daiichi Shobō, 1987), pp. 217–222.

43. Shintani, "Kasō to dosō," pp. 243–246.

44. Cremation was referred to not only as *kasō,* literally, "fire burial," but as *dabi,* a transliteration of *dhyāpayati,* the Sanskrit term for cremation. Anna Seidel, "Dabi," in *Hōbōgirin: Dictionaire encyclopédique du bouddhisme d'après les sources chinoises et japonaises,* vol. 6, Sylvain Lévi et al., eds. (Paris: Librairie d'amérique et d'orient, 1983), pp. 573–585.

45. The late-twelfth-century courtier Fujiwara Kanezane (1149–1207) perfunctorily noted in his diary, "Cremation is meritorious; earth burial is inadequate." Shiori Nobukazu, "Sōhō no hensen: toku ni kasō no juyō o chūshin to shite," in *Sōsen saishi to sōbo,* ed. Fujii Masao (Tokyo: Meicho Shuppan, 1988), pp. 133–134.

46. Another story in the *Shasekishū,* for example, features an itinerant priest carrying the cremated remains of his mother to Mt. Kōya, headquarters of the Shingon sect and the resting place of the sect founder and folk hero Kūkai (774–835); Morrell, *Sand and Pebbles,* p. 83.

47. Translation from Keene, *Anthology,* p. 232.

48. Bodiford, *Sōtō Zen,* pp. 201–202.

49. Ibid., p. 202.

50. Ibid., p. 203.

51. Michael Cooper, ed., *They Came to Japan* (Berkeley: University of California Press, 1965), p. 367.

52. The phrase "sixty-odd provinces" refers to the regions comprising Japan. Yasui Sanesuke, "Hikasōron" (1685), reproduced in *Kan'utei sōsho,* vol. 6, pt. 5, ed. Itakura Katsuaki (Annaka-han: Minobe Sei and Tajima Toyohisa, 1843), p. 2.

53. Shinno Toshikazu, "Shinshū ni okeru sōsō girei no keisei," *Kokuritsu rekishi minzoku hakubutsukan kenkyū hōkō* 49 (March 1993): 181–182.

54. Asaka Katsusuke, "Kasōba no rekishi to henyō," in *Sōsō bunkaron,* ed. Sōsō Bunka Kenkyūkai (Tokyo: Kokon Shoin, 1993), pp. 121–126.

55. Shihōshō, *Zenkoku minji kanrei ruishū,* reprint (Tokyo: Seishisha, 1976), pp. 162–163.

56. For example, a 1707 order in Kyoto stated that *hinin* (vagrants, literally, "nonhumans"), *kawata* (referred to here and in other legal documents as *eta,* "highly polluted"), and *onbō* were all prohibited from performing day labor; Kyōto Burakushi Kenkyūjo, ed., *Kyōto no burakushi,* vol. 4 (Kyoto: Kyōto Burakushi Kenkyūjo, 1986), p. 39.

57. *Sanmai* is Japanese for the Sanskrit term *samādhi,* meaning a state of deep meditation. From the medieval period it was popularly used to refer to graveyards and cremation grounds. The word *hijiri* was applied broadly to itinerant clerics and charismatic religious figures only loosely affiliated with monastic institutions; Kamibeppu Shigeru, "Sesshū sanmai hijiri no kenkyū: toku ni sennichi bosho sanmai hijiri o chūshin to shite," in *Sōsō bosei kenkyū shūsei,* vol. 1, Doi Takuji and Satō Yoneshi, eds. (Tokyo: Meicho Shuppan, 1979), pp. 58–76; and Yoshii Toshiyuki, "Sanmai hijiri to bosei no hensen," *Kokuritsu rekishi minzoku hakubutsukan kenkyū hōkō* 68 (March 1996): 109–131.

58. Yoshii, "Sanmai hijiri," pp. 109–131.

59. Asaka Katsusuke and Yagisawa Sōichi, *Kasōba* (Tokyo: Daimeidō, 1983), p. 56.

60. Before the late nineteenth century, burning corpses consumed a tremendous amount of wood, filled the air with noxious fumes, and ran the gruesome risk of not adequately finishing the appointed task.

61. Mori Kenji, *Haka to sōsō no shakaishi* (Tokyo: Kōdansha, 1993), pp. 71–72. The court had first instituted burial regulations as part of the Taika period (645–649) reforms. These were promulgated by Emperor Kōtoku as part of his effort to centralize state power through Chinese legal structures. The court mandated that "plots of ground be set apart for interments," as "it is not permitted to pollute the earth by dispersed interments in various places." The court also determined the sizes of tombs according to rank and forbade certain funerary customs, such as "burying valuables in the grave in honour of the dead" and "stabbing the thighs and pronouncing an eulogy on the dead (while in this condition)." *Nihongi,* vol. 2, pp. 217–220.

62. Tamamuro, *Sōshiki Bukkyō,* pp. 210–261.

63. See Date Mitsuyoshi, *Nihon shūkyō seido shiryō ruiju kō,* rev. ed. (Kyoto: Rinsen Shoten, 1974) for a listing of both Edo and Meiji regulations concerning temples and shrines. Regulations are organized chronologically and by subject. For English-lan-

guage discussions of the ways in which the Tokugawa shogunate dominated Buddhism in the seventeenth century, refer to Baroni, *Obaku Zen;* Vesey, "The Buddhist Clergy"; and Williams, *The Other Side of Zen.*

64. For a detailed account of the introduction and persecution of Christianity in English, see George Elison, *Deus Destroyed: The Image of Christianity in Early Modern Japan* (Cambridge, MA: Harvard University Press, 1991).

65. James C. Scott introduces the concept of "legibility" and the ways in which states seek to produce it in *Seeing Like a State: How Certain Schemes to Improve the Human Condition Have Failed* (New Haven: Yale University Press, 1998), pp. 2–3, 11–83.

66. Tamamuro Fumio, "Local Society and the Temple-Parishioner Relationship within the Bakufu's Governance Structure," *Japanese Journal of Religious Studies* 28: 3–4 (Fall 2001): 262.

67. The Fuju-fuse and Hiden subsects of Nichiren Buddhism were banned in 1669 and 1691, respectively; ibid., p. 265.

68. Ibid., pp. 265–269, 276–278. See Tamamuro Fumio's *Sōshiki to danka* (Tokyo: Furukawa Kōbunkan, 1999) for a book-length study of the origins and implementation of the parishioner household system.

69. John Hall called Tokugawa Japan a "container society" in "Rule by Status in Tokugawa Japan," *Journal of Japanese Studies* 1 (Autumn 1974): 39–49.

70. See William Bodiford, "Zen and the Art of Religious Prejudice: Efforts to Reform a Tradition of Social Discrimination," *Japanese Journal of Religious Studies* 23, 1–2 (1996): 1–27. Bodiford's article discusses measures taken since the 1980s by the Sōtō Zen sect, under pressure from the Buraku Liberation League, to rectify past discrimination. This includes the provision of new mortuary tablets and tombstones free of charge to replace those featuring derogatory titles. For a book-length historical treatment of discriminatory *kaimyō,* see Kobayashi Daiji, *Sabetsu kaimyō no rekishi* (Tokyo: Yūsankaku Shuppan, 1987).

71. Herman Ooms, *Tokugawa Village Practice: Class, Status, Power, Law* (Berkeley: University of California Press, 1996), p. 244.

72. The dead were often carried and buried in a seated position, since this gave them the appearance of meditating buddhas.

73. Most likely a reference to chanting of the *nembutsu* (calling the name of Amida Buddha) and *daimoku* (reciting the title of the Lotus Sutra).

74. Cooper, *They Came to Japan,* pp. 363–364.

75. Ibid., p. 366.

76. Seikanbō Kōa, *Imayo heta dangi, Kyōkun zoku heta dangi,* ed. Noda Hisao, 3rd ed. (Tokyo: Ōfūsha, 1977), pp. 38–46.

77. Also referred to as *koshiya* or *kagoya* during the Tokugawa period.

78. These were communal religious organizations, the former dedicated to praising Amida Buddha and the latter to chanting the title of the Lotus Sutra.

79. Seikanbō, *Imayo heta dangi,* p. 41.

80. Ibid.

81. Ibid., p. 43.

82. One *koku* of rice equals a little over five bushels. Throughout the Tokugawa period a samurai's status was determined by an annual stipend measured in *koku* of rice. Daimyo collected at least 10,000 a year.

83. Seikanbō, *Imayo heta dangi,* p. 44.

84. Jalland, *Death in the Victorian Family,* p. 195.

85. Ibid.

86. Ibid.

87. Robert W. Habenstein and William M. Lamers, *The History of American Funeral Directing* (Milwaukee: Bulfin Publishers, 1955), p. 182.

88. Ibid., p. 206.

89. Ibid., p. 204.

90. Ibid., p. 216.

91. *TSS, Sangyōhen,* vol. 3, p. 85.

92. Ibid., pp. 85–87.

93. *TSS, Shigaihen,* vol. 37, p. 385.

94. Again, the *rokudō* are the six transmigratory realms of the Buddhist cosmos, while "sen" is a unit of currency that also means "coin" in general. Coins were placed in coffins so that, in its journey into the afterlife, the dead soul could pay the ferryman of the Sanzu River. The Sanzu River resembles the River Styx of Greek mythology.

95. *TSS, Sangyōhen,* vol. 15, pp. 945–955.

96. In the story about Sōshichi, the pamphlet mentions that among the items that will be supplied are *rokudōsen* printed on paper; and when describing the practice of burying *rokudōsen,* a Christian missionary writing in 1925 noted, "In old Japan real money was placed in the coffin, but now India ink impressions are made of the six pieces on extra heavy, good paper, which, when cut out, are put in the coffin." William Hugh Erskine, *Japanese Customs: Their Origin and Value* (Tokyo: Kōbunkan, 1925), p. 95. It is also noteworthy that excavations in the 1980s of one former temple grave-yard in Tokyo unearthed coins dating from the late sixteenth to the late seventeenth century, but uncovered no coins from later periods, even though burials continued there through the eighteenth century; Tanigawa Akio, "Excavating Edo's Cemeteries: Graves as Indicators of Status and Class," *Japanese Journal of Religious Studies* 19, 2–3 (June–September 1992): 283.

97. A thorough survey of records throughout Japan would have to be made to determine more accurately the rate at which the practice of keeping *kōdenchō* spread in different regions and among different classes. The oldest *kōdenchō* that I have seen mentioned in the scholarly literature comes from a village in today's Yamanashi prefecture and dates from 1619; Amano Tsutomu, "Kōden," in *Sōsō bunkaron,* ed. Sōsō Bunka Kenkyūkai (Tokyo: Kokon Shoin, 1993), p. 54. Another seventeenth-century record

comes from a village in today's Nagano prefecture and dates from 1698. Listed gifts include money, white rice, miso, tofu, tea, incense, tobacco, and candles; Ariga Kizaemon, *Mura no seikatsu sōshiki* (Tokyo: Miraisha, 1968), p. 243.

98. The family, which lives in Yamagata prefecture, asked to remain anonymous.

99. Mori Kenji, *Hayama no bosei* (Research data published privately with funding from the Ministry of Education, 1997), p. 23.

100. Ibid., p. 36.

101. Tanigawa Akio, "Excavating Edo's Cemeteries," pp. 287–292.

102. Names that included the titles *ingō, koji,* and *daishi* were the most desirable, while *shinji* and *shinnyo* went to those of middling status and *zenjōmon* and *zenjōni* to those of still lower rank; Tamamuro Fumio, "The Temple-Parishioner Relationship," pp. 272–275.

103. There were also cases, conversely, in which priests resisted pressure from parishioners to award elite titles, putting them into conflict. See, for example, the case described in Vesey, "The Buddhist Clergy," pp. 376–383.

104. The text of the 1831 regulations appears in Date, *Nihon shūkyō seido,* p. 279.

CHAPTER 2   THE SHINTO CHALLENGE TO BUDDHIST DEATH

1. For a nuanced, book-length examination of the place of Confucian thought within the production of a wider political and ethical discourse in seventeenth-century Japan, see Herman Ooms, *Tokugawa Ideology: Early Constructs, 1570–1680* (Princeton: Princeton University Press, 1985).

2. Kumazawa Banzan, "Sōsai benron" (date unclear), in *Banzan zenshū,* vol. 5, ed. Masamune Atsuo, reprint (Tokyo: Meicho Shuppan, 1978), pp. 97–98.

3. Ibid.

4. It is worth noting that until survival rates improved in the mid-twentieth century, children in Japan, as in other parts of the world, were often disposed of unceremoniously. In 1873, for example, Wakayama prefecture found it necessary to ban the long-standing practice of casting dead infants into rivers; Tanigawa Ken'ichi, ed., *Nihon shomin seikatsu shiryō shūsei,* vol. 21 (Tokyo: San'ichi Shobō, 1979), p. 273. In a 1941 ritual manual for fellow clerics, a Sōtō Zen priest noted that rural families neglected to invest in death rites for young children because of their high mortality rate, observing that when babies died, parents did not hold funerals so much as "dispose" of them; Mogi Mumon, *Sōshiki, hōji no shikata* (Tokyo: Yoyogi Shoin, 1941), p. 41.

5. People in Tokugawa Japan rarely revealed their emotions in writing, but in Harold Bolitho's *Bereavement and Consolation* we encounter three such men who did, including a Confucian scholar. All three men recorded the grief they felt upon losing their children.

6. Kumazawa, "Sōsai benron," pp. 97–99.

7. Isabella Bird, *Unbeaten Tracks in Japan,* 3rd ed. (London: John Murray, 1888), p. 150.

8. Excavations of early Edo graveyards show that *hayaoke* accounted for the vast majority of graves; see Tanigawa Akio, "Excavating Edo's Cemeteries," pp. 282–284. Bodies of the more well-to-do were placed in square coffins in a seated position *(zakan)*, giving them the appearance of sitting in meditation.

9. Ibid., p. 101. In China too, Confucian thinkers encouraged respect for local gods, so Kumazawa's reminder to propitiate the *kami* reflected a continental tradition as much as any native belief system. It was just this sort of appeal to localized worship, however, that would contribute to the development of full-fledged Shinto funerals in the latter part of the Tokugawa period.

10. Kumazawa, "Sōsai benron," p. 100.

11. In fact Chinese Buddhist texts often referred to cremation by using compounds meaning "transformation of man" or "metamorphosis by fire"; J. J. M. De Groot, *The Religious System of China,* vol. 3, bk. 1, reprint (Taipei: Ch'eng-wen Publishing Co., 1967), p. 1391.

12. Confucian scholars in Song dynasty China (960–1280) fulminated passionately against cremation, which Cheng Yi (1033–1107), one of the founding fathers of neo-Confucianism, called "the worst of customs of our modern times . . . a rite which even filial sons and affectionate grandsons do not consider as heterodox." Translation from De Groot, *The Religious System of China,* p. 1396. Another Song-period scholar, this one a district magistrate, wrote, "a man who burns his parents commits the grossest possible sin against the *hsiao* [filial devotion]. . . . Taking them up to cast them into a fire is the very highest pitch of cruelty; there is in such deeds nothing that tallies with the natural feelings of man." Ibid., p. 1403. The anti-cremation position among Confucian scholars in China hardened over the next several centuries, and the Ming dynasty (1368–1644) placed a comprehensive ban on cremation that was later inherited by the Qing (1644–1912); ibid., pp. 1411–1413. See also Patricia Ebrey, "Cremation in Sung China," *American Historical Review* 95, 2 (April 1990): 406–428.

13. Kumazawa, "Sōsai benron," p. 101.

14. Saitō Tadashi, *Higashi Ajia sō bosei no kenkyū,* pp. 242–243.

15. Yasui, "Hikasōron," p. 1.

16. Ibid., p. 2.

17. Tsuji Zennosuke, *Nihon Bukkyōshi,* vol. 4 (Tokyo: Iwanami Shoten, 1955), p. 115.

18. "Busshū kōken," in *Kōbunko,* vol. 15, ed. Mozume Takami (Tokyo: Meicho Fukyūkai, 1928), p. 710.

19. Ooms, *Tokugawa Ideology,* p. 198.

20. Tamamuro Fumio, "Okayamahan no shaji seiri seisaku ni tsuite," *Meiji Daigaku jinbun kagaku kenkyūjo kiyō* 40 (1996), p. 368.

21. Ibid., pp. 370–371.

22. Ibid., p. 382.

23. Priests at the Ise shrine, which was (and still is) dedicated to the sun goddess, Amaterasu, scrupulously avoided the use of Buddhist rituals and terminology. Kuroda

Toshio, "Shinto in the History of Japanese Religion," p. 13; and Namihira Emiko, *Kegare* (Tokyo: Tōkyōdō Shuppan, 1985), pp. 80–81.

24. Kondō Keigo, "Tokugawa Mitsukuni no sōrei," in *SD*, p. 47.

25. Ibid., 48–49. See also Mito Shishi Hensan Iinkai, *Mito shishi*, vol. 2, bk. 1, reprint (Mitoshi: Mitoshi Yakusho, 1977), pp. 871–875.

26. Kondō Keigo, "Tokugawa Mitsukuni no sōrei," in *SD*, p. 48.

27. Saitō Tadashi, *Higashi Ajia sō bosei no kenkyū*, pp. 240–241. Before retired Emperor Gomizuno-o died in 1680, he asked to be cremated, but his request was denied.

28. Edmund Gilday, "Bodies of Evidence: Imperial Funeral Rites and the Meiji Restoration," *Japanese Journal of Religious Studies* 27, 3–4 (Fall 2000): 277, 285.

29. Asoya Masahiko and Tanuma Mayumi, eds., *Shinsōsai shiryō shūsei* (Tokyo: Perikan, 1995), p. 34. See also Allan G. Grapard, "The Shinto of Yoshida Kanetomo," *Monumenta Nipponica* 47, 1 (Spring 1992): 38.

30. Grapard, "The Shinto of Yoshida Kanetomo," p. 46.

31. Asoya and Tanuma, *Shinsōsai shiryō shūsei*, p. 35.

32. For a detailed discussion of Kanemigi's funeral in English, see Elizabeth Kenney, "Shinto Funerals in the Edo Period," *Japanese Journal of Religious Studies* 27, 3–4 (Fall 2000): 243–248.

33. Yoshida Kanemi, "Yuiitsu shintō sōsai shidai"; reproduced in *Shinsōsai shiryō shūsei*, eds. Asoya and Tanuma, pp. 14, 81–98. The original manuscript no longer exists. The text appearing in the *Shinsōsai shiryō shūsei* is based on a nineteenth-century copy.

34. *Nihongi*, vol. 1, pp. 33–34.

35. Yoshida, "Yuiitsu shintō sōsai shidai," p. 82.

36. The name is sometimes pronounced "Koretari."

37. Ooms, *Tokugawa Ideology*, p. 198.

38. Asoya and Tanuma, *Shinsōsai shiryō shūsei*, p. 35.

39. Suika was Yamazaki Ansai's Shinto name. It can be translated as "blessings from above."

40. Ooms, *Tokugawa Ideology*, p. 234. For a discussion of Yamazaki's development as a neo-Confucian/Shinto thinker, see pp. 194–232.

41. Ibid., p. 221.

42. Shigeru Matsumoto, *Motoori Norinaga* (Cambridge, MA: Harvard University Press, 1970), p. 172.

43. Ibid., pp. 172–173.

44. I am grateful to Anne Walthall for pointing out this fact.

45. Matsumoto, *Motoori Norinaga*, pp. 168–170.

46. Ryusaku Tsunoda et al., *Sources of Japanese Tradition*, vol. 2, revised edition (New York: Columbia University Press, 1964), p. 46; and Muraoka Tsunetsugu, *Studies in Shinto Thought*, trans. Delmer M. Brown and James T. Araki (Tokyo: Japanese

National Commission for UNESCO, 1964), p. 185. For a penetrating analysis of Hirata's teachings, see Harootunian, *Things Seen and Unseen*.

47. Kamata Tōji, "The Disfiguring of Nativism: Hirata Atsutane and Orikuchi Shinobu," in *Shinto in History: Ways of the Kami*, eds. John Breen and Mark Teeuwen (Honolulu: University of Hawai'i Press, 2000), p. 306.

48. Tsunoda et al., *Sources of Japanese Tradition*, vol. 2, pp. 44–46.

49. See Muraoka, *Studies in Shinto Thought*, pp. 190–196, for a summary of these different positions.

50. Asoya and Tanuma, *Shinsōsai shiryō shūsei*, pp. 355–468.

51. See, for example, the ritual format devised in 1769 by Shinto priest Sugawara Noboyuki, who, as Elizabeth Kenney puts it, "created a Shinto funeral that was free of Buddhist elements and brimming with Confucian ingredients"; Kenney, "Shinto Funerals in the Edo Period," p. 260. Sugawara's funeral manual appears as "Heiri Shinkan Shinshūki," in *Shinsōsai shiryō shūsei*, eds. Asoya and Tanuma, pp. 388–425. In Kenney's analysis of the symbols and actions of another eighteenth-century Shinto funeral, this one for a Shinto priest named Nemoto Tanemaro, she observes, "It must have been a vexing task for Edo-period Shintoists to enact (or even just to describe) concretely a funeral based on a mythic scenario that was part cryptic and part unintelligible"; see "Shinto Funerals in the Edo Period," p. 248.

52. Grapard, "The Shinto of Yoshida Kanetomo," p. 56.

53. Mito Shishi Hensan Iinkai, *Mito shishi*, vol. 2, bk. 1, p. 874.

54. Shimura Kimurō, "Shinsōsai mondai to sono hatten," *Shigaku zasshi* 41, 9:72–74.

55. *MSBS*, vol. 9, pp. 118–119.

56. Katō Takahisa, "Tsuwano han no shinsōsai fukkō undō to shinrei kenkyū," in *SD*, pp. 385–389.

57. For a book-length analysis of Mito thought, see J. Victor Koschmann, *The Mito Ideology: Discourse, Reform and Insurrection in Late Tokugawa Japan, 1790–1864* (Berkeley: University of California Press, 1987).

58. A seminal articulation of this emperor-centered ideology is "Shinron," or "The New Theses," by Mito thinker Aizawa Seishisai. An English translation and analysis of the famous text appears in Bob Tadashi Wakabayashi, *Anti-Foreignism and Western Learning in Early-Modern Japan: The New Theses of 1825* (Cambridge, MA: Council on East Asian Studies, Harvard University, 1986).

59. Ibid., pp. 167, 174.

60. Ketelaar, *Of Heretics and Martyrs*, p. 47.

61. Mito Shishi Hensan Iinkai, *Mito shishi*, vol. 2, bk. 3, pp. 289–300.

62. Ibid., p. 297.

63. Ibid., pp. 321–325.

64. Katō Hōkyō, "Sōsai ryakushiki: tenpō onsadame" (1844). Manuscript located in collection of family documents "Satomi shozō bunsho," set 1, compiled by Samukawa Chōshi Hensanka. There is no pagination.

65. Koschmann, *The Mito Ideology,* pp. 139–140.

66. Mito Shishi Hensan Iinkai, *Mito shishi,* vol. 2, bk. 4, pp. 224–226.

67. Katō Takahisa, "Tsuwano han no shinsōsai fukkō undō," p. 387.

68. Ibid., pp. 389–391.

69. The influential samurai Kido Kōin was the main author of this and the other articles of the so-called "Charter Oath" of 1868; John Breen, "The Imperial Oath of April 1868: Ritual, Politics, and Power in the Restoration," in *Meiji Japan: Political, Economic and Social History 1868–1912,* vol. 1, *The Emergence of the Meiji State,* ed. Peter Kornicki (London: Routledge, 1998), pp. 107–108.

70. For more on the role these men played in the Ministry of Rites, see John Breen, "Ideologues, Bureaucrats and Priests: On 'Shinto' and 'Buddhism' in early Meiji Japan," in *Shinto in History: Ways of the Kami,* eds. John Breen and Mark Teeuwen (Honolulu: University of Hawai'i Press, 2000), pp. 230–249.

71. Date, *Nihon shūkyō seido,* p. 576.

72. The separation edicts and other shrine and temple regulations passed in the first two years of Meiji are listed in ibid., pp. 576–586.

73. For an in-depth case study of this decision-making process, see Thal, *Rearranging the Landscape of the Gods.* Thal explains the political maneuverings that transformed a syncretic ritual complex devoted to the deity Konpira into the explicitly Shinto shrine Kotohira.

74. Ketelaar, *Of Heretics and Martyrs,* p. 9.

75. In addition to Ketelaar, see Martin Collcutt, "Buddhism: The Threat of Eradication," in *Japan in Transition: From Tokugawa to Meiji,* eds. Marius B. Jansen and Gilbert Rozman (Princeton: Princeton University Press, 1986), pp. 143–167, for an account of the Meiji persecution of Buddhism.

76. Ketelaar, *Of Heretics and Martyrs,* p. 44. The funeral for Emperor Kōmei in 1866 had included Buddhist sutra readings, although these were confined to private ceremonies held after the official Shinto funeral; Gilday, "Bodies of Evidence," p. 287.

77. *DJR,* vol. 1, bk. 135, sec. 1.

78. The decision to build the Kyoto *shōkonsha* was based on two previous examples: one set in 1853 by the Tsuwano domain, which performed a public Shinto ceremony to pacify the spirits of the deceased, and the other set in 1863 by a Shinto shrine in Kyoto, which constructed a subshrine specifically for the purpose of honoring the war dead. The shrine built in 1868 became, in turn, a model imitated throughout Japan; Mori Kenji, *Haka to sōsō shakaishi,* pp. 36–38.

79. Murata Antoku, "Meiji shonen ni okeru shinsōsai kara bussō e no tenkai," *Nihon kindai Bukkyōshi kenkyū* 3 (March 1996): 24.

80. Murata examines Shinto funeral campaigns at the grassroots level in "Meiji shonen ni okeru shinsōsai kara bussō e no tenkai." See also Murata Antoku, "Meiji ishinki shinsōsai undō no tenmatsu," *Nihonshi kōkyū* 22 (November 1996): 1–17.

81. Notto R. Thelle, *Buddhism and Christianity in Japan: From Conflict to Dialogue, 1854–1899* (Honolulu: University of Hawai'i Press, 1987), p. 13.

82. Ibid., pp. 14, 35–36.

83. Ibid., p. 30.

84. Ibid., p. 35.

85. *DJR,* vol. 1, bk. 135, sec. 3 (first request).

86. Ibid.

87. In 1870, however, a shrine parishioner system was implemented in Nagasaki in order to impose a new layer of control over Christians; Sakamoto Koremaru, *Kokka shintō keisei katei no kenkyū* (Tokyo: Iwanami Shoten, 1994), pp. 172–190.

88. Ibid., p. 427.

89. Ibid., p. 428.

90. *TKS,* 605.C5.08, "Sōgi, dai ichi hen dai san setsu sōgi no bu," item no. 1.

91. Matsumoto domain was absorbed into Chikuma prefecture, which was itself abolished in 1876, part of the short-lived prefecture devolving to Gifu prefecture and the rest to Nagano prefecture; Takayanagi Mitsutoshi and Takeuchi Rizō, eds., *Kadokawa Nihonshi jiten,* 2nd ed. (Tokyo: Kadokawa Shoten, 1995), p. 1274.

92. *MSBS,* vol. 5, pp. 361–362.

93. Katō Takahisa, "Tsuwano ni okeru soreisha to sōreisha," in *SD,* pp. 403, 414 n. 12.

94. The radically pro-Shinto but internally divided Ministry of Rites, dubbed the "Ministry of Afternoon Naps" *(hirunekan)* or "Ministry of Indecision" *(injunkan)* by its critics, came under particularly sharp attack from the eminent statesmen Saigō Takamori and Etō Shimpei; Ketelaar, *Of Heretics and Martyrs,* p. 98.

95. Ibid., p. 104.

96. Date, *Nihon shūkyō seido,* p. 622.

97. Murata, "Meiji shonen ni okeru shinsōsai kara bussō e no tenkai," pp. 27–28.

98. Ibid., p. 30.

99. Ibid., p. 31.

100. Date, *Nihon shūkyō seido,* p. 621. The new policy was extended to include nuns in 1873. The Shin sect had sanctioned meat-eating and marriage for centuries and had thus been treated separately from other Buddhist denominations. But the legalization of these practices for all Buddhist sects triggered anguished debates among the priests of other sects about how to properly respond. For a detailed treatment of the government decision to legalize marriage and the clerical response, see Jaffe, *Neither Monk nor Layman.*

101. Jaffe, *Neither Monk nor Layman,* pp. 73–78.

102. In 1869 the Ministry of Rites and the Council of State negotiated with city authorities to establish two such graveyards on suburban samurai estates. These were opened to "all classes of people" *(shimin ippan)* in 1872, with management placed in the hands of Shinto priests. A few months later four more Shinto cemeteries were designated for Tokyo, and the Ministry of Doctrine announced that it would legally recognize Shinto cemeteries established in other areas of Japan as well; *DJR,* vol. 1, bk. 135, sec. 31; and vol. 2, bk. 269, sec. 20–22.

103. Breen, "Ideologues, Bureaucrats and Priests," pp. 232–234.

104. Date, *Nihon shūkyō seido*, p. 622.

105. Furukawa Motoyuki, "Sōgiryaku" (1865); reproduced in *Shinsōsai shiryō shūsei*, eds. Asoya and Tanuma, pp. 454–468.

106. It is worth noting that the new policy was designed not to end discrimination so much as to standardize the registration and surveillance of all the emperor's subjects. It was, in other words, a measure designed less to liberate a minority than to dominate the majority; Hirota Masaki, *Sabetsu no shisō*, vol. 22, Nihon kindai shisō taikei, (Tokyo: Iwanami Shoten), p. 78.

107. Mori Kenji, "Meiji shonen no bukki, fukusō: Hitotsu no oboegaki to shite," in Kōmoto Mitsugi and Yagi Tōru, *Kazoku to shisha saishi* (Tokyo: Waseda Daigaku Shuppanbu, 1997), pp. 140–141.

108. For example, when the Tōshōgu shrine to Ieyasu was built in 1624, officials conducted checks among the construction workers to make sure that none of them was contaminated by death or birth *kegare*. Merchants were forbidden to visit Edo castle while in mourning, and when the shogun himself was in mourning, he too avoided making visits or sending proxies to Tokugawa-related shrines. The same rule applied to retainers, who were also supposed to refrain from their official duties, although the latter requirement could be lifted by special dispensation; Hayashi Yukiko, "Edo bakufu bukki rei no igi to tokushitsu," in *Kazoku to shisha saishi*, eds. Kōmoto Mitsugi and Yoshie Akio (Tokyo: Waseda Daigaku Shuppanbu, 1997), pp. 71, 95–109.

109. Date, *Nihon shūkyō seido*, p. 622.

110. Konoe Tadafusa and Senge Takatomi, *Sōsai ryakushiki* (1872); reproduced in SD, pp. 416–425.

111. Yasui Sanesuke, on p. 2 in his 1685 essay "Against Cremation" (Hikasōron), observed that, when bathing the dead *(yūkan)*, survivors mercilessly scrubbed the corpse "as if it were a burdock root or radish," ripping the skin in the process.

112. Furukawa Motoyuki, "Sōgiryaku"; reproduced in *Shinsōsai shiryō shūsei*, eds. Asoya and Tanuma, p. 465.

113. Shihōshō, *Zenkoku minji kanrei ruishū*, pp. 160, 179. Some areas devised symbolic strategies in order to allow for burial on *tomobiki no hi*. John Embree, in his 1936 study of Suyemura, wrote that villagers buried a doll along with the deceased; that way, no one else would be pulled into death; Embree, *Suye Mura: A Japanese Village* (Chicago: The University of Chicago Press, 1936), p. 216.

114. Mori, "Meiji shonen no bukki, fukusō," p. 143.

115. Ibid., pp. 143–144.

116. Ibid., p. 144.

117. According to the mythological text, Chūai reigned in the late second century; *Nihongi*, vol. 1, pp. 217–223.

118. Ibid., pp. 224–225.

119. Established in 1871, the Sa-in was an appointed body charged with considering

and devising policy changes. These were either accepted or rejected by the Sei-in, which reported/dictated to the emperor himself.

120. This was suggested in the earlier consultations leading to the February 7 ruling; Mori, "Meiji shonen no bukki, fukusō," p. 143.

121. Horiuchi Misao, ed., *Meiji zenki mibunhō taizen,* vol. 4 (Tokyo: Nihon Hikakuhō Kenkyūjo, 1981), pp. 351–352.

122. *Shinbun zasshi* was a newsbook founded in 1871 largely through funding provided by Meiji oligarch Kido Kōin. Its name changed to *Akebono shinbun* in 1875; Huffman, *Creating a Public,* p. 52.

123. *Shinbun zasshi,* 28 (July 1873); reproduced in *SSM,* vol. 2, p. 59.

124. Date, *Nihon shūkyō seido,* p. 640.

CHAPTER 3   THE GREAT CREMATION DEBATE

1. Kōseishō Seikatsu Eiseikyoku Kikakuka, *Chikujō kaisetsu: Bochi, maisō nado ni kan suru hōritsu* (Tokyo: Daiichi Hōki Shuppan Kabushiki Kaisha, 1991), pp. 240–243.

2. Date, *Nihon shūkyō seido,* p. 640.

3. Aoki Toshiya, "Meiji shoki hōrei shiryō kara mita sōsō shūzoku to kokka kisei no kenkyū," *Matsudo shiritsu hakubutsukan kiyō* 3 (March 1996): 48. In 1897, the first year for which nationwide statistics are available, 29.2 percent of the dead in Japan were cremated; Narumi Tokunao, *Aa kasō* (Niigatashi: Niigata Nippō Jigyōsha, 1995), p. 61.

4. Yoda made this observation during a debate among council members about the cremation ban. The proceedings were published in the *Yūbin hōchi shinbun,* June 24, 1874.

5. *DJR,* vol. 2, bk. 269, sec. 6 (May 29, 1873, letter to Justice Ministry).

6. *Tōkyō nichi nichi shinbun,* February 3, 1873.

7. Kyōto Burakushi Kenkyūjo, *Kyōto no burakushi,* vol. 6 (Kyoto: Kyōto Burakushi Kenkyūjo, 1984), p. 533.

8. Each domain provided one representative to the assembly. The assembly's name changed to the Shūgi-in a few months after its founding in 1869. It was then attached to the Sa-in in 1871 and replaced completely by the latter body in 1873.

9. Meiji Bunka Kenkyūkai, ed., *Meiji bunka zenshū,* vol. 1, reprint (Tokyo: Nihon Hyōronsha, 1969), pp. 98–99.

10. *DJR,* vol. 2, bk. 269, sec. 6 (May 22, 1873, letter to Justice Ministry).

11. The "red line" *(shubikisen)* was established by the Tokugawa shogunate's senior councilors in 1818. It denoted the "lord's city" *(gofunai);* and, in the words of Katō Takashi, "circumscribed an area that began at Sunemura, a village near the mouth of the Naka River; traveled upstream to Kige village, where it turned west to Senju; ran up the Ara River to Oji and swept out to Itabashi village; and then began a long bend south through the villages of Kami Ochiai, Yoyogi, and Kami Osaki before meeting the sea at

Minami Shinagawa." In 1869 the area within the red line was divided into six wards that comprised the inner city of Tokyo; see Katō Takashi, "Governing Edo," in *Edo and Paris: Urban Life and the State in the Early Modern Era*, eds. James L. McClain et al. (Ithaca, New York: Cornell University Press, 1997), p. 45. See also Edward Seiden-sticker, *Low City, High City* (Rutland, VT: Charles E. Tuttle, 1984), p. 29.

12. Asaka and Yagisawa, *Kasōba*, p. 55. The fumes released by burning bodies had been targeted by the opponents of cremation in China as well. In discussing the destruction of local crematories in a thunderstorm, a Song dynasty magistrate wrote, "It is my conviction that their foul stench had spread so far as to cause the offended spirits of the dead to conjointly lay their complaints before the Imperial Heaven, and that Heaven, convulsed with rage, destroyed those crematories, root and branch"; De Groot, *The Religious System of China*, p. 1402.

13. *Tōkyō nichi nichi shinbun*, February 13, 1873.

14. The Tokyo police prefaced their suggestion to relocate crematories with a qual-ifier: "It is not the business of this department to decide whether this practice [i.e., cre-mation] is proper or not," a clear recognition on their part that the proposal would be controversial. *DJR*, vol. 2, bk. 269, sec. 6 (May 22, 1873, letter to Justice Ministry).

15. *DJR*, vol. 2, bk. 269, sec. 6 (May 29, 1873, Council of State memo).

16. Ibid. (June 4, 1873, letter to Council of State).

17. Aoki, "Meiji shoki hōrei shiryō," pp. 48–49.

18. This debate is also taken up by Makihara Norio in *Meiji shichinen no daironsō*, pp. 79–117.

19. Memorial from Ōuchi Seiran to the Sa-in (August 19, 1874); reproduced in *MKS*, vol. 3, pp. 751–753.

20. To give just one more example, Kondō Shūrin, a Shinshū priest in Tokyo, ended his petition to the Sa-in by writing, "I wish that the choice of cremation or earth burial were left up to the desire of each chief mourner and that the feeling of depres-sion among the people were dispelled." Memorial from Kondō Shūrin to the Sa-in (December 1874). In *MKS*, vol. 4, p. 312.

21. Memorial from Oe Koryū to the Shūgi-in (February 8, 1873); reproduced in *MKS*, vol. 2, pp. 439–443.

22. De Groot, *The Religious System of China*, p. 1412.

23. Tsuji, *Nihon Bukkyōshi*, vol. 4, p. 116.

24. Petition to Ōkubo Ichiō, governor of Tokyo, from Tamura Ryōyū, Matsumoto Chigen, and Niwa Kyōjin, representing the fourteen cremation temples of Senju (November 7, 1874). *TKS*, 605.C5.08, "Sōgi, dai ichi hen dai san setsu sōgi no bu," item no. 91, pp. 397–398.

25. Memorial from Shimaji Mokurai to the Sa-in (October 1874). In Shimaji Mokurai, *Shimaji Mokurai zenshū*, vol. 1, ed. Futaba Kenkō and Mineshima Hideo (Kyoto: Honganji Shuppan, 1973), p. 70.

26. Memorial from Tokunaga Kanmyō to the Sa-in (August 1874); reproduced in *MKS*, vol. 3, p. 813.

27. *TKS*, 605.C5.08, item no. 91, pp. 395–396.

28. *DJR*, vol. 2, bk. 269, sec. 6 (May 22, 1873, letter to Justice Ministry).

29. Ibid, sec. 6 (June 1873 letters to Council of State).

30. Ibid., sec. 26 (August 1873 communications between the Finance Ministry and Council of State).

31. Ibid.

32. Asaka and Yagisawa, *Kasōba*, p. 59.

33. Kanda Takahira, *Tōkyō nichi nichi shinbun*, July 29, 1874; reproduced in *MKS*, vol. 3, pp. 753–754.

34. *DJR*, vol. 2, bk. 269, sec. 23.

35. Memorial from Tokunaga Kanmyō to the Sa-in (August 1874); reproduced in *MKS*, vol. 3, pp. 812–813.

36. Memorial from Ōuchi Seiran to the Sa-in (August 19, 1874). In *MKS*, vol. 3, p. 752.

37. Shimaji, *Shimaji Mokurai zenshū*, vol. 1, p. 69.

38. Founded in 1872 by the secretary for the minister of posts and telecommunications, this newspaper competed head-to-head with the *Tōkyō nichi nichi shinbun;* Huffman, *Creating a Public*, pp. 53–54.

39. Letter submitted by Ogura "so-and-so," letter to the editor, *Yūbin hōchi shinbun*, October 3, 1873.

40. Satake Keishō, "Kasō ben'ekiron," *Yūbin hōchi shinbun*, July 9, 1874.

41. Hiramatsu Kaname, letter to the editor, *Yūbin hōchi shinbun*, October 3, 1873.

42. For example, during the great cholera epidemic of 1858, when "not thirty or forty days would pass without several people dying in one household," families in Edo who usually preferred earth burial turned en masse to cremation. As a result, crematories were overwhelmed with thousands of bodies stacked in huge piles; Satake, "Kasō ben'ekiron."

43. *TKS*, 605.C5.08, item no. 91, pp. 398–400.

44. Satake, "Kasō ben'ekiron."

45. *Tōkyō nichi nichi shinbun*, August 30, 1874.

46. *Yūbin hōchi shinbun*, June 24, 1874.

47. Sakatani Shiroshi, "Kasō no utagai," *Meiroku zasshi* 18 (October 1874), pp. 5–6.

48. On December 6, 1876, an Austrian nobleman and theosophist, Baron De Palm, was cremated in Washington, Pennsylvania, in a facility designed by Dr. Francis Julius Le Moyne, a reformist physician. The well-publicized event drew journalists from "as far away as England, France, and Germany." It also "attracted local residents staunchly opposed to incineration who, according to *The New York Times*, lent to the occasion the raucous air of a prizefight (or an execution)." Prothero, *Purified by Fire*, p. 32.

49. Bird, *Unbeaten Tracks*, p. 325.

50. Prothero, *Purified by Fire*, pp. 15–17.

51. Ariès, *The Hour of Our Death*, p. 493.

52. Ibid., pp. 495–496.

53. Prothero, *Purified by Fire*, pp. 17–18.

54. Ibid. p. 19.

55. Sabata Toyoyuki, *Kasō no bunka* (Tokyo: Shinchōsha, 1990), p. 27.

56. From the 1960s, however, cremation has steadily grown in popularity. In the 1990s approximately a quarter of those who died in the United States were cremated; Mitford, *The American Way of Death Revisited*, p. 111.

57. Memorial from Ōuchi Seiran to the Sa-in (August 19, 1874); reproduced in *MKS*, vol. 3, p. 752.

58. *Yūbin hōchi shinbun*, August 5, 1874.

59. Memorial from Tokunaga Kanmyō to the Sa-in (August 1874); reproduced in *MKS*, vol. 3, pp. 812–813.

60. *Yūbin hōchi shinbun*, October 3, 1873.

61. Takagi Naokage, letter to the editor, *Yūbin hōchi shinbun*, September 26, 1873.

62. Konishi Mokuichi, letter to the editor, *Tōkyō nichi nichi shinbun*, December 7, 1873.

63. Mr. Yokozawa, letter to the editor, *Tōkyō nichi nichi shinbun*, December 27, 1873.

64. *MKS*, vol. 3, p. 753.

65. Letter to the editor from "just someone from Seinan," *Tōkyō nichi nichi shinbun*, August 30, 1874.

66. *DJR*, vol. 2, bk. 269, sec. 7 (January 1875 letter to Home Ministry).

67. Ibid. (Undated letter to Council of State).

68. Ibid. (January 28, 1875, Sa-in policy statement).

69. Ibid. (Council of State Edict no. 89).

70. "Kasō jinmin no jiyū to naru," *Chōya shinbun*, May 25, 1875; cited in Asaka and Yagisawa, *Kasōba*, p. 120.

71. Aoki, "Meiji shoki hōrei shiryō," p. 49.

72. Asaka and Yagisawa, *Kasōba*, p. 88.

73. When Nagasaki outlawed full-body burial in its city center in 1888, the *Asahi shinbun* reported that the measure was intended "to protect against epidemics." This does not mean that Nagasaki mandated cremation; in fact, the newspaper noted that the municipal government would set aside alternative cemeteries for burial in the suburbs. Because citizens could continue to bury cremated remains inside the city, however, cremation became all the more attractive to those who wanted to keep the dead close at hand. *Asahi shinbun*, June 5, 1888; reproduced in Hosono Ungai, *Fumetsu no funbo* (Tokyo: Ganshōdō Shoten, 1932), p. 96.

74. Mori Kenji, "Kindai no 'kegare'—sabetsu to haka," *Buraku kaihō* 418 (March 1997): 204–205. Cholera killed hundreds of thousands of Japanese during the course of the Meiji period. The number of people killed by cholera in 1877 was 8,027; in 1879, 105,786; in 1882, 33,784; and in 1886, 108,405; Kawakami Takeshi, *Gendai Nihon iryōshi* (Tokyo: Keisō Shobō, 1965), p. 131.

75. Asaka and Yagisawa, *Kasōba*, p. 31.

76. *DJR*, vol. 2, bk. 269, sec. 7 (January 28, 1875, Sa-in policy statement).

77. Ibid. (June 24, 1875, Home Ministry proclamation).

78. The building was constructed around pits much like the ones dug in the open air and filled with brush and firewood.

79. Asaka and Yagisawa, *Kasōba*, p. 121.

80. Ibid.

81. Report from Dr. Tjarko Beukema to the governor of Tokyo (February 21, 1878). In *TSS*, Shigaihen 60, pp. 419–423.

82. Asaka and Yagisawa, *Kasōba*, p. 124.

83. Yoshii Toshiyuki notes that the collapse of the feudal order left cremators bereft of tax exemptions and monopolistic privileges. However, his research does not show how *onbō* in different areas of Japan navigated the new political and economic environment of early Meiji. Yoshii, "Sanmai hijiri to bosei no hensen," pp. 129–131.

84. *Asahi shinbun*, December 23 and 25, 1888; reproduced in Hosono, *Fumetsu no funbo*, p. 205.

85. Keene, *Anthology*, p. 232

86. Asaka and Yagisawa, *Kasōba*, pp. 88–90.

87. Ibid., pp. 33–36. Also see Aoki, "Meiji shoki hōrei shiryō," pp. 49–50.

88. Asaka and Yagisawa, *Kasōba*, p. 69.

89. Bird, *Unbeaten Tracks*, pp. 327–328.

90. Edward J. Bermingham, *The Disposal of the Dead: A Plea for Cremation* (New York: Bermingham & Co., 1881), pp. 45–48.

91. *Tōkyō Yokohama mainichi shinbun*, October 9, 1883.

92. Asaka and Yagisawa, *Kasōba*, p. 91.

93. *RR* (1884), vol. 2, pp. 367–369 (January 7, 1881, inquiry). In the end the Home Ministry refused to let the renegade parishioners establish their own graveyard, not because it would harm public health, but because the ministry opposed the establishment of sectarian burial grounds in general.

94. "Kasō en'yu no koto," *Myōmyō bunko* 10 (October 1883): 6–8.

CHAPTER 4   DIVESTING SHINTO FUNERALS

1. In the negotiations leading to this shift in policy, translators invented the modern Japanese word for "religion," *shūkyō*. It comprises the Chinese characters for "lineage" and "teaching." During the Tokugawa period and earlier, boundaries had been drawn between different systems of belief and practice, but without reference to a universal, autonomous category of "religion" as developed in the Enlightenment West. Just as there was a "way of the Buddha" and a "way of the *kami*" (i.e., Shinto), there was also a "way of the warrior" *(bushidō)*, a "way of calligraphy" *(shodō)*, and a "way of tea" *(chadō)*. In all these cases, "*dō*," or "way," referred not just to one way of doing something but the right way of doing it, excluding other possible approaches as wrong or completely other to the point of being beyond comparison. When emissaries of the

Western powers entered Japan just prior to the Restoration, they brought with them a new paradigm of distinction-making, one that grouped together relativized religions and collectively distinguished them from such phenomena as science, superstition, and, most importantly, the state.

2. Muraoka, *Studies in Shinto Thought*, p. 235.

3. Ketelaar, *Of Heretics and Martyrs*, p. 122.

4. Ibid., p. 128.

5. Translation from Nitta Hitoshi, "Shinto as a 'Non-religion': The Origins and Development of an Idea," in *Shinto in History: Ways of the Kami*, eds. John Breen and Mark Teeuwen (Honolulu: University of Hawai'i Press, 2000), p. 255.

6. Ketelaar, *Of Heretics and Martyrs*, p. 105.

7. Murata, "Meiji ni okeru shinsōsai kara bussō e no tenkai," p. 33.

8. Ketelaar, *Of Heretics and Martyrs*, p. 99; and Collcutt, "Buddhism," p. 155.

9. *DJR*, vol. 2, bk. 269, sec. 2.

10. *DJR*, vol. 2, bk. 269, sec. 4. The series of consultations leading to the Council of State decision originated with an inquiry to the Home Ministry from Saga prefecture.

11. Memorial from Yoshitake Shizuo to the Sa-in (December 12, 1874); reproduced in *MKS*, vol. 4, pp. 320–323.

12. Helen Hardacre, *Shintō and the State* (Princeton: Princeton University Press 1989), p. 66.

13. Translation from Nitta, "Shinto as a 'Non-religion,'" p. 255.

14. Ibid., pp. 263–264.

15. For more on the "pantheon dispute," see Hardacre, *Shintō and the State*, pp. 48–51; and Ketelaar, *Of Heretics and Martyrs*, pp. 115–116.

16. Date, *Nihon shūkyō seido*, p. 728.

17. Hardacre, *Shintō and the State*, p. 76. It is worth noting that some Shinto priests had opposed Shinto funerals as early as the eighteenth century. For example, in a privately circulated essay, the priest of Umemiya shrine in Kyoto, Hashimoto Tsunesuke, opposed them on the grounds that the newfangled, "detestable" ceremonies had no basis in ancient practice; Kenney, "Shinto Funerals in the Edo Period," pp. 266–267.

18. Hardacre, *Shintō and the State*, pp. 48, 50.

19. See Chapter Five, p. 112.

20. Tsuwano was incorporated into Hamada prefecture in 1871, which then merged with Shimane prefecture in 1876; Takayanagi Mitsutoshi, and Takeuchi Rizō, eds. *Kadokawa Nihonshi jiten*, 2nd ed. (Tokyo: Kadokawa Shoten, 1995), pp. 1276–1277.

21. Katō Takahisa, "Tsuwano ni okeru soreisha to sōreisha," p. 404.

22. Ibid.

23. Ibid.

24. Ibid., pp. 405–406.

25. Memorial from Moriya Makiyo and Narukawa Tetchū to Prime Minister Sanjō Sanetomi (March 12, 1882); reproduced in *MKS*, vol. 6, pp. 699–700.

26. Date, *Nihon shūkyō seido*, p. 733.

27. From 1875 onward, Christian funerals had, in practice, been allowed, even though the law against performing funerals without a Shinto or Buddhist officiant was still on the books.

28. *RR* (1887), vol. 3, p. 300; *TSS,* Shigaihen 63, pp. 624–631.

29. *RR* (1887), vol. 3, p. 300.

30. Thelle, *Buddhism and Christianity in Japan,* p. 115.

31. *Kōbun ruishū* (microfilm at Meiji University, Tokyo), vol. 7, bk. 63, sec. 6–16.

32. François Macé, "The Funerals of the Japanese Emperors," *Nanzan Bulletin* 13 (1989): pp. 27–29.

33. In the consultations leading to the state funeral of Iwakura Tomomi, the word "Shinto" did not appear even once; *Kōbun ruishū,* vol. 7, bk. 13, sec. 11.

34. "Kokusō no koto," *Reichikai zasshi* 84 (March 1891): 36.

35. "Kokusō ni tsuite," *Zenkoku shinshoku kaikaihō* 133 (November 1909): 1–4.

36. Ibid., p. 2.

37. Ibid.

38. "Kaitō" (Questions and answers), *Jinja kyōkai zasshi* 4, 1 (January 1905): 45–46.

39. Sugawara Mōsei, "Shinshoku to sōgi to no kankei," *Jinja kyōkai zasshi* 33 (November 1904): 49.

40. Ibid.

41. Fujita Meitarō, "Shinshoku to sōgi no kankei ni tsuite," *Jinja kyōkai zasshi* 34 (December 1904): 52–53.

42. Tōkyōto Kōbunshokan, *Nisshin sensō to Tōkyō,* vol. 1, bk. 2 of *Toshi shiryō shūsei* (Tokyo: Tōkyōto Kōbunshokan Shuppan, 1998), p. 491.

43. Ibid., pp. 492–496.

44. Ibid., pp. 487–490.

45. Ibid., p. iii.

46. Tōkyōto Kōbunshokan, *Nisshin sensō to Tōkyō,* vol. 1, bk. 1, pp. 432–433.

47. Ogata Itsuo, "Senshi gunjin no sōgi ni tsuite," *Jinja kyōkai zasshi* 4, 1 (January 1905): 41–42.

48. "Kaitō," *Jinja kyōkai zasshi* 4, 1 (January 1905): 44–45.

49. Ibid., p. 45.

50. Ibid., pp. 45–46.

51. Ono Kiyohide, *Kokka sōdōin* (Tokyo: Kokufūkai, 1937), p. 229.

52. Ibid., pp. 230–231.

53. Ibid.

54. Ibid., p. 230.

55. Mogi, *Sōshiki, hōji no shikata,* p. 115.

56. Ibid., p. 116.

57. Disputes over the ownership and use of temple graveyards will be covered in Chapter Five.

58. Dōon Koji, "Seizen ni hōmyō o ukezu shite sōshiki o nasubekarazu," *Reichikai zasshi* 30 (January 1886): 28.

59. Ibid., pp. 29–30.

60. Ibid., pp. 30–32.

61. For a full-length study of "new Buddhism" see Ikeda Eishun, *Meiji no shinbuk-kyō undō* (Tokyo: Yoshikawa Kōbunkan, 1976). Also see Ketelaar's account of Japanese participation in the 1893 World Parliament of Religions in Chicago; Ketelaar, *Of Heretics and Martyrs*, pp. 136–173.

62. Jaffe, *Neither Monk nor Layman*, p. 169.

63. Satomi Kishio, *Japanese Civilization: Its Significance and Realization* (London: Kegan Paul, Trench, Trubner & Co., 1923), pp. 4, 6.

64. *Tōkyō nichi nichi shinbun*, November 18, 1892; reproduced in *KD*, p. 84.

65. *Tōkyō nichi nichi shinbun*, February 5, 1901; reproduced in *SKH*, p. 496.

66. Helen Hardacre, *Kurozumikyō and the New Religions of Japan* (Princeton: Princeton University Press, 1986), p. 118.

CHAPTER 5   GRAVE MATTERS

1. Nishiki Kōichi, "Bohi naki bochi no kōkei: Toshi kasō minshū no shi to maisō o megutte," in *Kinsei toshi Edo no kōzō*, ed. Takeuchi Makoto (Tokyo: Sanseidō, 1997), pp. 31–54.

2. Hitomi Tatsuo, "Kokoro to shizen o hakai suru reien kaihatsu," in Sōsō no Jiyū o Susumerukai, ed., *"Haka" kara no jiyū: Chikyū ni kaeru shizensō* (Tokyo: Shakai Hyō-ronsha, 1994), pp. 101–124.

3. See Epilogue, pp. 174–175.

4. The term *ryōbosei* itself was coined by Omachi Tokuzō and popularized by Yana-gita Kunio after 1929. Since then scholars have offered varying explanations of the significance and origins of the double-grave system, but by and large they all recognize the belief in *kegare* (pollution) to be a crucial factor; Mori Kenji, *Haka to sōsō no genzai: Sosen saishi kara sōsō no jiyū e* (Tokyo: Tōkyōdō Shuppan, 2000), p. 159.

5. *DJR*, vol. 2, bk. 269, sec. 22.

6. Ibid., sec. 23. Management was subsequently transferred to Tokyo prefecture in 1876 and to the city of Tokyo in 1889; Tanaka Kiyoshi, *Aoyama reien* (Tokyo: Tōkyōto Kōen Kyōkai, 1994), pp. 31–34.

7. Kobayashi Katsushō, *Bochi toriatsukai kisoku* (Tokyo: Bunkeidō, 1874), p. 3.

8. Date, *Nihon shūkyō seido*, p. 626.

9. Although the Finance Ministry declared in the fall of 1872 that it was following precedent by confirming graveyards to be tax free, under the Tokugawa regime some graveyards had, in fact, been located on taxable land. Soon after the policy was announced, the ministry's Land Tax Reform Bureau (Chiso Kaisei Kyoku) received an inquiry from Tochigi prefecture asking what to do about such burial grounds. Should they be made tax free or continue to be taxed? The bureau answered that if graves had been built "without permission" before the Restoration, the land on which they were

located would continue to be taxed. If, however, a communal graveyard were located on taxable land, that land would be made tax free; *CKKS,* vol. 1, p. 63.

10. Mori Kenji, "Meiji shonen no bochi oyobi maisō ni kan suru hōsei no hatten," in Fujii Masao et al., eds., *Kazoku to haka* (Tokyo: Waseda Daigaku Shuppanbu, 1996), p. 205.

11. *DJR,* vol. 2, bk. 269, sec. 27.

12. Ibid. Edict 355 also appears in Date, *Nihon shūkyō seido,* p. 641. The concern about haphazard burial was shared by provincial authorities. In August 1873, several months before the Council of State announced this edict, Shiga prefecture outlawed the building of private burial plots and ordered villages to establish communal grave-yards—preferably in wilderness areas that produced no tax revenue; Aoki, "Meiji shoki hōrei shiryō kara mita sōbo shūzoku to kokka kisei no kenkyū," p. 60.

13. *CKKS,* vol. 1, pp. 399–400.

14. *RR* (1884), vol. 2, pp. 375–377.

15. Ibid., pp. 362–363 (April 24, 1876, inquiry).

16. Ibid.

17. *RR* (1887), vol. 4, pp. 290–291 (May 6, 1885, inquiry).

18. *RR* (1884), vol. 2, p. 392 (February 20, 1878, inquiry).

19. Ibid., pp. 393–395 (May 22 and November 4, 1878, inquiries). Yamanashi pre-fecture also challenged the ministry in a November 1882 communication, writing that there was no available land for communal burial grounds in towns and villages, so it wanted to allow families to continue burying in the scattered private plots that they had used for generations. The reply from Tokyo was unequivocal: establish communal cemeteries. *RR* (1884), vol. 2, pp. 372–373 (November 9, 1882, inquiry).

20. Mori, *Haka to sōsō no shakaishi,* pp. 79–84.

21. *RR* (1884), vol. 2, pp. 377–378.

22. *RR* (1887), vol. 2, p. 410 (June 2, 1883, inquiry).

23. *RR* (1887), vol. 3, pp. 286–287 (February 6, 1884, inquiry).

24. *RR* (1884), vol. 2, pp. 367–369 (January 7, 1881, inquiry).

25. Date, *Nihon shūkyō seido,* p. 733.

26. *RR* (1887), vol. 3, pp. 297–301.

27. *Kōbun ruishū,* vol. 8, sec. 27.

28. *RR* (1887) vol. 3, pp. 297–298.

29. The variety of reporting systems was recorded by the Justice Ministry in its 1880 nationwide survey of customs; Shihōshō, *Zenkoku minji kanrei ruishū,* pp. 150–153.

30. *RR* (1887), vol. 3, p. 300; *TSS,* Shigaihen, vol. 63, pp. 624–631.

31. *RR* (1887), vol. 3, pp. 298–301.

32. The office was established jointly by the Finance and Home ministries in 1875. It superseded the Finance Ministry's Land Tax Reform Bureau (Chiso Kaisei Kyoku).

33. Arakawa Genki, *Jiin handobukku: Bochi hen.* Revised edition (1978; rev. ed., Tokyo: Sansei Shobō, 1988), p. 468.

34. Hōjō Hiroshi, "Meiji shonen no bochi shoyūken to riyō," part 1, *Teikyō Daigaku hōgaku kiyō* 14, 2 (September 1984), pp. 71–72. In certain instances a deed would display the name of one individual serving as a representative for his neighborhood.

35. The structural ambiguities of the Meiji land reform occupied lawyers even in the late twentieth century. In the preface to his article, Hōjō wrote that he began investigating the process of establishing property rights for graveyards in early Meiji because of his participation as a legal expert in current disputes over their use; ibid., pp. 29–30. Digests and an analysis of eight court cases from the 1960s to the 1980s appear in Nakao Eishun, "Bochi shiyōken to seikaku," *Gendai zaisan kenron no kadai* (Tokyo: Keibundō, 1988), pp. 36–54. Some disputes involved temple priests, temple parishioners, and former parishioners, while others arose between "ancestral households of origin" *(honke)* and their collateral "branch households" *(bunke)*.

36. The Finance Ministry published a volume in 1954 to explain the redistribution and management of temple and shrine lands from the Restoration onward; Ōkurashō Kanzai Kyoku, ed., *Shaji keidaichi shobunshi* (Tokyo: Ōkura Zaimu Kyōkai, 1954). Implementation of the 1870 Council of State order is covered from pp. 30–57, the order itself appearing on p. 31. The order also appears in Arakawa, *Jiin handobukku,* pp. 462–463, and is discussed in Murayama Hirō, "Bochi hō no kiso," *Minshō hō zasshi* 68, 1 and 3 (1973), part 1, pp. 51–54.

37. Ōkurashō, *Shaji keidaichi shobunshi,* p. 39. This second order also instructed local officials to calculate the average income of remaining properties over a six-year period.

38. Ibid., pp. 62–64.

39. Arakawa, *Jiin handobukku,* p. 468.

40. *CKKS,* vol. 1, p. 4.

41. Ōkurashō, *Shaji keidaichi shobunshi,* p. 72.

42. An inquiry sent from Miyagi prefecture to the Home Ministry in June 1879, for example, stated that Miyagi officials planned to disburse deeds for graveyards carved from temple lands to villages and not to individual owners (who would include priests or parishioners) because "even if extra space were available, there is no guarantee that those with property rights would not, in the future, refuse new burials." *RR* (1884), vol. 2, pp. 380–382.

43. Tonooka Mojurō, ed., *Meiji zenki kazokuhō shiryō,* vol. 1, bk. 2 (Tokyo: Waseda Daigaku, 1967), pp. 638–639.

44. *RR* (1884), vol. 2, pp. 394–396.

45. *RR* (1887), vol. 3, p. 299.

46. In 1887 the Home Ministry responded to an inquiry from Aomori prefecture concerning one such dispute that "disputes over rights between grave owners are not the concern of administrative officials [in Tokyo]." Ibid., vol. 6, pp. 348–352 (March 4, 1887, inquiry).

47. "Ikyōsha maisō jiken," *Mitsugon Kyōhō* 71 (12 September 1892): 16–17.

48. Ibid., p. 16.

49. Ibid.

50. Ibid., pp. 16–17.

51. *TSS*, Shigaihen, vol. 74, pp. 241–243.

52. Ibid., pp. 243–244.

53. Ibid., pp. 239–241, 245.

54. Ibid., pp. 245–246.

55. Ibid., pp. 240–241.

56. Ibid., vol. 81, p. 214.

57. In January 1889 the Home Ministry also ordered local officials to determine jurisdictions for the management of public assets; ibid., p. 240 (Home Ministry Order no. 1, January 24).

58. Ibid., p. 214.

59. Ibid., pp. 226–240. These pages contain drafts of letters as well as those actually sent.

60. Ibid., pp. 229–231.

61. The August regulations, as well as those later announced in November, were compiled into a booklet that was published in January 1893; Tōkyōfu, *Jiin keidai bochi kanrisha kokoroe* (Tokyo: Sawa Jitsukyō, 1893).

62. Ibid., pp. 9–10.

63. *TSS*, Shigaihen, vol. 84, p. 351.

64. Ibid., p. 352.

65. Tōkyōfu, *Jiin keidai bochi kanrisha kokoroe*, p. 7.

66. *TSS*, Shigaihen, vol. 84, p. 354.

67. *Yomiuri shinbun*, November 20, 1892; ibid., p. 363.

68. *TSS*, Shigaihen, vol. 84, pp. 352–357.

69. Arguments made before the court and the eventual decision (with which Maruyama disagrees) are discussed in Maruyama, "Bochi hō no kiso," part 2, pp. 411–417. See also Yoshida Hisashi, *Bochi shoyūkenron to bochi shiyōkenron* (Tokyo: Shinseisha, 1962), pp. 26–27.

70. *TSS*, Shigaihen, vol. 84, pp. 349–363. This was published as a pamphlet in November 1892; Tōkyōfuka Kakushū Jiin Sōdai Bochi Iin, ed., *Tōkyōfuka moto jiin keidai kyōyū bochi ni kan suru ikensho* (Tokyo: Kakushū Bochi Iin Jimusho).

71. *TSS*, Shigaihen, vol. 84, pp. 359–360. During the land reform process of 1875 and 1876, most temples in Japan also failed to take advantage of a rule allowing them to register state-owned precincts as private property. This rule required temples to present pre-Restoration evidence of ownership. The Finance Ministry speculated in its 1954 manual that in the 1870s temples perhaps wanted to hold onto their state-land status because they feared becoming the object of taxation in the future. The ministry also suggested that local officials may have pressured them to forego privatization; Ōkurashō, *Shaji keidaichi shobunshi*, pp. 71–72. However, another reason may have been

the aforementioned concern about letting either clerics or parishioners gain too much power.

72. *TSS*, Shigaihen, vol. 84, pp. 358–359.

73. *TKS*, 621.A4.14, "Bochi ni kan suru shorui," item no. 7 (September 27, 1895, petition from Seigenji temple in Akasaka ward). This petition was one of fifteen compiled by Tokyo officials in the 1895 "Bochi ni kan suru shorui" (Documents concerning graveyards).

74. Tanaka, *Aoyama reien*, pp. 34–35.

75. In 1882, for example, Tokyo prefecture informed the Home Ministry that it was moving 175 gravesites in Yanaka village out of the path of a railroad under construction, with plans to relocate them to a new "common burial" graveyard on state land appropriated from nearby Tennōji temple; *RR* (1884), vol. 2, p. 390 (December 15, 1882, inquiry). In 1886 Aichi prefecture communicated with the Home Ministry regarding the removal of a Nagoya temple and its graveyard due to roadwork; *RR* (1887), vol. 5, pp. 451–452 (December 3, 1886, inquiry).

76. *Ōsaka asahi shinbun*, July 5, 1917; reproduced in Hosono, *Fumetsu no funbo*, p. 102.

77. *Asahi shinbun*, December 19, 1886; reproduced in Hosono, *Fumetsu no funbo*, pp. 204–205.

78. *TKS*, 623.B4.5, "Dai ni ka bunsho, chiri, bochi," item no. 25 (July 11, 1889, request from Senryūji temple, Shitaya ward). Tokyo harnessed the profit motive to encourage other temple communities to consolidate voluntarily and remove graves from city-owned "common burial graveyards." The city could force relocations, and it did, but it was preferable to secure the cooperation of priests and parishioners. So in what essentially amounted to robbing Peter to pay Paul, the city announced in 1903 that temple cemeteries it had claimed as "common burial graveyards" in 1891 would be transferred to temples if they removed the graves and turned them into vacant lots. These lots could then be developed at the temples' discretion into housing or other profit-making enterprises. The logic of the city's offer was apparently not to make space for centrally guided projects like roadwork, but to encourage economic development in general and to speed the process of expelling the dead from its core. Some temples apparently took the city's bait, profiting from the displacement of ancestral tombs. From available records it is difficult to gauge how many temples actually took advantage of Tokyo's offer and to what extent the decision to do so was made by priests or parishioners. At the very least, documents show six temples acting on the Tokyo offer in 1908. *TKS*, 602.A4.11 (1908), "Tochi, bochi, dai isshu, dai go go," items no. 1–6. The requests all noted City Order no. 45 (1903), which allowed for the transfer of cemeteries free of charge as long as they were vacated of graves. Also in 1903, an updated urban renewal plan was announced that reiterated the goal of removing graveyards scattered throughout the city; Arakawa, *Jiin handobukku*, p. 472.

79. Nishio Ujizō, ed., *Bochi kokoroe* (Osaka: Nishio, 1885), p. 21.

80. Ibid., p. 19.

81. Literally, "grave without bonds." The dead who go uncared for are commonly referred to as *muenbotoke* (buddhas without bonds).

82. Tōkyōfu, *Jiin keidai bochi kanrisha kokoroe*, pp. 7–8.

83. *TKS*, 623.B4.5, "Dai ni ka bunsho, bochi," item no. 6 (March 7, 1899, petition).

84. "Haka o gomakasu akusō o kenkyo," *Yorozu chōhō,* August 21, 1927; reproduced in Hosono, *Fumetsu no funbo,* p. 104.

85. For an overview of the "rural" and "lawn" cemetery movements in nineteenth-century America, see James Farrell, *Inventing the American Way of Death: 1830–1920* (Philadelphia: Temple University Press, 1980), pp. 99–145.

86. Murakoshi Tomoyo, *Tama reien* (Tokyo: Tōkyōto Kōen Kyōkai, 1994), p. 10.

87. Ibid., pp. 8–10.

88. Ibid., p. 27.

89. Ibid., p. 10.

90. Tanaka, *Aoyama reien*, p. 41.

91. Inoshita Kiyoshi, "Toshi no teienteki kyōsō bochi ni tsuite," *Toshi mondai* 25, 6 (December 1937), p. 85.

92. Inoue Yasumoto, *Bochi keiei* (Tokyo: Kokon Shoin, 1941), pp. 66–67.

93. Newspaper articles describing plans for park-like cemeteries in Nagoya and Kobe appear in Hosono, *Fumetsu no funbo,* pp. 209–214.

94. Asaka and Yagisawa, *Kasōba,* pp. 59, 91.

95. Ibid., pp. 100–101.

96. A menagerie of grisly tales appears in Hosono, *Fumetsu no funbo,* under the successive chapter headings "Horrors of Frightful Crematory Hell" (Senritsu subeki kasōba jigoku), "Those Who Extract Gold Teeth and Rip Clothes Off the Deceased" (Shisha iryō o hagitori kinha o egurinuku mono), and "Those Who Squeeze Brains from the Dead, Remove Livers, and Eat the Flesh of Corpses" (Shisha no nōshō o shibori himo o nuki shiniku o kuu), pp. 311–317. The theft of body parts from grave-yards and crematories was evidently so widespread that the Home Ministry found it necessary in 1903 to announce specific penalties, including jail time, for the crime; Miyazaki Taiichi, "Bochi no torishimari ni tsuite," part 2, *Sōtai* 1, 2 (February 1932): 37–38.

97. *Kobe yūshin,* March 27, 1925; reproduced in Hosono, *Fumetsu no funbo,* p. 301.

98. *Ōsaka asahi shinbun,* July 26, 1928; reproduced in Hosono, *Fumetsu no funbo,* p. 302.

99. *Keijō nippō,* June 29, 1929; reproduced in Hosono, *Fumetsu no funbo,* p. 302.

100. Natsume Sōseki, *Natsume Sōseki zenshū,* vol. 9, ed. Etō Jun and Yoshida Sei-ichi (Tokyo: Kadokawa Shoten, 1974), pp. 340–341.

101. *Fukuoka nichi nichi,* April 16, 1930; reproduced in Hosono, *Fumetsu no funbo,* pp. 303–304.

102. *Tōkyōshi kōhō,* April 16, 19, 21, and 23, 1938.

103. *Tōkyōshi kōhō,* April 21, 1938.

104. Ibid.

105. Inoue Yasumoto, *Bochi keiei,* p. 64.

106. One *tsubo* equals 3.95 square yards. Figures taken from Tōkyō Shiyakusho, *Tōkyōshi bochi gaikyō* (1933), p. 3; and Statistical Bureau of the Municipal Office of Tokyo, *Twentieth Annual Statistics of the City of Tokyo* (1924), pp. 32–33.

107. Inoue Yasumoto, *Bochi keiei,* pp. 288–290.

108. *Hinode shinbun,* June 3, 1929; reproduced in Hosono, *Fumetsu no funbo,* pp. 203–204.

109. *Hōchi shinbun,* July 17, 1930; reproduced in Hosono, *Fumetsu no funbo,* p. 286.

110. Hozumi, *Ancestor Worship and Japanese Law,* p. 170.

111. *Kokumin shinbun,* April 23, 1927; reproduced in Hosono, *Fumetsu no funbo,* p. 197.

112. Inoue Seijun, "Meibo hōzon no igi," *Sōtai* 1 (November 1932), p. 2.

113. Inoshita Kiyoshi, "Bochi no seiri to hōzon," *Sōtai* 2 (December 1932), pp. 32–33.

114. Each locale developed its own rules for dealing with *muen* graves. In his 1941 work on graveyard management, Inoue Yasumoto noted that the abandoned deceased in Tokyo's publicly administered cemeteries were exhumed and reburied in a section for *muenbotoke* at Tama *reien.* Before moving a set of remains, the city tried to track down relatives through municipal records, and if that was unsuccessful, placed ads in five different daily newspapers. If no one responded within three months, the discarded dead were shipped out to Tama *reien,* where, Inoue observed, the dead could be honored together "regardless of class." The rate of abandonment in Tokyo was apparently quite high: as of 1941, approximately one-third of all graves in Aoyama cemetery had gone *muen,* according to Inoue Yasumoto, *Bochi keiei,* pp. 261–263, 266–267.

115. Scores of these articles appear throughout Hosono's book.

116. Hosono, *Fumetsu no funbo,* pp. 1–7.

117. Ibid., pp. 353–356, 372–373.

118. Ibid., p. 3.

119. Ibid., p. 1 (of preface).

120. Ibid., pp. 439–440.

121. Benedict Anderson, *Imagined Communities: Reflections on the Origin and Spread of Nationalism,* 2nd edition (New York: Verso, 1991).

122. Yanagita Kunio, *Japanese Culture in the Meiji Era,* vol. 4, *Manners and Customs,* trans. Charles E. Terry (Tokyo: Toyo Bunko, 1957), p. 198.

123. *Kokumin shinbun,* May 17, 1927; reproduced in Hosono, *Fumetsu no funbo,* p. 235.

124. *Ōsaka mainichi shinbun,* April 18, 1928; reproduced in Hosono, *Fumetsu no funbo,* p. 222.

125. Inoue Yasumoto noted this trend in 1941; *Bochi keiei,* p. 3.

126. Yanagita, *Japanese Culture,* p. 198.

CHAPTER 6   DYING IN STYLE

1. To explain the Japanese funeral in terms of its social logic is in no way meant to imply that attendees do not experience deeply personal emotions. It is precisely because those feelings are so individual and varied, however, that they cannot account for the ritual system as a whole. The same can be said, of course, for death rites in any time and place.

2. In 1872, for example, Niigata officials announced, "It is prohibited to use artificial flowers for a funeral procession," and Gunma authorities in the following year inveighed against the custom of tossing money to children during funeral processions. The prefectural order pointed out that the relatively well-off competed in the amounts they disbursed and that even the poor were tempted to follow suit; Tanigawa Ken'ichi, *Nihon shomin,* pp. 19, 344.

3. Noguchi Katsuichi, "Sōshiki no heifū o aratamubeshi," *Fūzoku gahō* 172 (September 1898): 2.

4. I use the male pronoun because men, and ideally, eldest sons, were the ones who inherited patriline headships.

5. The ministry added that, in communities along the Tōkaidō, the *ihai* was placed on top of the coffin in cases where no successor had been designated; Shihōshō, *Zenkoku minji kanrei ruisan,* pp. 157–158.

6. *Tōkyō e-iri,* July 25, 1882; reproduced in *SSM,* vol. 5, p. 104.

7. *Tōkyō nichi nichi shinbun,* February 15, 1885; reproduced in *KD,* pp. 113–114.

8. Hōkōsha, ed., *Sōsai gojū nen: Kabushiki Kaisha Kōekisha no ayumi* (Osaka: Hōkōsha, 1982), p. 480.

9. Doves and sparrows were carried in cages and released at temples as meritorious acts of "mercy," only to be captured and used again.

10. Hirade Kōjirō, *Tōkyō fūzokushi,* 3 vols. in one, reprint (1901; repr., Tokyo: Hara Shobō, 1968), vol. 3, pp. 22–23.

11. Shirai Mitsuo, *Shukusai sōgei sōgi konrei junbi annai* (Tokyo: En'ya Shoten, 1905), pp. 53, 59.

12. These consisted of *manjū,* confectionaries made with sweet bean paste, and *kowameshi,* a mixture of rice and sweet beans.

13. Haga, *Sōgi no rekishi,* pp. 284–285.

14. *Chōya shinbun,* July 7, 1880; reproduced in *SSM,* vol. 4, p. 230.

15. Kata Sunsha, "Sōshiki sagen," *Fūzoku gahō* (October 1898): 17.

16. See Chapter One, p. 36.

17. *Chōya shinbun,* January 7, 1886; reproduced in *SSM,* vol. 6, p. 222.

18. Ōno Kazufusa, ed., *Ichiyanagi Sōgu Sōhonten sōgyō hyakunenshi* (Nagoya: Ichiyanagi Sōgu Sōhonten, 1977), pp. 66, 70, 93.

19. Hōkōsha, *Sōsai gojūnen,* p. 486.

20. Kojima Katsuji, "Shōto Ōsaka no sōshiki," *Kamigata* 96 (December 1938): 29.

21. In a work on Japanese customs published in 1925, when in fact processions in

major cities were nearing extinction, an American doing missionary work in Osaka claimed that "it would take a book to describe the movements of the professional mourners, some of whom are acrobats, and perform all the way from the house to the crematory"; Erskine, *Japanese Customs*, p. 99.

22. It was not uncommon to offer a branch of *shikimi* (star anise) to the dead. It was also regular practice to stuff *shikimi* leaves in the coffin not only to disguise the smell emitted by the corpse but also to keep the corpse from shaking during transport.

23. *Tōkyō asahi shinbun*, March 2, 1894; reproduced in *SSM*, vol. 9, p. 34.

24. Inoue Shōichi, *Reikyūsha*, pp. 93–94.

25. Noguchi, "Sōshiki no heifū," p. 2. Another avenue for advertising, although it escaped the scorn of this particular critic, was to piggyback the newspaper obituaries of celebrities. For example, when a member of the Tokugawa family died in 1893, Sugimoto Shōten placed an ad on the same page as the obituary, announcing that it was supplying the funeral and listing its address and telephone number. It offered a "special discount price" to those who placed orders for flowers and other gifts in memory of the deceased. *Tōkyō nichi nichi shinbun*, February 2, 1893; reproduced in *KD*, p. 112.

26. Arthur Hyde Lay, "Japanese Funeral Rites," *Transactions of The Asiatic Society of Japan*, vol. 19 (Tokyo: Hakubunsha, 1891), p. 543. He also made the following prognostication, with perhaps a bit too much confidence: "As to the funeral ceremonies of the future, they will of course depend upon the respective places taken by the three religions at present striving for mastery in the country. Everything, however, seems to point unmistakably to the conclusion that Christianity, or at least a form of it, influenced perhaps to some extent by Shintō and Buddhism, will be the future faith of Japan."

27. *KD*, p. 111.

28. Shirai, *Shukusai*, p. 53.

29. Hosono, *Fumetsu no funbo*, p. 338.

30. Hōkōsha, *Sōsai gojūnen*, p. 488.

31. Ibid., pp. 493–495.

32. *Tōto Seiten Kyōdō Kumiai sanjūnenshi* (Tokyo: Tōto Seiten Kyōdō Kumiai, 1981), p. 18.

33. Shirai, *Shukusai*, pp. 53–56.

34. Ibid., pp. 52–53.

35. Ibid., pp. 53–58.

36. Hirade, *Tōkyō fūzokushi*, vol. 3, p. 20.

37. These numbers do not include the substitute porters (used for both *kago* and *koshi*), who were frequently on hand to provide relief at certain intervals; Murakami Kōkyo, "Taishō ki Tōkyō ni okeru sōsō girei no henka to kindaika," *Shūkyō kenkyū* 64, 1 (June 1990), p. 40.

38. During the Tokugawa period, even the rich often chose to be buried in a seated position, since this gave them the appearance of either meditating buddhas or guardian deities. The decline in the popularity of *zakan* among the Tokyo elite can therefore

be attributed not only to the desire to use *koshi* instead of *kago*, but also to the Shinto funeral movement, which, drawing on Confucian precedent, encouraged horizontal burial.

39. Hirade, *Tōkyō fūzokushi*, vol. 3, p. 20.

40. Ibid., p. 19.

41. Ishikawa Takuboku, "Sōretsu," in *Takuboku zenshū*, vol. 4, ed. Ishikawa Masao (Tokyo: Iwanami Shoten, 1953), p. 69.

42. Shirai, *Shukusai*, p. 58.

43. Uchida Roan, "Bakudan," in *Uchida Roan zenshū*, supplemental vol. 2, ed. Nomura Takashi (Tokyo: Yumani Shobō, 1987), p. 217.

44. Toi Masataka, *Nihon fūzoku kairyōron* (Tokyo: Fūzoku Kairyō Zasshisha, 1891), pp. 32–33.

45. Noguchi, "Sōshiki no heifū," p. 1.

46. Ibid., p. 2.

47. Kata Sunsha, "Sōshiki sagen," *Fūzoku gahō* 174 (October 1898): 17.

48. Yamashita Jūmin, "Sōgiron," *Fūzoku gahō* 174 (October 1898): 1.

49. Toi, *Nihon fūzoku kairyōron*, p. 30.

50. Noguchi, "Sōshiki no heifū," p. 1.

51. Toi, *Nihon fūzoku kairyōron*, p. 32.

52. Noguchi, "Sōshiki no heifū," p. 1.

53. Sakai Toshihiko, "Sōshiki no kairyō," *Yorozu chōhō*, September 7, 1903; reproduced in *Sakai Toshihiko zenshū*, vol.1, ed. Kawaguchi Takehiko (Tokyo: Hōritsu Bunkasha, 1971), p. 284.

54. Yamashita, "Sōgiron," p. 1.

55. Hirade, *Tōkyō fūzokushi*, vol. 3, p. 23. Several decades earlier, in fact, a contributor to the *Shinbun zasshi* expressed reservations about mourners riding in wheeled vehicles. He noted the case of someone who, upon his mother's death, had rented rickshaws from a business just opened that year (1873) in Tokyo to provide vehicles specifically for funerals. Because "all of the blood relatives rode in rickshaws, there was not one person who walked," he said, adding, "there are those who gossip about whether this very convenient method is not mistaken," apparently because it kept mourners from adequately exerting themselves on behalf of the dead. *Shinbun zasshi* 155 (October 1873); reproduced in *SSM*, vol. 2, p. 83.

56. Yamashita, "Sōgiron," p. 1.

57. Noguchi, "Sōshiki no heifū," p. 1.

58. Ibid., p. 1. Kata praised the simplicity of samurai funerals and noted that even the processions of the well-to-do townspeople of Edo were not nearly as lavish as their Meiji successors; Kata, "Sōshiki sagen," pp. 16–17.

59. Shirai, *Shukusai*, p. 61. Hirade also noted, "because funerals are made grand by those outside of the relatives and close acquaintances who give *kōden*, families looking to keep things simple communicate in obituaries their intent to refuse offerings of artificial flowers and birds for release." Hirade, *Tōkyō fūzokushi*, p. 20.

60. *SKH,* p. 482.

61. *Jiji, Tōkyō nichi nichi shinbun, Yomiuri shinbun,* February 5, 1901; reproduced in *SKH,* p. 496.

62. *KD,* p. 107.

63. Noguchi, "Sōshiki no heifū," p. 2.

64. *Tōkyō nichi nichi shinbun,* March 30, 1908; reproduced in *KD,* p. 100.

65. Ibid., March 22 and April 22, 1896; reproduced in *KD,* p. 61.

66. Noguchi, "Sōshiki no heifū," p. 2.

67. Uchida, "Bakudan," p. 218.

68. Emi Suiin, *Jiko chūshin Meiji bundanshi* (Tokyo: Nihon Tosho, 1982), pp. 401–402.

69. Sakai, "Sōshiki no kairyō," p. 284.

70. Inoue Shōichi, *Reikyūsha,* p. 116.

71. Ibid., p. 120.

72. *Tōkyō nichi nichi shinbun,* July 19, 1909; reproduced in *KD,* pp. 101–102.

73. Inoue Shōichi, *Reikyūsha,* p. 110.

74. *KD,* p. 163.

75. Kojima, "Shōto Ōsaka no sōshiki," p. 28.

76. Mogi, *Sōshiki, hōji no shikata,* p. 72.

77. *Yomiuri shinbun,* April 21,1914; reproduced in *SKH,* p. 358.

78. Haga, *Sōgi no rekishi,* p. 291.

79. Inoue Shōichi, *Reikyūsha,* pp. 111–113.

80. Hōkōsha, *Sōsai gojūnen,* p. 502.

81. The *Hōchi shinbun* characterized the funeral as "eccentric"; December 15, 1901.

82. *SKH,* pp. 497–498.

83. *Tōkyō asahi shinbun,* August 28, 1894. *SKH,* p. 489.

84. *Mitsugon kyōhō* 130 (February 1895): 7.

85. *KD,* pp. 88–89.

86. *Yomiuri shinbun,* December 15, 1901; reproduced in *SKH,* p. 498.

87. *Hōchi shinbun,* December 15, 1901.

88. Shirai, *Shukusai,* pp. 111–112.

89. *Asahi shinbun,* February 10, 1916, p. 5.

90. *KD,* p. 163.

91. Murakami, "Taishō ki ni okeru sōsō girei," p. 44.

92. The counterpart for Shinto funerals was the presenting of *tamagushi.*

93. Mogi, *Sōshiki, hōji no shikata,* p. 7.

94. Ibid., p. 8.

95. Sakai Noboru, "Kaimyō rakugo," *Hyakkaen* 1, 17 (January 5, 1890): 19–21.

96. Uchida, "Bakudan," p. 210.

97. For example, an obituary appearing in an October 1926 issue of the *Tōkyō nichi nichi shinbun* announced that while there would be sutra readings at Kichijōji temple

starting at 2:00, the *kokubetsushiki* would occur from 3:00 to 4:00. *Tōkyō nichi nichi shinbun,* October 23, 1926; reproduced in *KD,* p. 126.

98. Bukkyō Shōshōkai, *Sōgi no kokoroe* (Tokyo: Bukkyō Shōshōkai, 1932) p. 30.

99. Ibid., p. 28.

100. Mogi, *Sōshiki, hōji no shikata,* p. 67.

101. This phenomenon is mentioned in both the 1932 and 1941 funeral manuals; ibid., p. 7. Bukkyō Shōshōkai, *Sōgi no kokoroe,* p. 8.

102. Mogi, *Sōshiki, hōji no shikata,* p. 7.

103. Bukkyō Shōshōkai, *Sōgi no kokoroe,* pp. 50–51.

104. Ibid., p. 24.

105. Mogi, *Sōshiki, hōji no shikata,* pp. 3–4.

106. Ōno, *Ichiyanagi,* pp. 126–127.

107. Shirai, *Shukusai,* p. 55.

108. Bukkyō Shōshōkai, *Sōgi no kokoroe,* pp. 9–15.

109. Sōsō Bunka Kenkyūkai, *Sōsō bunkaron,* p. 38.

110. For centuries the funerals of abbots and abbesses had featured their portraits, but it was not until photography became readily available that the practice of displaying images of the deceased became popular. Pictures of funeral altars in Ichiyanagi's company history show that they held photographs, as well as spirit tablets, from the first few years of Shōwa. Photos grew much larger over the following decades. Ōno, *Ichiyanagi,* pp. 301–529.

111. Yamada Shin'ya, "Shi o jūyō saseru mono: Koshi kara saidan e," *Nihon minzokugaku* 207 (August 1996), pp. 35–36.

112. Kitakushi Hensan Chōsakai, *Kitakushi,* vol. 1 (Tokyo: Tōkyōto, Kitaku, 1992), pp. 444–445.

113. Sōsō Bunka Kenkyūkai, *Sōsō bunkaron,* p. 42.

114. Yamada, "Shi o jūyū saseru mono," pp. 37–40.

115. Inoue Shōichi, *Reikyūsha,* p. 132.

116. Walter Weston, *A Wayfarer in Unfamiliar Japan* (London: Methuen & Co., 1925), p. 177.

117. Inoue Shōichi, *Reikyūsha,* pp. 31–32.

118. Ibid., p. 43.

119. Ibid., p. 49.

120. Ibid., p. 44.

121. Ibid., p. 46.

122. Mogi, *Sōshiki, hōji no shikata,* p. 72.

123. Natsume, *Natsume Sōseki zenshū,* vol. 9, p. 339.

124. Murakami, "Taishō ki Tōkyō ni okeru sōsō girei," p. 46.

125. Bukkyō Shōshōkai, *Sōgi no kokoroe,* p. 10.

126. Interview held on October 6, 1997.

127. Abe Isoo, "Kyorei to jōhi o hai shita no sōgi," *Shufu no tomo* (April 1917): 10–13.

128. Sheldon Garon, *Molding Japanese Minds* (Princeton: Princeton University Press, 1997), p. 9.

129. Ibid., pp. 10–12. See also Garon, "Fashioning a Culture of Diligence and Thrift: Savings and Frugality Campaigns in Japan, 1900–1931," in *Japan's Competing Modernities,* ed. Sharon A. Minichiello (Honolulu: University of Hawai'i Press, 1998), pp. 312–331.

130. Erskine, *Japanese Customs,* p. 92.

131. Watanabe family records at the Edo-Tokyo Museum, item no. 90013417.

132. Abe calculated that, including the rickshaws used in going to the crematory and a death notice in the newspaper, the total for his father's funeral came to 120 yen and 94 sen.

133. Watanabe records, item no. 90013413.

134. Ibid., item no. 90013427.

135. Reproduced in Hosono, *Fumetsu no funbo,* p. 460.

136. Reproduced in ibid., p. 456.

137. Reproduced in ibid., p. 455.

138. Reproduced in ibid., p. 453.

139. Embree, *Suye Mura,* pp. 217–218.

140. Ibid., p. 216.

141. The investigation was reported in the December 25, 1929 issues of the *Hōchi shinbun* and *Jiji shinbun;* reproduced in Hosono, *Fumetsu no funbo,* pp. 453–454.

142. *KD,* p. 166.

143. *Tōto Seiten Kyōdō Kumiai,* p. 51.

144. During the 1970s, however, a number of department stores, including Mitsukoshi, jumped at the chance to set up funeral advice corners in their stores, right next to the items purchased as return presents for *kōden.*

145. Hōkōsha, *Sōsai gojūnen,* p. 28.

146. Ibid., pp. 44–45.

147. Ibid., p. 45.

148. Fifty yen apparently bought the rental of a shrine-style hearse made from white wood (this style being popular in the Kansai region); an upright coffin; bunting; a pair of star anise branches; a pair of artificial flowers; a pair of paper flowers; a pair of live flowers in baskets; a three-level spirit tablet made from white wood; a bag, box, and stand to hold cremated remains; a cover for the coffin; a stand to hold incense; an incense burner and related items; wooden horses to hold up the coffin; and coins, a rosary, and star anise leaves to put in the coffin; ibid., pp. 78–81.

149. Nakamaki Hirochika, "Memorial Monuments and Memorial Services of Japanese Companies: Focusing on Mount Kōya," in *Ceremony and Ritual in Japan,* ed. Jan Van Breman and D. P. Martinez (New York: Routledge, 1995).

150. Hōkōsha, *Sōsai gojūnen,* pp. 57–60.

151. Ōno, *Ichiyanagi,* p. 128. The funeral Ichiyanagi coordinated for Toyota in 1930 was its first *shasō.* During the 1960s company funerals grew more lavish in line with

rapid economic growth. For the 1967 funeral of a top Toyota executive (which was conducted as a Shinto ceremony) Ichiyanagi used as many as 50,000 chrysanthemum blossoms in the altar; pp. 145, 419.

152. Bukkyō Shōshōkai, *Sōgi no kokoroe*, p. 9.

153. Driven by a "desire for an origin that could never be reached," these researchers sought out the shrinking puddles of a supposedly bona fide Japan in order to channel them into a "reservoir of authentic meaning" for all Japanese; H. D. Harootunian, "Figuring the Folk: History, Poetics, and Representation," in *Mirror of Modernity: Invented Traditions of Modern Japan,* ed. Stephen Vlastos (Berkeley: University of California Press, 1998), pp. 145, 155. Over the course of the twentieth century this effort generated a vast literature devoted to cataloging the minutest details of local custom. Produced most often in the form of "local history" *(chihōshi),* this nostalgic scholarship gives a prominent place to funerary rituals, since it is through them that communities most actively assert the continuity held dear by folklorists and their readers.

154. Washio Masahisa, "Nishinomiya chihō no sōsai shūzoku," *Kamigata* 96 (December 1938): 34–36.

155. *Tōkyō asahi shinbun,* August 22, 1940, p. 5.

156. Ibid., p. 7.

157. Interview held on October 6, 1997.

158. *Tōto Seiten Kyōdō Kumiai,* p. 20.

159. Hōhōsha, *Sōsai gojūnen,* pp. 116–188.

160. Ōno, *Ichiyanagi,* p. 134.

161. Garon, *Molding Japanese Minds,* p. 184.

162. Zen Gorenshi Henshū Iinkai, ed., *Zenkoku Kankon Sōsai Gojokaishi* (Tokyo: Zenkoku Kankon Sōsai Gojokai Dōmei, 1974), pp. 33–35.

163. In its 1880 survey of Japanese customs the Justice Ministry noted the presence of these funds throughout Japan; Shihōshō, *Zenkoku minji kanrei ruishū,* pp. 165–171.

164. Zen Gorenshi Henshū Iinkai, ed., *Zenkoku Kankon Sōsai Gojokaishi,* pp. 155–157.

165. Interestingly, the statement uses the katakana version of the English word "outsider," perhaps to emphasize the foreignness of their enemies; Zensōren Nijūgoneshi Henshū Iinkai, ed., *Zensōren nijūgonenshi* (Tokyo: Zen Nihon Sōsaigyō Kyōdō Rengōkai, 1982), p. 64.

166. See Hōkōsha, *Sōsai gojūnen,* p. 383, for example.

167. Yamada, "Shi o jūyū saseru mono," p. 37.

168. Ibid., p. 45.

169. Yamada, "Sōsei no bunka to chiiki shakai."

170. Ibid., p. 35.

171. Ibid., p. 36.

172. Ibid., p. 27.

173. Tokyo Co-op, "Anshin to nattoku copsesō," February 1997.

174. Suzuki, *The Price of Death,* pp. 207–208.

175. Since the 1960s a number of researchers have noted that Japanese tend to be "doers" rather than "believers" when it comes to interactions with the dead. For example, Herman Ooms reported the following response from a householder who was asked about the significance of ancestral offerings: "It is a bother and does not have any special meaning, but I probably will make the offerings. Doesn't one do these things naturally?" Herman Ooms, "A Structural Analysis of Japanese Ancestral Rites and Beliefs," in *Ancestors,* ed. William H. Newell (The Hague: Mouton Publishers, 1976), p. 67. Matthew Hamabata, writing in 1990, shared the following realization: "After they performed some rite pertaining to death and ancestorhood, I would collar my informants and ask, 'Do you really believe that the dead still continue to exist, that they are around somewhere?' Invariably, the answers would be to the effect: 'Gee, I wonder.' Or, 'I don't know.' Makoto Moriuchi's irritable reply, however, seemed right on target: 'It really doesn't matter, does it?' Makoto was absolutely right. I was barking up the wrong tree." Matthew Hamabata, *Crested Kimono: Power and Love in the Japanese Business Family* (Ithaca, NY: Cornell University Press, 1990), p. 83; quoted in Jane M. Bachnik, "Orchestrated Reciprocity: Belief versus Practice in Japanese Funeral Ritual," in *Ceremony and Ritual in Japan: Religious Practices in an Industrialized Society,* ed. Jan van Bremen and D. P. Martinez (New York: Routledge, 1995), p. 109. For a book-length study of ancestor worship in postwar Japan, see Robert J. Smith, *Ancestor Worship in Contemporary Japan* (Stanford: Stanford University Press, 1974).

176. Interviews in 1997 with employees of Kōekisha, Sugimoto, and Ceremony Miyazaki.

EPILOGUE

1. See, for example, the ethnographic reports collected in Kokuritsu Rekishi Minzoku Hakubutsukan Minzoku Kenkyūbu, ed., *Shi, sōsō, bosei shiryō shūsei,* 3 vols. (Chiba: Kokuritsu Rekishi Minzoku Hakubutsukan, 1999–2000).

2. Suzuki, *The Price of Death,* pp. 205, 221.

3. Arikawa Ichihō, *Shitai wa shōhin!! Warui sōgiya* (Tokyo: Deita Hausu, 1992).

4. Shibuya Kishū, *Anata no sōshiki, anata no ohaka* (Tokyo: San'ichi Shobō, 1993).

5. Tony Walter, *The Revival of Death* (London: Routledge, 1994), pp. 2–3.

6. Mori, *Haka to sōsō no genzai,* p. 3.

7. Ibid., pp. 7, 14–16.

8. Ibid., pp. 115–130.

9. Sōsō no Jiyū o Susumerukai, *"Haka" kara no jiyū,* pp. 176–177.

10. Inoue Haruo, *Ima sōgi, ohaka ga kawaru* (Tokyo: Sanseidō, 1993), pp. 232–233.

11. Ibid., pp. 8–16.

Bibliography

Abe Isoo. "Kyorei to jōhi o hai shita no sōgi." *Shufu no tomo* (April 1917): 10–13.

Akashi Kazunori. "Kodai no sōrei to fukukasei." In *Kazoku to shisha saishi*, edited by Kōmoto Mitsugi and Yoshie Akio. Tokyo: Waseda Daigaku Shuppanbu, 1997.

Amano Tsutomu. "Kōden." In *Sōsō bunkaron*, edited by Sōsō Bunka Kenkyūkai. Tokyo: Kokon Shoin, 1993.

Ambros, Barbara, and Duncan Williams. "Local Religion in Tokugawa History." *Japanese Journal of Religious Studies* 28, 3–4 (2001): 209–225.

Analects, The. Translated by D. C. Lau. New York: Penguin Books, 1979.

Anderson, Benedict. *Imagined Communities: Reflections on the Origin and Spread of Nationalism.* 2nd edition. New York: Verso, 1991.

Aoki Toshiya. "Meiji shoki hōrei shiryō kara mita sōsō shūzoku to kokka kisei no kenkyū." *Matsudo shiritsu hakubutsukan kiyō* 3 (March 1996): 37–71.

Arakawa Genki. *Jiin handobukku: Bochi hen.* 1978. Revised edition. Tokyo: Sansei Shobō, 1988.

Ariès, Philippe. *L'Homme devant la Mort.* Paris: Éditions du Seuil, 1977.

———. *The Hour of Our Death.* Translated by Helen Weaver. Oxford: Oxford University Press, 1991.

———. "The Reversal of Death: Changes in Attitudes Toward Death in Western Societies." Translated by Valerie M. Stannard. In *Death in America*, edited by David E. Stannard. Philadelphia, PA: University of Pennsylvania Press, 1975.

Ariga Kizaemon. *Mura no seikatsu sōshiki.* Tokyo: Miraisha, 1968.

Arikawa Ichihō. *Shitai wa shōhin!! Warui sōgiya.* Tokyo: Deita Hausu, 1992.

Asaka Katsusuke. "Kasōba no rekishi to henyō." In *Sōsō bunkaron*, edited by Sōsō Bunka Kenkyūkai. Tokyo: Kokon Shoin, 1993.

Asaka Katsusuke and Yagisawa Sōichi. *Kasōba.* Tokyo: Daimeidō, 1983.

Asoya Masahiko and Tanuma Mayumi, eds. *Shinsōsai shiryō shūsei.* Tokyo: Perikan, 1995.

Bachnik, Jane M. "Orchestrated Reciprocity: Belief versus Practice in Japanese Funeral Ritual." In *Ceremony and Ritual in Japan: Religious Practices in an Industrialized Society*, edited by Jan van Bremen and D. P. Martinez. New York: Routledge, 1995.

Baroni, Helen. *Obaku Zen: The Emergence of the Third Sect of Zen in Tokugawa Japan.* Honolulu: University of Hawai'i Press, 2000.

Bermingham, Edward J. *The Disposal of the Dead: A Plea for Cremation.* New York: Bermingham & Co., 1881.

Berry, Mary. "Public Life in Authoritarian Japan." *Daedalus* 127, 3 (Summer 1988): 138.

Bird, Isabella. *Unbeaten Tracks in Japan.* 3rd edition. London: John Murray, 1888.

Bloch, Maurice, and Jonathan Parry, eds. *Death and the Regeneration of Life.* Cambridge: Cambridge University Press, 1982.

Bodiford, William M. *Sōtō Zen in Medieval Japan.* Honolulu: University of Hawai'i Press, 1993.

———. "Zen and the Art of Religious Prejudice: Efforts to Reform a Tradition of Social Discrimination." *Japanese Journal of Religious Studies* 23, 1–2 (1996): 1–27.

Bolitho, Harold. *Bereavement and Consolation: Testimonies from Tokugawa Japan.* New Haven: Yale University Press, 2003.

Book of Filial Duty, The. Translated by Ivan Chēn. London: John Murray, 1908.

Breen, John. "Ideologues, Bureaucrats and Priests: On 'Shinto' and 'Buddhism' in early Meiji Japan." In *Shinto in History: Ways of the Kami*, edited by John Breen and Mark Teeuwen. Honolulu: University of Hawai'i Press, 2000.

———. "The Imperial Oath of April 1868: Ritual, Politics, and Power in the Restoration." In *Meiji Japan: Political, Economic and Social History 1868–1912.* Vol. 1, *The Emergence of the Meiji State*, edited by Peter Kornicki. London: Routledge, 1998.

Breen, John, and Mark Teeuwen, eds. *Shinto in History: Ways of the Kami.* Honolulu: University of Hawai'i Press, 2000.

Bukkyō Shōshōkai. *Sōgi no kokoroe.* Tokyo: Bukkyō Shōshōkai, 1932.

Burns, Susan. *Before the Nation: Kokugaku and the Imagining of Community in Early Modern Japan.* Durham, NC: Duke University Press, 2003.

"Busshū kōken." In *Kōbunko.* Vol. 15, edited by Mozume Takami. Tokyo: Meicho Fukyūkai, 1928.

Cannadine, David. "War and Death, Grief and Mourning in Modern Britain." In *Mirrors of Mortality: Studies in the Social History of Death*, edited by Joachim Whaley. New York: St. Martin's Press, 1982.

Chiso Kaisei Shiryō Kankōkai. *Chiso kaisei kiso shiryō.* 3 vols. Tokyo: Yūhikaku, 1953.

Collcutt, Martin. "Buddhism: The Threat of Eradication." In *Japan in Transition: From Tokugawa to Meiji*, edited by Marius B. Jansen and Gilbert Rozman. Princeton: Princeton University Press, 1986.

Cooper, Michael, ed. *They Came to Japan.* Berkeley: University of California Press, 1965.

Dajō ruiten. Records of the Council of State, 1868–1881. 5 vols. Microfilm at Meiji University, Tokyo.

Danforth, Loring M. *The Death Rituals of Rural Greece.* Princeton: Princeton University Press, 1982.

Date Mitsuyoshi. *Nihon shūkyō seido shiryō ruiju kō.* 1930. Revised edition. Kyoto: Rinsen Shoten, 1974.

De Groot, J. J. M. *The Religious System of China.* Vol. 3, bk. 1. Reprint. Taipei: Ch'eng-wen Publishing Co., 1967.

Dōon Koji. "Seizen ni hōmyō o ukezu shite sōshiki o nasubekarazu." *Reichikai zasshi* 30 (January 1886): 27–32.

Ebersole, Gary L. *Ritual Poetry and the Politics of Death in Early Japan.* Princeton: Princeton University Press, 1989.

Ebrey, Patricia. "Cremation in Sung China." *American Historical Review* 95, 2 (April 1990): 406–428.

Elison, George. *Deus Destroyed: The Image of Christianity in Early Modern Japan.* Cambridge, MA: Harvard University Press, 1991.

Embree, John. *Suye Mura: A Japanese Village.* Chicago: University of Chicago Press, 1936.

Emi Suiin. *Jiko chūshin Meiji bundanshi.* Tokyo: Nihon Tosho, 1982.

Erskine, William Hugh. *Japanese Customs: Their Origin and Value.* Tokyo: Kōbunkan, 1925.

Farrell, James. *Inventing the American Way of Death: 1830–1920.* Philadelphia: Temple University Press, 1980.

Fujii Masao, ed. *Sōgi daijiten.* Tokyo: Kamakura Shinsho, 1995.

Fujita Meitarō. "Shinshoku to sōgi no kankei ni tsuite." *Jinja kyōkai zasshi* 34 (December 1904): 52–53.

Fujita Yukio. *Shinbun kōkokushi hyakuwa.* Tokyo: Shinsensha, 1970.

Furukawa Motoyuki. "Sōgiryaku." 1865. Reproduced in *Shinsōsai shiryō shūsei,* edited by Asoya Masahiko and Tanuma Moyumi. Tokyo: Perikan, 1995.

Garon, Sheldon. "Fashioning a Culture of Diligence and Thrift: Savings and Frugality Campaigns in Japan, 1900–1931." In *Japan's Competing Modernities,* edited by Sharon A. Minichiello. Honolulu: University of Hawai'i Press, 1998.

———. *Molding Japanese Minds.* Princeton: Princeton University Press, 1997.

Gilday, Edmund. "Bodies of Evidence: Imperial Funeral Rites and the Meiji Restoration." *Japanese Journal of Religious Studies* 27, 3–4 (Fall 2000): 273–296.

Gluck, Carol. *Japan's Modern Myths: Ideology in the Late Meiji Period.* Princeton: Princeton University Press, 1985.

———. "Meiji for Our Time." In *New Directions in the Study of Meiji Japan,* edited by Helen Hardacre and Adam L. Kern. New York: Brill, 1997.

Goodwin, Janet. *Alms and Vagabonds: Buddhist Temples and Popular Patronage in Medieval Japan.* Honolulu: University of Hawai'i Press, 1994.

Gorer, Geoffrey. *Death, Grief, and Mourning.* New York: Doubleday, 1965.

Grapard, Allan G. "The Shinto of Yoshida Kanetomo." *Monumenta Nipponica* 47, 1 (Spring 1992): 27–55.

Habenstein, Robert W., and William M. Lamers. *The History of American Funeral Directing.* Milwaukee, WI: Bulfin Publishers, 1955.

Haga Noboru, *Sōgi no rekishi.* 1970. Revised edition. Tokyo: Yūzankaku Shuppan, 1991.

Hall, John. "Rule by Status in Tokugawa Japan." *Journal of Japanese Studies* 1 (Autumn 1974): 39–49.

Hamabata, Matthew. *Crested Kimono: Power and Love in the Japanese Business Family.* Ithaca, NY: Cornell University Press, 1990.

Hardacre, Helen. *Kurozumikyō and the New Religions of Japan.* Princeton: Princeton University Press, 1986.

———. *Religion and Society in Nineteenth-century Japan: A Study of the Southern Kantō Region, Using Late Edo and Early Meiji Gazetteers.* Ann Arbor: Center for Japanese Studies, University of Michigan, 2002.

———. *Shintō and the State, 1868–1988.* Princeton: Princeton University Press, 1989.

Harootunian, H. D. "Figuring the Folk: History, Poetics, and Representation." In *Mirror of Modernity: Invented Traditions of Modern Japan,* edited by Stephen Vlastos. Berkeley: University of California Press, 1998.

———. *Things Seen and Unseen: Discourse and Ideology in Tokugawa Nativism.* Chicago: University of Chicago Press, 1988.

Hayashi Yukiko. "Edo bakufu bukki rei no igi to tokushitsu." In *Kazoku to shisha saishi,* edited by Kōmoto Mitsugi and Yoshie Akio. Tokyo: Waseda Daigaku Shuppanbu, 1997.

Hirade Kōjirō. *Tōkyō fūzokushi.* 3 vols. in one. 1901. Reprint. Tokyo: Hara Shobō, 1968.

Hirota Masaki. *Sabetsu no shisō.* Vol. 22, Nihon kindai shisō taikei. Tokyo: Iwanami Shoten, 1990.

Hitomi Tatsuo. "Kokoro to shizen o hakai suru reien kaihatsu." In *Haka kara no jiyū,* edited by Sōsō no Jiyū o Susumerukai. Tokyo: Shakai Hyōronsha, 1994.

Hobsbawm, Eric J., and Terence O. Ranger, eds. *The Invention of Tradition.* Cambridge: Cambridge University Press, 1983.

Hōjō Hiroshi. "Meiji shonen no bochi shoyūken to riyō." Part 1. *Teikyō Daigaku hōgaku kiyō* 14, 2 (September 1984): 29–75.

Hōkōsha, ed. *Sōsai gojūnen: Kabushiki Kaisha Kōekisha no ayumi.* Osaka: Hōkōsha, 1982.

Horiuchi Misao, ed. *Meiji zenki mibunhō taizen.* Vol. 4. Tokyo: Nihon Hikakuhō Kenkyūjo, 1981.

Hosono Ungai. *Fumetsu no funbo.* Tokyo: Ganshōdō Shoten, 1932.

Hozumi Nobushige. *Ancestor Worship and Japanese Law.* 1912. 6th edition. Tokyo: Hokuseido Press, 1940.

Huffman, James L. *Creating a Public: People and Press in Meiji Japan.* Honolulu: University of Hawai'i Press, 1997.

Hur, Nam-lin. *Prayer and Play in Late Tokugawa Japan.* Cambridge, MA: Harvard University Press, 2000.

Ikeda Eishun. *Meiji no shinbukkyō undō.* Tokyo: Yoshikawa Kōbunkan, 1976.

"Ikyōsha maisō jiken." *Mitsugon Kyōhō* 71 (September 12, 1892): 16–17.

Inada Tsutomu and Ōta Tenrei, *Sōshiki muyōron.* Tokyo: Sōshiki o Kaikakusurukai, 1968.

Inagaki, Hisao. *A Dictionary of Japanese Buddhist Terms.* Union City, CA: Heian International, 1988.

Inoshita Kiyoshi. "Bochi no seiri to hozon." *Sōtai* 1, 2 (December 1932): 31–34. Reprint. Vol. 1. Tokyo: Yumani Shobō, 1984.

———. "Toshi no teienteki kyōsō bochi ni tsuite." *Toshi mondai* 25, 6 (December 1937): 84–90.

Inoue Haruo. *Ima sōgi, ohaka ga kawaru.* Tokyo: Sanseidō, 1993.

Inoue Seijun. "Meibo hozon no igi." *Sōtai* 1, 1 (November 1932): 2–3. Reprint. Vol. 1. Tokyo: Yumani shobō, 1984.

Inoue Shōichi. *Reikyūsha no tanjō.* Tokyo: Asahi Shinbunsha, 1990.

Inoue Yasumoto. *Bochi keiei.* Tokyo: Kokon Shoin, 1941.

Irokawa Daikichi and Gabe Masao, eds. *Meiji kenpakusho shūsei.* Tokyo: Chikuma Shobō, 1986–.

Ishikawa Takuboku. *Takuboku zenshū.* Vol. 4, edited by Ishikawa Masao. Tokyo: Iwanami Shoten, 1953.

Itami Jūzō. *The Funeral.* 1987. Produced by Tamaoki Yasushi and Okada Yutaka. Los Angeles: Republic Pictures Home Video, 1988.

Ivy, Marilyn. *Discourses of the Vanishing: Modernity, Phantasm, Japan.* Chicago: University of Chicago Press, 1995.

Jaffe, Richard. *Neither Monk nor Layman: Clerical Marriage in Modern Japanese Buddhism.* Princeton: Princeton University Press, 2001.

Jalland, Pat. *Death in the Victorian Family.* Oxford: Oxford University Press, 1999.

Jupp, Peter. "Cremation or Burial? Contemporary Choice in City and Village." *The Sociology of Death,* edited by David Clark. Oxford: Blackwell Publishers, 1993.

Kakehata Minoru. "Chūgoku shūdai no sōfuku seido." In *Kazoku to shisha saishi,* edited by Kōmoto Mitsugi and Yoshie Akio. Tokyo: Waseda Daigaku Shuppanbu, 1997.

Kamata Tōji. "The Disfiguring of Nativism: Hirata Atsutane and Orikuchi Shinobu." In *Shinto in History: Ways of the Kami,* edited by John Breen and Mark Teeuwen. Honolulu: University of Hawai'i Press, 2000.

Kamibeppu Shigeru. "Sesshū sanmai hijiri no kenkyū: Toku ni sennichi bosho sanmai hijiri o chūshin to shite." In *Sōsō bosei kenkyū shūsei.* Vol. 1, edited by Doi Takuji and Satō Yoneshi. Tokyo: Meicho Shuppan, 1979.

"Kasō en'yu no koto." *Myōmyō bunko* 10 (1883): 6–8.

Kata Sunsha. "Sōshiki sagen." *Fūzoku gahō* 174 (October 1898): 16–17.

Katō Hōkyō. "Sōsai ryakushiki: tenpō onsadame." 1844. Manuscript in collection of family documents, "Satomi shozō bunsho," set 1, compiled by Samukawa Chōshi Hensanka.

Katō Takahisa, ed. *Shinsōsai daijiten.* Tokyo: Ebisu Kōshō Shuppan, 1997.

———. "Tsuwano ni okeru soreisha to sōreisha." In *SD.*

Katō Takashi. "Governing Edo." In *Edo and Paris: Urban Life and the State in the Early Modern Era,* edited by James L. McClain et al. Ithaca, NY: Cornell University Press, 1997.

Kawakami Takeshi. *Gendai Nihon iryōshi.* Tokyo: Keisō Shobō, 1965.

Keene, Donald, ed. *Anthology of Japanese Literature.* 1955. 20th edition. Rutland, VT: Charles E. Tuttle, 1988.

Kenney, Elizabeth. "Shinto Funerals in the Edo Period." *Japanese Journal of Religious Studies* 27, 3–4 (Fall 2000): 239–271.

Ketelaar, James. *Of Heretics and Martyrs in Meiji Japan: Buddhism and Its Persecution.* Princeton: Princeton University Press, 1990.

Kitakushi Hensan Chōsakai. *Kitakushi.* Vol. 1. Tokyo: Tōkyōto, Kitaku, 1992.

Kobayashi Daiji. *Sabetsu kaimyō no rekishi.* Tokyo: Yūsankaku Shuppan, 1987.

Kobayashi Katsushō. *Bochi toriatsukai kisoku.* Tokyo: Bunkeidō, 1874.

Kōbun ruishū. Vol. 7. Microfilm at Meiji University, Tokyo.

Kojiki. Translated by Donald L. Philippi. Tokyo: Tokyo University Press, 1968.

Kojima Katsuji. "Shōto Ōsaka no sōshiki." *Kamigata* 96 (December 1938): 28–32.

Kokuritsu Rekishi Minzoku Hakubutsukan Minzoku Kenkyūbu, ed. *Shi, sōsō, bosei shiryō shūsei.* 3 vols. Chiba: Kokuritsu Rekishi Minzoku Hakubutsukan, 1999–2000.

"Kokusō ni tsuite." *Zenkoku shinshoku kaikaihō* 133 (November 1909): 1–4.

"Kokusō no koto." *Reichikai zasshi* 84 (March 1891): 36.

Konoe Tadafusa and Senge Takatomi. *Sōsai ryakushiki.* 1872. Reproduced in SD.

Kōseishō Seikatsu Eiseikyoku Kikakuka, ed. *Chikujō kaisetsu: Bochi, maisō nado ni kan suru hōritsu.* Tokyo: Daiichi Hōki Shuppan Kabushiki Kaisha, 1991.

Koschmann, J. Victor. *The Mito Ideology: Discourse, Reform and Insurrection in Late Tokugawa Japan, 1790–1864.* Berkeley: University of California Press, 1987.

Kotani Midori. *Senzō saishi no genjō to ohaka no kongo.* Tokyo: Raifu Dezainu Kenkyūjo, 1997.

Kumazawa Banzan. "Sōsai benron." In *Banzan zenshū.* Vol. 5, edited by Masamune Atsuo. 1942. Reprint. Tokyo: Meicho Shuppan, 1978.

Kuroda Toshio. "Shinto in the History of Japanese Religion." *The Journal of Japanese Studies* 7, 1 (Winter 1981): 1–21.

Kyōto Burakushi Kenkyūjo, ed. *Kyōto no burakushi.* Vols. 4, 6. Kyoto: Kyōto Burakushi Kenkyūjo, 1986.

Lay, Arthur Hyde. "Japanese Funeral Rites." *Transactions of the Asiatic Society of Japan,* vol. 19. Tokyo: Hakubunsha, 1891: 507–544.

Lu, David. *Japan: A Documentary History*. 2 vols. Armonk, New York: M. E. Sharpe, 1997.

Macé, François. "The Funerals of the Japanese Emperors." *Nanzan Bulletin* 13 (1989): 26–37.

Makihara Norio. *Meiji shichinen no daironsō*. Tokyo: Nihon Keizai Hyōronsha, 1990.

Masugi Takayuki. *Kurowaku no dorama: Shibō kōkoku monogatari*. Tokyo: Sōyōsha, 1985.

Matsumoto Shigeru. *Motoori Norinaga*. Cambridge, MA: Harvard University Press, 1970.

Meiji Bunka Kenkyūkai, ed. *Meiji bunka zenshū*. Vol. 1. 1928. Reprint. Tokyo: Nihon Hyōronsha, 1969.

Mitford, Jessica. *The American Way of Death Revisited*. New York: Vintage Books, 2000.

Mito Shishi Hensan Iinkai. *Mito shishi*. Vol. 2. 1968. Reprint. Mitoshi: Mito Shiyaku-sho, 1977.

Miyazaki Taiichi. "Bochi no torishimari ni tsuite." 2 parts. *Sōtai* 1, 1–2 (1932): 21–23, 35–38. Vol. 1. Reprint. Tokyo: Yumani Shobō, 1984.

Mogi Mumon. *Sōshiki, hōji no shikata*. Tokyo: Yoyogi Shoten, 1941.

Mori Kenji. *Haka to sōsō no shakaishi*. Tokyo: Kōdansha, 1993.

———. *Haka to sōsō no genzai: Sōsen saisha kara sōsō no jiyū e*. Tokyo: Tōkyōdō Shuppan, 2000.

———. *Hayama no bosei*. Research data published privately with funding from the Japanese Ministry of Education, 1997.

———. "Kindai no 'kegare': Sabetsu to haka." *Buraku kaihō* 418 (March 1997): 199–206.

———. "Meiji shonen no bochi oyobi maisō ni kan suru hōsei no hatten." In *Kazoku to haka*, edited by Fujii Masao, Kōmoto Mitsugi, and Yoshie Akio. Tokyo: Waseda Daigaku Shuppanbu, 1996.

———. "Meiji shonen no bukki, fukusō: Hitotsu no oboegaki to shite." In *Kazoku to shisha saishi*, edited by Kōmoto Mitsugi and Yagi Tōru. Tokyo: Waseda Daigaku Shuppanbu, 1997.

Morrell, Robert E. *Sand and Pebbles (Shasekishū): The Tales of Mujū Ichien, A Voice for Pluralism in Kamakura Buddhism*. Albany: State University of New York Press, 1985.

Murakami Kōkyō. "Taishō ki Tōkyō ni okeru sōsō girei no henka to kindaika." *Shūkyō kenkyū* 64, 1 (June 1990): 37–52.

Murakoshi Tomoyo. *Tama reien*. Tokyo: Tōkyōto Kōen Kyōkai, 1994.

Muraoka Tsunetsugu. *Studies in Shinto Thought*. Translated by Delmer M. Brown and James T. Araki. Tokyo: Japanese National Commission for UNESCO, 1964.

Murata Antoku. "Meiji ishin ki shinsōsai undō no tenmatsu." *Nihonshi kōkyū* 22 (November 1996): 1–17.

————. "Meiji shonen ni okeru shinsōsai kara bussō e no tenkai." *Nihon kindai Bukkyōshi kenkyū* 3 (March 1996): 23–37.

Murayama Hirō. "Bochi hō no kiso." 2 parts. *Minshō hō zasshi* 68, 1 and 3 (1973): 45–65, 400–420.

Naimushō Chirikyoku, ed. *Reiki ruisan.* Records of Home Ministry Land Office, 1872–1887. Reprint in 10 vols. Tokyo: Tachibana Shoin, 1981.

Nakagawa Yasuaki, ed. *Shinbun shūsei: Meiji hennenshi.* 15 vols. Tokyo: Honpō Shoseki, 1982.

Nakamaki Hirochika. "Memorial Monuments and Memorial Services of Japanese Companies: Focusing on Mount Kōya." Translated by Scott Schnell. In *Ceremony and Ritual in Japan,* edited by Jan Van Breman and D. P. Martinez. New York: Routledge, 1995.

Nakao Eishun. "Bochi shiyōken to seikaku." In *Gendai zaisan kenron no kadai,* ed. Kobayashi Mitsue Sensei Taikan Kinen Ronbushū Kankō Iinkai. Tokyo: Keibundō, 1988.

Namihira Emiko. *Kegare.* Tokyo: Tōkyōdō Shuppan, 1985.

Narumi Tokunao. *Aa kasō.* Niigatashi: Niigata Nippō Jigyōsha, 1995.

Natsume Sōseki. *Natsume Sōseki zenshū.* Vol. 9, edited by Etō Jun and Yoshida Seiichi. Tokyo: Kadokawa Shoten, 1974.

Nihongi: Chronicles of Japan from the Earliest Times to A.D. 697. Edited by W. G. Aston. 2 vols. in one. Rutland, VT: Charles E. Tuttle, 1972.

Nishiki Kōichi. "Bohi naki bochi no kōkei: Toshi kasō minshū no shi to maisō o megutte." In *Kinsei toshi Edo no kōzō,* edited by Takeuchi Makoto. Tokyo: Sanseidō, 1997.

Nishio Ujizō, ed. *Bochi kokoroe.* Osaka: Nishio, 1885.

Nitta Hitoshi. "Shinto as a 'Non-religion': The Origins and Development of an Idea." In *Shinto in History: Ways of the Kami,* edited by John Breen and Mark Teeuwen. Honolulu: University of Hawai'i Press, 2000.

Noguchi Katsuichi. "Sōshiki no heifū o aratamubeshi." *Fūzoku gahō* 172 (September 1898): 1–2.

Nosco, Peter. *Remembering Paradise: Nativism and Nostalgia in Eighteenth-Century Japan.* Cambridge, MA: Council on East Asian Studies, Harvard University, 1990.

Ogata Itsuo. "Senshi gunjin no sōgi ni tsuite." *Jinja kyōkai zasshi* 4, 1 (January 1905): 41–42.

Ōkurashō Kanzai Kyoku, ed. *Shaji keidaichi shobunshi.* Tokyo: Ōkura Zaimu Kyōkai, 1954.

Ōno Kazufusa, ed. *Ichiyanagi Sōgu Sōhonten sōgyō hyakunenshi.* Nagoya: Ichiyanagi Sōgu Sōhonten, 1977.

Ono Kiyohide. *Kokka sōdōin.* Tokyo: Kokufūkai, 1937.

Ooms, Herman. "A Structural Analysis of Japanese Ancestral Rites and Beliefs." In *Ancestors,* edited by William H. Newell. The Hague: Mouton Publishers, 1976.

———. *Tokugawa Ideology: Early Constructs, 1570–1680.* Princeton: Princeton University Press, 1985.

———. *Tokugawa Village Practice: Class, Status, Power, Law.* Berkeley: University of California Press, 1996.

Piggot, Joan R. *The Emergence of Japanese Kingship.* Stanford: Stanford University Press, 1997.

Prothero, Stephen. *Purified by Fire: A History of Cremation in America.* Berkeley: University of California Press, 2001.

Pyle, Kenneth B. "Meiji Conservatism." In *The Cambridge History of Japan.* Vol. 5, *The Nineteenth Century,* edited by Marius B. Jansen. Cambridge: Cambridge University Press, 1989.

Rawski, Evelyn S. "A Historian's Approach to Chinese Death Ritual." In *Death Ritual in Late Imperial and Modern China,* edited by James L. Watson and Evelyn S. Rawski. Berkeley: University of California Press, 1988.

Reader, Ian, and George Tanabe, eds. *Practically Religious: Worldly Benefits and the Common Religion of Japan.* Honolulu: University of Hawai'i Press, 1998.

Rowe, Mark. "Stickers for Nails: The Ongoing Transformation of Roles, Rites, and Symbols in Japanese Funerals." *Japanese Journal of Religious Studies* 27, 3–4 (Fall 2000): 353–378.

Sabata Toyoyuki. *Kasō no bunka.* Tokyo: Shinchōsha, 1990.

Saitō Tadashi. *Higashi Ajia sō, bosei no kenkyū.* Tokyo: Daiichi Shobō, 1987.

Sakai Noboru. "Kaimyō rakugo." *Hyakkaen* 1, 17 (January 5, 1890): 19–26.

Sakai Toshihiko. *Sakai Toshihiko zenshū.* Vol. 1, edited by Kawaguchi Takehiko. Tokyo: Hōritsu Bunkasha, 1971.

Sakamoto Koremaru. *Kokka shintō keisei katei no kenkyū.* Tokyo: Iwanami Shoten, 1994.

Sakatani Shiroshi. "Kasō no utagai." *Meiroku zasshi* 18 (October 1874): 4–6.

Satake Keishō. "Kasō ben'ekiron." *Yūbin hōchi shinbun,* July 9, 1874.

Satomi Kishio. *Japanese Civilization: Its Significance and Realization.* London: Kegan Paul, Trench, Trubner & Co., 1923.

Scott, James C. *Seeing Like a State: How Certain Schemes to Improve the Human Condition Have Failed.* New Haven: Yale University Press, 1998.

Seidel, Anna. "Dabi." In *Hōbōgirin: Dictionaire encyclopédique du bouddhisme d'après les sources chinoises et japonaises.* Vol. 6, edited by Sylvain Lévi et al. Paris: Librairie d'amérique et d'orient, 1983.

Seidensticker, Edward. *Low City, High City.* Rutland, VT: Charles E. Tuttle, 1984.

Seikanbō Kōa. *Imayo heta dangi, Kyōkun zoku heta dangi.* 3rd edition, edited by Noda Hisao. Tokyo: Ōfūsha, 1977.

Shibuya Kishū. *Anata no sōshiki, anata no ohaka.* Tokyo: San'ichi Shobō, 1993.

Shihōshō. *Zenkoku minji kanrei ruishū.* 1880. Reprint. Tokyo: Seishisha, 1976.

Shimaji Mokurai. *Shimaji Mokurai zenshū.* Vol. 1, edited by Futaba Kenkō and Mineshima Hideo. Kyoto: Honganji Shuppan, 1973.

Shimura Kimurō. "Shinsōsai mondai to sono hatten." *Shigaku zasshi* 41, 9 (1929): 70–85.

Shinno Toshikazu. "Shinshū ni okeru sōsō girei no keisei." *Kokuritsu rekishi minzoku hakubutsukan kenkyū hōkō* 49 (March 1993): 176–193.

Shintani Takanori. "Kasō to dosō." In *Minshū seikatsu no Nihonshi: ka,* edited by Hayashiya Tatsusaburō. Tokyo: Dōmeisha, 1996.

Shiori Nobukazu. "Sōhō no hensen: Toku ni kasō no juyō o chūshin to shite." In *Sōsen saishi to sōbo,* edited by Fujii Masao. Tokyo: Meicho Shuppan, 1988.

Shirai Mitsuo. *Shukusai sōgei konrei sōgi junbi annai.* Tokyo: En'ya Shoten, 1905.

Shoku Nihongi. Edited by Aoki Kazuo et al. *Shin Nihon koten bungaku taikei.* Book 1, vol.12, edited by Satake Akihiro. Tokyo: Iwanami Shoten, 1989.

Silver, J. M. W. *Sketches of Japanese Manners and Customs.* London: Day and Son, 1867.

Smith, Robert J. *Ancestor Worship in Contemporary Japan.* Stanford: Stanford University Press, 1974.

Sōsō Bunka Kenkyūkai, ed. *Sōsō bunkaron.* Tokyo: Kokon Shoin, 1993.

Sōsō no Jiyū o Susumerukai, ed. *"Haka" kara no jiyū: Chikyū ni kaeru shizensō.* Tokyo: Hyōronsha, 1994.

Statistical Bureau of the Municipal Office of Tokyo. *Twentieth Annual Statistics of the City of Tokyo,* 1924.

Sugawara Mōsei. "Shinshoku to sōgi to no kankei." *Jinja kyōkai zasshi* 33 (November 1904): 49–50.

Sugawara Noboyuki. "Heiri shinkan shinshūki." 1769. Reproduced in *Shinsōsai shiryō shūsei,* edited by Asoya Masahiko and Tanuma Mayumi. Tokyo: Perikan, 1995.

Suzuki, Hikaru. *The Price of Death: The Funeral Industry in Contemporary Japan.* Stanford: Stanford University Press, 2000.

Takayanagi Mitsutoshi and Takeuchi Rizō, eds. *Kadokawa Nihonshi jiten.* Second edition. Tokyo: Kadokawa Shoten, 1995.

Takemi Momoko. "'Menstruation Sutra' Belief in Japan." Translated by W. Michael Kelsey. *Japanese Journal of Religious Studies* 10, 2–3 (1983): 229–246.

Tamamuro Fumio. "Bakuhan taisei to Bukkyō." In *Nihon Bukkyōshi: Edo jidai,* edited by Tamamuro Fumio. Tokyo: Yūsankaku Shuppan, 1986.

———. "Okayamahan no shaji seiri seisaku ni tsuite." *Meiji Daigaku jinbun kagaku kenkyūjo kiyō* 40 (1996): 364–382.

———. *Sōshiki to danka.* Tokyo: Furukawa Kōbunkan, 1999.

———. "Local Society and the Temple-Parishioner Relationship within the Bakufu's Governance Structure." *Japanese Journal of Religious Studies* 28, 3–4 (Fall 2001): 261–292.

Tamamuro Taijō. *Sōshiki Bukkyō.* 1963. 11th edition. Tokyo: Daihōrinkaku, 1993.

Tanaka Kiyoshi. *Aoyama reien.* Tokyo: Tōkyōto Kōen Kyōkai, 1994.

Tanigawa Akio. "Excavating Edo's Cemeteries: Graves as Indicators of Status and Class." *Japanese Journal of Religious Studies* 19, 2–3 (June–September 1992): 271–297.

Tanigawa Ken'ichi, ed. *Nihon shomin seikatsu shiryō shūsei.* Vol. 21. Tokyo: San'ichi Shobō, 1979.

Teeuwen, Mark, and Fabio Rambelli, eds. *Buddhas and Kami in Japan: Honji Suijaku as a Combinatory Paradigm.* London: Routledge-Curzon Press, 2003.

Teiser, Stephen F. *The Ghost Festival in Medieval China.* Princeton: Princeton University Press, 1988.

Thal, Sarah. *Rearranging the Landscape of the Gods: The Politics of a Pilgrimage Site in Japan.* Chicago: University of Chicago Press, 2005.

Thelle, Notto R. *Buddhism and Christianity in Japan: From Conflict to Dialogue, 1854–1899.* Honolulu: University of Hawai'i Press, 1987.

Toi Masataka. *Nihon fūzoku kairyōron.* Tokyo: Fūzoku Kairyō Zasshisha, 1891.

Tōkyō Co-op. "Anshin to nattoku copsesō" (video). February 1997.

Tōkyō Shiyakusho, ed. *Tōkyōshi shikō.* 1911–.

Tōkyōfu. *Jiin keidai bochi kanrisha kokoroe.* Tokyo: Sawa Jitsukyō, 1893.

Tōkyōfuka Kakushū Jiin Sōdai Bochi Iin, ed. *Tōkyōfuka moto jiin keidai kyōyū bochi ni kan suru ikensho.* Tokyo: Kakushū Bochi Iin Jimusho, 1892.

Tōkyōto Kōbunshokan, ed. *Nisshin sensō to Tōkyō.* Vol. 1, *Toshi shiryō shūsei.* Tokyo: Tōkyōto Kōbunshokan Shuppan, 1998.

Tōkyōto kōbunshokan shiryō. Records of the Tokyo Metropolitan Government Archives.

Tōkyō Shiyakusho. *Tōkyōshi bochi gaikyō.* 1933.

Tonooka Mojurō, ed. *Meiji zenki kazokuhō shiryō.* Vol. 1, bk. 2. Tokyo: Waseda Daigaku, 1967.

Tōto Seiten Kyōdō Kumiai sanjūnenshi. Tokyo: Tōto Seiten Kyōdō Kumiai, 1981.

Tsuji Zennosuke. *Nihon Bukkyōshi.* Vol. 4. Tokyo: Iwanami Shoten, 1955.

Tsuji Zennosuke, Junkyō Washio, and Murakami Senshō, eds. *Meiji ishin shinbutsu bunri shiryō.* 1926. New Edition. 10 vols. Tokyo: Meicho Shuppan, 1983.

Tsunoda, Ryusaku, et al., eds. *Sources of Japanese Tradition.* 2 vols. 1958. Revised edition. New York: Columbia University Press, 1964.

Uchida Roan. *Uchida Roan zenshū.* Supplemental vol. 2, edited by Nomura Takashi. Tokyo: Yumani Shobō, 1987, p. 217.

Vesey, Alexander. "The Buddhist Clergy and Village Society in Early Modern Japan." Ph.D. dissertation, Princeton University, 2003.

Vlastos, Stephen, ed. *Mirror of Modernity: Invented Traditions of Modern Japan.* Berkeley: University of California Press, 1998.

Wakabayashi, Bob Tadashi. *Anti-Foreignism and Western Learning in Early-Modern Japan: The New Theses of 1825.* Cambridge, MA: Council on East Asian Studies, Harvard University, 1986.

Walter, Tony. *The Revival of Death.* London: Routledge, 1994.

Walthall, Anne. *The Weak Body of a Useless Woman: Matsuo Taseko and the Meiji Restoration.* Chicago: University of Chicago Press, 1998.

Washio Masahisa. "Nishinomiya chihō no sōsai shūzoku." *Kamigata* 96 (December 1938): 34–35.

Watson, James L. "Of Flesh and Bones: The Management of Death Pollution in Cantonese Society." In *Death and the Regeneration of Life,* edited by Maurice Bloch and Jonathan Parry. Cambridge: Cambridge University Press, 1982.

———. "The Structure of Chinese Funerary Rites: Elementary Forms, Ritual Sequences, and the Primacy of Performance." In *Death Ritual in Late Imperial and Modern China,* edited by James L. Watson and Evelyn S. Rawski. Berkeley: University of California Press, 1988.

Watson, James L., and Evelyn S. Rawski, eds. *Death Ritual in Late Imperial and Modern China.* Berkeley: University of California Press, 1988.

Weston, Walter. *A Wayfarer in Unfamiliar Japan.* London: Methuen & Co., 1925.

Williams, Duncan. *The Other Side of Zen: A Social History of Sōtō Zen Buddhism in Tokugawa Japan.* Princeton: Princeton University Press, 2005.

Yamada Shin'ya. "Shi o jūyō saseru mono: Koshi kara saidan e." *Nihon minzokugaku* 207 (August 1996): 29–37.

———. "Sōsei no bunka to chiiki shakai." *Nihon minzoku gaku* 203 (August 1995): 23–59.

Yamashita Jūmin. "Sōgiron." *Fūzoku gahō* 174 (October 1898): 1–3.

Yanagita Kunio. *Japanese Culture in the Meiji Era.* Vol. 4, *Manners and Customs.* Translated by Charles S. Terry. Tokyo: Toyo Bunko, 1957.

Yasui Sanesuke. "Hikasōron." 1685. Reproduced in *Kan'utei sōsho,* vol. 6, pt. 5, edited by Itakura Katsuaki. Annaka-han: Minobe Sei and Tajima Toyohisa, 1843.

Yoshida Hisashi. *Bochi shoyūkenron to bochi shiyōkenron.* Tokyo: Shinseisha, 1962.

Yoshida Kanemi. "Yuiitsu shintō sōsai shidai." Reproduced in *Shinsōsai shiryō shūsei,* edited by Asoya Masahiko and Tanuma Mayumi. Tokyo: Perikan, 1995.

Yoshii Toshiyuki. "Sanmai hijiri to bosei no hensen." *Kokuritsu rekishi minzoku hakubutsukan kenkyū hōkō* 68 (March 1996): 109–131.

Zen Gorenshi Henshū Iinkai, ed. *Zenkoku Kankon Sōsai Gojokaishi.* Tokyo: Zenkoku Kankon Sōsai Gojokai Dōmei, 1974.

Zensōren Nijūgonenshi Henshū Iinkai, ed. *Zensōren nijūgonenshi.* Tokyo: Zen Nihon Sōsaigyō Kyōdō Kumiai Rengōkai, 1982.

Index

Abe Isoo, 160–161, 162, 214n. 132
Adachi Tatsujun, 59
afterlife: Buddhist limbo *(chūin* or *chūu),* 6, 24, 25; Jizō, 25; nativist views of, 41, 49–51, 95; Pure Land (Jōdo), 3, 25, 182n. 27; skepticism about, 21, 153, 169–170, 215–216n. 175; ten kings belief, 25
Aizawa Seishisai, 53–54
altars: biers and, 157–158; Buddhist household *(butsudan),* 21, 50; in contemporary funerals, 1; evolution of designs, 8, 19, 157–158, 167–168; for farewell ceremonies, 157; photographs of deceased, 157, 167, 213n. 110; sizes, 157
Amaterasu, 15, 22, 27, 95
Amida Buddha, 3, 152–153, 182n. 27
ancestor reverence (worship): as argument for cremation, 76–77, 84, 90; attitudes toward, 215–216n. 175; Buddhist household altars *(butsudan),* 21, 50; eternal tombs, 130; increase in, 39; spirit shrines, 96; traditions blended with modernity, 12–13
ancestral graves. *See* family graves
Aoyama cemetery, 151, 208n. 114
Ariès, Philippe, 10, 11
aristocracy: Buddhist funerals, 104; cremations, 28, 29–30. *See also* imperial court
Atsumi Keien, 95
automobiles. *See* hearses

bathing corpses, 143, 160, 194n. 111
beggars, 137–138, 143
Bermingham, Edward J., 88
Beukema, Tjarko, 86–87
biers, 141, 157–158

Bird, Isabella, 45, 80, 87–88
bodies: bathing corpses, 143, 160, 194n. 111; donated to medical research, 150; sold to university hospitals, 162. *See also* burials; cremation
Book of Filial Duty, The (Xiao jing), 23
Boshin Imperial Rescript of 1908, 161
British Cremation Society, 88
buddha, as term for deceased *(hotoke/hotokesama),* 2, 26, 152, 173
Buddhism: in China, 23; entry to Japan, 6, 22, 177n. 6; Indian, 23; limbo period *(chūin* or *chūu),* 6, 24, 25; merit transfer ceremonies *(ekō),* 24–25, 99; nativist campaign against, 15–16, 53–55; new, 104; Nichiren sect, 88, 104; persecution, 56, 57; Pure Land (Jōdo) sect, 3; Rinzai Zen, 25–26; ritual offerings *(kuyō),* 24–25, 27; separation from state, 14, 15, 42, 56, 61; Sōtō Zen, 25–26, 27, 28, 122. *See also* afterlife; priests, Buddhist; Shin sect (Jōdo Shinshū); sutra-chanting/reading; temples
Buddhist funerals: in China, 26; clerical, 26; Confucian criticism of, 43–45; contemporary, 1–6; cremations, 28–29; as defense against vengeful spirits, 25; in early Meiji period, 60–61, 97, 98, 103–104; farewell ceremonies *(kokubetsushiki),* 152–157; of imperial court, 24, 47, 98, 182n. 29, 183n. 31; locations, 154–155; Mito campaign against, 53–55; pre-Tokugawa, 6–7, 22–27, 28, 29, 30, 32; rituals following, 5, 6, 21, 25, 128; roles of priests, 23–24, 156, 173; seventh-day ceremony, 5, 128; for soldiers, 100–102, 103; standardization, 25–26, 27, 32, 171; in Tokugawa period, 33–35, 38,

About the Author

Andrew Bernstein received his doctorate from Columbia University in 1999. He is presently assistant professor of history at Lewis and Clark College in Portland, Oregon.

Studies of the Weatherhead East Asian Institute Columbia University

SELECTED TITLES

(Complete list at www.columbia.edu/cu/weai/publications/html)

Rearranging the Landscape of the Gods: The Politics of a Pilgrimage Site in Japan, 1573–1912, by Sarah Thal. Chicago: University of Chicago Press, 2005.

The Merchants of Zigong: Industrial Entrepreneurship in Early Modern China, by Madeleine Zelin. New York: Columbia University Press, 2005.

Science and the Building of a Modern Japan, by Morris Low. New York: Palgrave Macmillan, Ltd., 2005.

Kinship, Contract, Community, and State: Anthropological Perspectives on China, by Myron L. Cohen. Stanford, CA: Stanford University Press, 2005.

Reluctant Pioneers: China's Expansion Northward, 1644–1937, by James Reardon-Anderson. Stanford, CA: Stanford University Press, 2005.

Japan's Colonization of Korea: Discourse and Power, by Alexis Dudden. Honolulu: University of Hawai'i Press, 2005.

Contract and Property in Early Modern China, ed. Madeleine Zelin, Jonathan K. Ocko, and Robert P. Gardella. Stanford, CA: Stanford University Press, 2004.

Gutenberg in Shanghai: Chinese Print Capitalism, 1876–1937, by Christopher A. Reed. Vancouver: University of British Columbia Press, 2004.

Divorce in Japan: Family, Gender, and the State, 1600–2000, by Harald Fuess. Stanford, CA: Stanford University Press, 2004.

The Communist Takeover of Hangzhou: The Transformation of City and Cadre, 1949–1954, by James Gao. Honolulu: University of Hawai'i Press, 2004.

Taxation without Representation in Rural China, by Thomas P. Bernstein and Xiaobo Lü. Modern China Series. Cambridge: Cambridge University Press, 2003.

The Reluctant Dragon: Crisis Cycles in Chinese Foreign Economic Policy, by Lawrence Christopher Reardon. Seattle: University of Washington Press, 2002.

Cadres and Corruption: The Organizational Involution of the Chinese Communist Party, by Xiaobo Lū. Stanford, CA: Stanford University Press, 2000.

Japan's Imperial Diplomacy: Consuls, Treaty Ports, and War in China, 1895–1938, by Barbara Brooks. Honolulu: University of Hawai'i Press, 2000.

China's Retreat from Equality: Income Distribution and Economic Transition, ed. Carl Riskin, Zhao Renwei, and Li Shi. Armonk, NY: M.E. Sharpe, 2000.

Nation, Governance, and Modernity: Canton, 1900–1927, by Michael T. W. Tsin. Stanford, CA: Stanford University Press, 1999.

Assembled in Japan: Electrical Goods and the Making of the Japanese Consumer, by Simon Partner. Berkeley: University of California Press, 1999.

Civilization and Monsters: Spirits of Modernity in Meiji Japan, by Gerald Figal. Durham, NC: Duke University Press, 1999.

The Logic of Japanese Politics: Leaders, Institutions, and the Limits of Change, by Gerald L. Curtis. New York: Columbia University Press, 1999.

Contesting Citizenship in Urban China: Peasant Migrants, the State and Logic of the Market, by Dorothy Solinger. Berkeley: University of California Press, 1999.

Bicycle Citizens: The Political World of the Japanese Housewife, by Robin LeBlanc. Berkeley: University of California Press, 1999.

Alignment despite Antagonism: The United States, Japan, and Korea, by Victor Cha. Stanford, CA: Stanford University Press, 1999.

PRODUCTION NOTES

Bernstein   *Modern Passings*

Interior design by the University of Hawai'i Press Design &
Production Department
Jacket design by Heather Truelove Aiston

Composition by Josie Herr
Text set in Minion with display in GillSans

Printing and binding by The Maple-Vail Book Manufacturing Group
Printed on 60# Sebago Eggshell, 420 ppi